MODERNIZATION AND
KIN NETWORK

MONOGRAPHS AND THEORETICAL STUDIES
IN SOCIOLOGY AND ANTHROPOLOGY
IN HONOUR OF NELS ANDERSON

General Editor: K. Ishwaran

Publication 7

MODERNIZATION AND KIN NETWORK

DANESH A. CHEKKI
University of Winnipeg, Canada

WITH A FOREWORD by K. ISHWARAN

LEIDEN
E. J. BRILL
1974

ISBN 90 04 03922 8

To
my Parents

TABLE OF CONTENTS

Kinship, Modernization and the Populistic Model in Karnataka

K. ISHWARAN

I AM VERY HAPPY to introduce this timely and valuable monograph on modernization and kinship in Karnataka by D. A. Chekki. Chekki belongs to the younger generation of sociologists in Karnataka with some of whose work I was associated while I was Chairman of the Department of Social Anthropology and Sociology, Karnataka University, Dharwar, Karnataka State. This monograph was to have been part of a comprehensive and long-term research project on the society and culture of North Karnataka that I had planned, but, as things turned out, this remains the only tangible outcome of that project, at any rate, for the moment.

Chekki's focus of study is Dharwar, a medium-sized town in Karnataka, with a population of around a hundred thousand. Essentially an educational and cultural centre, unlike the more busy and commercial city of Hubli, just twelve miles away, Dharwar has occupied, and still occupies, a central place in the educational, cultural and literary development of North Karnataka. In 1963, however, Dharwar and Hubli were amalgamated into a single municipal corporation. It has a full-fledged university, a radio station, and such culturally active organizations as the Karnataka Vidyavardhaka Sangha (a pioneer in the revival of Kannada literary scholarship). Therefore, Chekki's study is an important contribution to the understanding of the socio-cultural growth of modern Karnataka, the land of the Kannada-speaking people.

To appreciate adequately Chekki's study, one should place it in the broader theoretical perspective of Indian sociology as a whole. It would be no exaggeration to suggest that this study throws light on an aspect of Indian social processes that has been hardly touched by the dominant tradition in Indian sociological research today, bogged down as it has been in general concepts like the Great Tradition or Sanskritization. I am not suggesting that these concepts have been of no help or that they should be abandoned. Far from it, I am only arguing that even to use these concepts meaningfully one needs to make a radical shift in research emphasis as well as in theoretical framework. To be more specific, there is now a greater need for a more careful and detailed examination of the complex heterogeneity and pluralism of India's socio-cultural reality. This means, in operational terms, an increasing focus on regional socio-cultural patterns and processes. It is only after a reasonable accumulation of such regionally-oriented studies that one can see in sharper relief and significance such all-India phenomena as the Great Tradition, Sanskritization, and modernization.

Studies such as this are now a prime necessity to restore a balance in Indian sociology between grand abstract theory and detailed accounts of concrete, local, socio-cultural structures, processes and patterns. Chekki's work illustrates that, even within a part of a linguistic region, there are different models of modernization. Addressing himself to the specific areas of kinship and family, he demonstrates that the pattern of kinship modernization for the two key caste groups in the area, the Brahmans of Gokul and the Lingayats of Kalyan, was different but also related to an overall process of modernization. Rightly locating the main parameter of this process in the fact that the Lingayats, as a community, are more rurally-oriented, Chekki finds that, in some ways, the Brahmans appeared to be modernizing at a slightly faster rate. At the same time he draws attention to the more modern and egalitarian aspects of the Lingayat tradition, both in ideological and institutional terms, which include equality between the sexes, emphasis on individual self-effort and achievement-orientation, and emphasis on a cultural system securely embedded in the life of the common people. Hence, the situation he presents and analyses is complex and demands a complex theoretical explanation.

In what follows, I shall propose certain theoretical models and provide a broad framework that might hopefully yield a better theoretical insight into this complexity. Though Chekki does not elaborate on these aspects, they are implicit in his account. Since his concern was quite specific and limited, he does not go into the theoretical issues raised by what he regards as differential rates of modernization between the Brahmans and Lingayats. In my view, a fuller appreciation of the significance of this finding is possible only if we talk not in terms of differential rates of social change but of different models of social change.

The Lingayat Model of Modernization as a Populistic Model

The history of the Lingayat community in Karnataka goes back to the twelfth century. Its founder, Basava, was very much in advance of his times when he offered to his followers a programme of radical restructuring of society and culture on the basis of what can now be seen as an explicit ideology of universalistic humanism. He proposed a model of society and culture that challenged the existing Brahmanical model of a Sanskritized, caste-hierarchical social order. Thus, the Lingayat tradition of modernization can claim to be one of the oldest in India. Basava backed up his ideology with an organizational structure that underpinned his popular, reformist movement. The original ideology of Lingayat socio-cultural reform involved: (1) a shift in the basis of social structure from the principle of hierarchy to a principle of equality, including the equality of sexes; (2) a shift in the ideology from an institutionalized downgrading of manual labour to an elevation of it in moral terms (the notion of *Kayaka*), implying a work ethic of the kind Weber identified in Calvinism; and (3) a cultural shift from Sanskrit to Kannada, the language of the local people, as the language of culture and ritual. In religious terms, this programme could be called a Protestant version of Hinduism and, in sociological terms, an ideology of modernism.

Even when it is admitted that this ideal became somewhat eroded in the course of subsequent history, it has continued to this day as a potential source of ideology from which the community can draw its inspiration and legitimize its modernization efforts. An excellent example of this adaptation is the active involvement of the traditional religious organizations, *Mathas*, in the growth of modern education in the community. Another example is that one of its leaders, Hardekar Manjappa, won over fellow Lingayats in the 1920's and 1930's to the nationalistic movement by propagating that Gandhiji was merely re-formulating the ideas of their founder, Basava. I suggest that it is this important fact that marks the changes in this community from the recent Brahmanical model of modernization (historically traceable from the mid-nineteenth century), which is less indigenous and closer to Westernization. Against this background, it can be seen that Brahman kinship patterns appeared more modern in some ways than that of the Lingayats because the latter began its modernization from a different set of antecedent conditions. The Lingayats were historically driven to seek a more indigenous model of modernization.

The indigenous, Lingayat model (I use model and pattern as interchangeable terms) was not only true to the local historical traditions of modernization, but also more sensitive to the local socio-economic context. If this much is granted, then, it can be seen that, in the long run, the Lingayat model is more relevant than the Brahmanical model to the Indian national process of modernization. The latter is basically a process that involves an interaction between a rurally-oriented regional system and a more cosmopolitan system radiating from the urban-oriented national centers. In this process, the very size of the rural population (80% of India's population) has been a decisive critical factor and its change-potential[1] becomes a strategic issue for the modern nation-building process. Currently dominant models of modernization in India have failed to take adequate account of this aspect. The Lingayat model of modernization has the merit of having emerged historically in the context of such a rural change-potential. This is because it has been a populistic model.[2] At this point, two questions arise: What is a populistic model? In what way is the Lingayat model a populistic model?

To take up the first question, the populistic model in the sense in which it is used here has certain basic characteristics. It presupposes a populistic

---

1 For a recent examination of rural change-potential, see K. Ishwaran (ed.), *Change and Continuity in India's Villages*. (Columbia, 1970).
2 A tentative formulation is offered here. I am working on an extended theoretical formulation of this model.

society, which has to be conceptually distinguished from what Kornhauser[3] has defined as a "mass society", that is, a society in which the elite and the masses are not mediated by intermediate groups and structures but tend to confront each other directly. It should also be distinguished from the Brahman model of society in which ritual status overshadows all other social attributes. It is more helpful to see it as a product of the historical encounter between an agrarian social system and the "modern", urban, industrial system. In Karnataka, as, of course, in India as a whole, it has to be seen as specifically related to the process of colonial impact on the peasant society and culture. It was a response to the combined impact of Westernization and modernization of a predominantly elitist type, both during the colonial period and the early post-independence years.

The populistic model, unlike the elitist models of modernization, involves a responsive and responsible elite, but is devoid of elitism. Conceptually, elitism can be defined as a situation which legitimizes the control and dominance of a select group of persons over the members of a society. It is not merely the presence of an elite but the nature of an elite that is at stake in this distinction. The elite in the populistic model are part of a non-elitist, horizontal, integrative principle, those of *Dharma* or the moral principle of mutuality. Even if it were demonstrated that there is asymmetry in the exchange between the elite and the non-elite in such a system, such asymmetry is an extrasystemic, not an intra-systemic, evaluation. Asymmetry is, in the final analysis, an external category to the populistic society.

I think that this absence of elitism in the populistic, Lingayat model has made it a better basis for integrating the rural society of Karnataka into the wider processes of regionalism and nationalism. In short, both in fact and in ideology, the Lingayat, populistic model has made such a process less de-stabilizing than would have the Brahman or western models of modernization.

The second characteristic of the populistic society is that it involves a plurality of functional-cultural units, which enjoy a substantial measure of autonomy within an integrated system. No single group can dominate or dictate, as in the case of a dominant caste model, and all social activity is grounded eventually in a mutually bargained inter-group understanding. The totality of inter-group relationships is built into the plurality of groups in a way that would be difficult to comprehend for an observer accustomed to the atomistic, elitist values of the western model or the elitism of the Brahman model.

Summing up, I would say that the Lingayat model of modernization is populistic in two senses—in its being devoid of elitism and in its basis on a pluralistic principle of social integration.

On the contrary, the Brahman model represents a limited, elitist model of modernization. As a small community with a tradition of elitism, the Brahmans

---

3   William Kornhauser, *The Politics of Mass Society.* (Routledge and Kegan Paul, London: 1965).

could "westernize" early and more easily. But I assume that westernization is not modernization. The former process confuses a specific historical manifestation of modernization for a universal process of modernization. It implies, in fact, a process of transferring the western models of modernization uncritically, whereas modernization is a process of which universalistic goals and values of the modern ideology—equality, freedom and progress—are realized through indigenous efforts in indigenous contexts. Westernization is imitative, while modernization is creative. The thrust of my argument is that the Lingayats represent a model of modernization that is more creative and more relevant to the Indian situation.

Populistic Lingayat Model of Modernization in Application

The populistic Lingayat model is not a static model. In fact, its strength lies in the fact that it is a model with great potentiality for change. In the post-independence period, this potentiality has been creatively used in the processes of nationalistic and democratic political transformations. The penetration of the modern, national political system has been made more peaceful and socially less costly because of the presence of the populistic regional model in Karnataka. The fact that India was able to carry on as a political democracy owes considerably to the existence of non-elitist, populistic socio-cultural models at the regional level. At any rate, in Karnataka the Lingayat populistic model was able to absorb the impact of national political inputs in an orderly manner.

This process of integration has taken place, and is taking place, at the rural grass-roots level. It is related to, but distinguishable from, the urban accommodation processes. It was not part of Chekki's study to examine these processes directly, but even then he demonstrates clearly the need for such a distinction in one dimension of social change, that of kinship. The Lingayat model of socio-cultural change has persisted not only in this dimension, but has extended to the general process of modernization in the Karnataka region. The populistic Lingayat model, therefore, may be a useful concept in understanding wider regional politics as well national politics.

The movement for regional-linguistic states in the post-1947 period may be seen as part of an interactive process between the populistic model, on the one hand, and, on the other hand, the western or Brahman models, at the political level. If what I have argued so far is valid, then no simplistic model of interaction between tradition and modernity (whether a polarized one or a continuum one) would seem to explain the Indian process of modernization. Within the continuum, one finds a more complex interaction between different types of modernization—in this case, the western or Brahman model, and the populistic Lingayat model.

The development, stabilization and maintenance of a modern, national political community in India cannot be reduced to a simplistic process of tradition-modernity interaction, even when it is conceived of as a continuum model. Continuum is a step further than polarity, but it is not in itself sufficient.

What one needs is a more complex model within a continuum framework. The purpose of introducing the populistic Lingayat model of modernization as an explanation of the differential modernization between Lingayats and Brahmans, as exemplified in Chekki's study, has been to do precisely this—to offer a more complex continuum model than the ones currently dominant. A fuller empirical validation of the thesis here presented cannot be done in the present context. One has to wait for a good number of empirical studies focussed specifically on the more intricate and now ignored interaction processes between the regional and national systems in India.

In the meanwhile, Chekki's monograph can be regarded as a significant contribution to the much-needed study of the structural and functional interrelationships that have gone into the modernization of the ancient society, culture and civilization of India.

PREFACE

AMONG THE MANY forces influencing human society today, the process of modernization stands out both for its magnitude and universality. Almost everywhere in Asia, Africa, and Latin America traditional societies and cultures are being transformed from several directions with new technology, modern education, new occupations, laws, ideas, and values. This metamorphosis seems to be unique in that most traditional societies in transition, it appears, have tried to synthesize their cultural heritage of the past with the present and to link it with the future.

This book attempts to give a descriptive analysis of social interaction among kin and how modernization has been influencing kin relationships in a medium-size city in the Southwestern region of India—the land of the Kannada speaking people. During the British period the people who spoke Kannada were divided into five major administrative units—provinces, princely states, etc. With the formation of an enlarged Mysore state in 1956 an overwhelming majority, more than 20 million of these people, bound by a common language achieved their long cherished dream of a single administrative unit—the state. However, it was in November 1973 that the state was renamed as "Karnataka" which truly depicts the cultural heritage of the region.

While I was studying (1956-1958) sociology at the University of Bombay under Professors G. S. Ghurye, K. M. Kapadia and A. R. Desai, among others, and later (1958-1961) when I was teaching sociology at the Government Law College, Bombay, I nourished the idea of undertaking research of the kind reported here. However, I could not translate this intention into action until (1961) when I joined the faculty of the Department of Sociology, Karnatak University, Dharwar.

This volume has emerged from a research project originally designed in 1961. The field research was undertaken during 1962-1963. A preliminary draft, based on this study, was completed in 1964. I did not have an opportunity to revise the entire manuscript for publication until last year. Notations for kinship terminologies used in this book follow the same method found in G. P. Murdock's "Social Structure" (1949). In this study I have used the terms "kin network" and "kin group" to refer to all the relatives whom a person knows to exist in all his/her related families.

The title of this volume is of my own choosing. I am not—nor, I suspect, will others be—completely at ease with it. The present title may not accurately convey the content of this book. The appropriate title should have been "Modernization and Kin Network Among the Lingayats and Brahmans of

Kalyan and Gokul in Dharwar, India." Because of its unusual length I have retained the present title. In any event, this research does not pretend to be more than the beginning of the study of the impact of modernization on the family and kinship as observed in the two suburbs of Dharwar.

While I have been specifically concerned with one region of India, the problem I have investigated is to a large extent common to traditional-transitional societies in general. One of my concerns has been not merely to illuminate the specific case but also to make a contribution to the growing literature on modernization of developing societies as a whole. Therefore, I hope that my modest endeavour will be of interest both to those concerned with the practical problems of legislative and socio-economic change, and to those involved in a variety of more theoretical pursuits in such fields as sociology of the family, modernization, comparative sociology, social change, urban sociology, social stratification, sociology of law, and traditional-modern societies and cultures.

I owe a special debt of gratitude to Professor K. Ishwaran, York University Toronto. His thoughtful comments and encouragement at various stages of this study are acknowledged with deep appreciation. Needless to say, his seminal foreword has enhanced the value of this book. Professors William McCormack and I. P. Desai read an earlier version of this book and made a number of valuable critical comments. I am extremely grateful to them. My thanks are due to those members of the faculty and staff of the Karnatak University, too many to mention here, who have helped in my research in various ways.

A great debt of gratitude must be acknowledged to the people of the two suburbs of Dharwar where this study was conducted. I thank them all for their patience and interest, and for their warm hospitality, and above all for the information they gave. Also, I am grateful to Dr. K. S. Kamalapur and Mr. B. V. Ghanekar, both respondents from Gokul, for allowing me to include their genealogies in my book.

In 1968 I joined the faculty of the Department of Sociology, University of Winnipeg. It was here through interaction with my colleagues and extensive exposure to recent sociological research that my ideas on the subject began to crystallize, and eventually enabled me to revise the manuscript. I am thankful to Professors William A. Morrison and John R. Hofley for their interest in my research and continuing encouragement of my academic work. I take this opportunity to express my thanks to Dr. B. G. Hogg, Dean of Research, and the Research Committee of the University of Winnipeg for a Research Grant which facilitated revision of the manuscript for publication.

During the last six years some portions of this book were published in a different form in various professional journals. Grateful acknowledgements are due to the editors of the following journals: The Journal of Marriage and the Family (30:4, Nov. 1968, 31:1 Feb. 1969), Journal of Asian and African Studies (III Nos. 3-4, July-Oct. 1968), Indian Sociological Bulletin (5:4, July 1968), The Journal of the Karnatak University (Humanities & Social

Science, IV, 1968), Man in India (48:4, Oct. Dec. 1968), Contributions to Asian Studies, (I, 1971), Sociologus (XX:2, 1970, and XXIII:1, 1973). I acknowledge my intellectual gratitude to all scholars cited in the bibliography.

This book is dedicated to my parents, who over the years have been imaginatively and ably adapting to modernization, as a token of my affection and regard to them. To my wife, Sheela, and son, Mahantesh, must go a heart-felt thank-you for their patience and tolerance during the several months when I worked on the manuscript for publication.

University of Winnipeg   DANESH A. CHEKKI
February 5th, 1974

CHAPTER ONE

Problem and Theory

MODERNIZATION of traditional societies in recent decades has assumed tremendous significance and, especially since the end of World War II, it has drawn the attention of social scientists, policy-makers, administrators and others interested in socio-cultural change. The popular understanding of "the modern" and the "modernized society" is usually associated with automation, atomic energy, computers, space travel, and similar instances of a rapidly changing technology. But they represent only a relatively recent phase of modernization which had a modest beginning. During the eighteenth century in England, critical changes in technology, economy, polity, values and behaviour slowly released the forces of modernization which gradually spread to other countries of Europe and North America. It has now become almost a world-wide process.

Over the last two decades or so, developing societies have been gripped by modernization in a myriad ways which have generated a number of problems and controversies regarding the nature and the rate of modernization in these societies. However, it is becoming clear that modernization is a continuing process of great complexity and empirical studies[1] are beginning to throw doubt on the assumption that the Western model of modernization would prevail in the modernizing non-western societies.

This exploratory study attempts to present the structure and role of family and kinship among two castes, Lingayats and Brahmans, exposed to modernization in a middle-sized Indian city. Hopefully, it may help one to understand similarities and differences of Hindu family and kinship with familial institutions among tribal, peasant and urban-industrial communities elsewhere. This study also seeks to analyse the process of modernization and its influence on family and kin network. Variables such as urbanization, education, occupational mobility, and law which seem to be important in precipitating some changes in values, attitudes and behavior have received special consideration.

During the last two decades, researchers in the sociology of the family seem to have focused their attention mainly on the examination of classical nuclear family theory advanced by a series of sociologists[2] from Emile Durkheim

---

1 Singer, M. 1972; Shah, A. M. 1972; Vatuk, S. 1972.
2 Refer, Durkheim, E. 1947; Simmel, G. 1950; Toennies, F. 1957; Weber, M. 1950; Mannheim, K. 1940; Wirth, L. 1938; Linton, R. in Anshen, R. (ed.), 1959, pp. 45–46; Ogburn, W. & Nimkoff, M. 1950; Burgess & Locke, 1953; Parsons, T. in Bendix, R. & Lipset S. M. (eds.), 1953. pp. 166ff; Parsons, T. 1958; Parsons, T. in Anshen, R. (ed.) 1959, pp. 263ff.; Parsons, T. et al (eds.), 1961, p. 257; Sorokin, P. 1957; Zimmerman, C. 1947.

to Talcott Parsons. The theory assumes that the family in urban society is a relatively isolated unit and that the nuclear family form is functionally appropriate for a modern industrial-urban economy. However, enough empirical data[3] have been gathered by social scientists mostly in America and in England which demonstrate that in modern industrial urban societies of the West the isolated nuclear family is a fiction. The fact is that many families maintain widespread extrafamilial kin ties. Studies on the family in developing nations, such as India, have been mainly concerned with changes in the traditional joint or extended family. However, recent studies[4] emphasize the absence of baseline quantitative evidence on the distribution of earlier family types and question the thesis of a transformation of the joint family into a nuclear family as a result of a number of variables that may be subsumed under the rubric of modernization. On account of lack of conceptual clarification, the family life-cycle process of fusion and fission, rural-urban differentials and a host of other complex variables, it is no wonder that researchers have arrived at different and sometimes seemingly contradictory conclusions.

Social scientests and laymen alike believe that the culture of the Indian people is undergoing a rapid change and that changing values and social institutions will affect all, especially Hindus. The process of modernization, it is said, has led to important changes in the joint family, caste and village community. Observations such as follows are not uncommon:

> With industrialization and urbanization the joint family in India is fast dis-integrating and the nuclear family is becoming the modal family in urban areas. There is increasing process of mutation in extrafamilial kin relationships. Although in a sense the entire country is undergoing Westernization, the educated and urbanized sections are becoming more Westernized than the others and this process seems to have increased after the withdrawal of the British from India. By and large, Indians are still a religious people but large areas of life are becoming secularised.[5]

In the light of the foregoing observations it is of great significance to examine the nature and role of the family and kin network and various modernizing forces impinging upon them in contemporary Indian society. This study is confined to the following relatively neglected problems of modernization and extended kin network in urban India: they appear to be of crucial importance especially in the present context of induced or non-induced modernization of traditional societies. The present study seeks to answer these questions;

  (a)   Does the nuclear family tend to be an isolated unit relatively cut off

---

3   Among others mention may be made of the works of Sussman, M. B., 1953, pp. 22–28, 1959, pp. 333–340, 1962, 1965; Litwak, E. 1960, pp. 9–21, 1960 a, pp. 385–394; Adams, B. N. 1968, Firth R., 1956, 1970; Young, M. & Wilmott, P., 1957; Bott, E. 1957; Ishwaran, K. (ed.). 1971.

4   Desai, I. P. 1956, pp. 144–156, 1964; Kapadia, K. M., 1954, 1955, 1966; Morrison, W. A. 1959, pp. 45–67; Ross, A. D. 1961; Gore, M. S. 1968; Singer, M. 1972; Shah, A. M. 1972; Vatuk, S. 1972.

5   Srinivas, M. N. 1962, passim, 1962a, pp. 131ff.

from its extended kin network? This question is posed in the light of Parsons[6] general theory that there has been a historic trend to whittle down the size of kinship units in the general direction of isolating the nuclear family.

(b) Do the patterns of urbanization and effects of urbanization in the developing nations follow exactly the same or similar lines as in the industrialized nations of the West?

(c) Does the transition from pre-urban to urban living necessarily involve stresses and strains, conflicts, and socio-cultural maladjustments?

Since the main theme of our inquiry is concerned with the impact of modernization on kin network, the following section will be devoted to an explication of concepts such as modernity and modernization.

According to Lerner[7] modernity is primarily a state of mind—expectation of progress, propensity to growth, readiness to adapt oneself to change. He writes: "The 'Western Model' is only historically Western; sociologically it is global". On the basis of the data from the Middle East he asserts that "the same basic model reappears in virtually all modernizing societies on all continents of the world, regardless of variations in race, color, or creed." In his view modernization is "a secular trend unilateral in direction—from traditional to participant lifeways." Lerner's basic typology of modernization includes variables such as urbanization, literacy, media participation and political participation.

In a cross-national comparative study of modernization among peasants Rodgers and Svenning[8] consider modernization as "the process by which individuals change from a traditional way of life to a more complex, technologically advanced, and rapidly changing style of life." They recognize modernization as essentially a communication process and use literacy, mass media exposure and cosmopoliteness as main antecedents; empathy, achievement motivation and fatalism as intervening variables; innovativeness, political knowledge and aspirations as main consequences. The authors explore the inter-relations of a number of social-psychological variables in order to determine the nature of modernization and the role of directed social change. Their goal is to seek commonly occurring patterns of behavior among peasants that regulate their paths toward modernization.

A review of the works[9] of social scientists like Smelser, Moore ,Inkeles, Eisenstadt, McClelland, Ithiel Pool, Levy, Weiner suggests in general some of

---

6 Parsons, T. et al (eds.), 1961, p. 257.
7 Lerner, 1964, pp. viii-ix.
8 Rodgers, E. M. & Svenning L., 1969, p. 14.
9 Smelser, N. in Hoselitz & Moore W. E. (eds.), 1963, pp. 32–48 and in Weiner (ed.), 1966, pp. 119–130; Moore W. E. in Hoselitz & Moore (eds.), 1963, pp. 299–368; Ithiel Pool in Hoselitz & Moore (eds.), 1963, pp. 279–293; Levy, M. J. 1966; Inkeles, A. in Weiner (ed.), 1966, pp. 151–163; Eisenstadt, 1966; McClelland, D. 1961. In addition, the following scholars, among others, have contributed to the field of modernization of society and culture, politics and government, and economy: Bendix, R., Black C. E., Galanter, M, Gusfield, J, Hunter, Lambert, R, Morse, Pye, Shils, E, Singer, M.

the major characteristics of modernization. These include: high achievement motivation, empathy, secularism, ever-rising aspirations to improve material conditions, advanced science and technology, extensive use of formal organizations, structural differentiation, faith in the desirability and possibility of change, rational ends-means calculations, lessening control of traditions, and customs and increasing control of state laws, importance of achieved status rather than the ascribed, demographic revolution (i.e. declining birth and death rates), increasing spatial and social mobility, increasing literacy and education, industrialization, urbanization, high national production, high standards of living, mass media exposure, political participation, innovativeness, cosmopoliteness and the like. Modernization as viewed by Ithiel Pool means, among other things, the acquisition of an image of limitless progress and growth as the normal character of life. He considers the psychic initiation of vast numbers of people as an essential step in the process of modernization.

Some scholars[10] have used Westernization to describe social change in non-Western countries. The concept of modernization, as used in the present study, is not synonymous with the concept of Westernization. To designate the change-process as Westernization is to imply that the source for change necessarily comes from the Western countries. Furthermore, it implies that societies adopting Western values become to a certain degree like the West. The concept of Westernization, therefore, is too narrow to stand for the wider and complex process of modernization in developing countries.

The assumption that modernization will have the same effects wherever it occurs and that modernity will necessarily replace tradition is not empirically valid since timing, sequence and cultural milieu vary enormously. These variables make it almost impossible for modernization to occur in the same way twice. While emphasizing the distinction between "modernization" and "modernity" Bendix indicates that many attributes of modernization like widespread literacy or modern medicine have appeared, or have been adopted, in isolation from the other attributes of a modern society. Hence, he says, modernization in some sphere of life *may* occur without resulting in "modernity". According to him recognition of this uncertainty provides a better basis for the comparative study of modernization.

Modernization is a value-neutral and a multi-dimensional concept. Intrinsically it is neither "good" nor "bad". Nevertheless, it brings change, and along with this change there may be beneficial and/or adverse effects. In other words, modernization may not be an unmixed blessing for all. Conceptually we can distinguish between individual and societal modernization. These two are markedly different social phenomena since individual modernity does not necessarily correlate with societal modernity. When a society is modern, it does not necessarily follow that all individuals living in that society are also modern. Some individuals, on the contrary, may be modern even when the total society is yet traditional. Lerner's "transitionals" is a good illustration

---

10   Refer, for example, Srinivas, M. N. 1962. "A Note on Sanskritization and Westernization".

of this point. The society in the latter case may undergo a period of transition before it finally emerges as a modern society. However, it is difficult to locate the "cutting-off" point in societies that are in a transitional stage.

Conceptual formulations of the contrast between tradition and modernity as presented by Toennies' *Gemeinschaft* and *Gesellschaft,* Maine's status and contract, Durkheim's mechanical and organic societies, Becker's sacred and secular, Redfield's folk-urban, Parsons' universalism and particularism have been used in sociological analysis. However, these sets of dichotomous concepts have not proved to be very fruitful in empirical analysis.

As already stated Lerner's model of modernization is based on four dimensions, namely, urbanization, literacy, media participation, and political participation which are systematically related to one another. According to Lerner, societies can be classified according to the degree to which they exhibit one set of attributes rather than another, and societies can be ranked in accordance with their degree of tradition, transition, or modernity.

Bendix[11] correctly points out that attribute-checklists of the relative modernization of countries do not easily avoid the implication that change once initiated must run its course along the lines indicated by the "Western model", and in the transition to modernity all aspects of the social structure change in some more or less integrated and simultaneous fashion. Furthermore, he argues that the timing and sequence of modernization of countries, which are often ignored, can make a crucial difference.

Since studies on social change have to rely on historical experience, theories of social evolution have influenced the formulation of contrasting "ideal types" of tradition and modernity. Often this contrast has been used to make contingent generalizations about the transition from tradition to modernity. Many sociologists seem to have ignored Max Weber's caution and they not only tend to confuse the ideal type and reality with one another but also tend to regard the ideal type as a generalization. More importantly, the usage of "tradition" and "modernity" as mutually exclusive concepts and as a generalized descriptive statement about two, contrasting types of society, has led to the recognition of "traditional" and "modern" societies as two distinct types, each with its own, more or less "built-in tendency towards self-maintenance of equilibrium."

For our purposes modernization is a process of change from a traditional social order to certain types of modern technology, economy, polity and associated forms of social structure, norms, value orientations, motivations and behaviour patterns. The traditional and the modern social systems are not regarded by us as mutually exclusive or conflicting systems. It is assumed that there may be a considerable degree of interaction between the two. Modern values and behaviour need not necessarily always replace the traditional values and behaviour. There may be a process of synthesis or adaptation and in some cases both the traditional and the modern may exist side by side.

---

11   Bendix, R., 1967, p. 311.

For us, modernization is not just a matter of imitation or adoption of foreign technology and cultural values; it is a unique process of fusion of old and new cultural systems and, as such, differs in different societies. The new cultural trait need not necessarily come from the West. It may originate within a society or may originate outside a society. Moreover adoption of innovations from another country need not make the recipient country a carbon copy of the original because the requirements of adjustment to differing cultural settings of receiving countries usually modify cultural elements.

The following brief review of research on family and kinship and the subsequent discussion on theoretical aspects of modernization and kin network are intended to place the present study within the perspective of present knowledge on the subject.

Previous Research

Besides some classical studies[12] on family and kinship among tribal and rural communities we have in recent decades several contributions made by sociologists and social anthropologists about family and extended kin among urban-industrial communities as well. Firth's study of kinship in London[13] deals with various facets of kinship among the English and the Italians. It sets aside the systematic study of kinship terminology and prefers "to give content to the genealogical material, primarily through the non-verbal kinship behaviour."

The studies of Mogey[14] in Oxford and Young and Willmott[15] in East London analyse the social effects of housing on the behaviour and attitude of the people towards their relatives. They were surprised to discover that the wider family, far from having disappeared, was very much alive in these cities.

A study of family life in the Netherlands by Ishwaran[16] reveals strong ties of kinship and extrafamilial relationships and obligations in normal and in difficult times. As observed by him the urban family in Holland despite spatial mobility has maintained a strong "team spirit" through kinship and other common interests. Studies in urban Canada by Garigue[17] and Piddington[18] reveal close kin relationships, intra-kin marriage, importance attached to constellations of kin and impact of urbanism on French Canadian Kinship. Sussman, Litwak and Adams among several others[19] have presented evidence

---

12 Refer the works of L. H. Morgan, W. H. R. Rivers, Malinowski, Firth, R., Schapera, Fortes, M., Evans-Pritchard, Radcliffe-Brown, R., Murdock, G. P., Hsu, Lang, Freedmon, M., Embree, Geertz, Arensberg. For details see Chekki, D. A. *J.K.U.* vol. VII, 1963, pp. 134–144.
13 Firth, R. 1956, p. 26.
14 Mogey, J. 1956.
15 Young, M. & Wilmott, P., 1957.
16 Ishwaran, K. 1959.
17 Garigue, 1956.
18 Piddington, R., 1961.
19 Sussman M. B., 1953, 1959, 1965; Litwak, E. 1960, 1960a; Adams, B. N. 1968.

showing the existence of "an American kin family system with complicated matrices of aid and service activities which link together the component units into a functioning network."

Kapadia's study on "Hindu kinship" based on the classical literature is an analysis of the relevant legal system in relation to other institutions. As he points out, his work is a synthesis of the principles underlying different institutions of Hindus to evolve a proper meaning of the kinship terminologies which are the very backbones of these institutions.

Karve's study of "Kinship Organization in India" considers relations within the family and its extensions, and, in addition inter-relations between families, kinship terminologies, marriage regulations and attitudes. It is based on classical and modern literature, ethnographic work and geneological studies. Karve's work is a rapid survey of kinship of different linguistic regions of India. Mayer in his "Caste and Kinship in Central India" gives us a picture of the way the caste system works in a multi-caste village of Central India and its surrounding region and he deals with kinship as subsidiary to the main theme of his book.

The studies made by Dube, Lewis, Marriot, Srinivas and others[20] are concerned with an account of kinship as it exists in their respective single "study village" or a limited region. In all these studies the main emphasis is on the study of intra-family relationships. Little attention has been paid by social scientists to the study of extrafamilial kinship network in Indian society.

However, studies of family and kinship in urban India are few and far between. Kapadia[21] and Desai[22] have studied the joint family in small towns of Gujarat, and Ross[23] has studied Hindu Family in the Bangalore region. Gore's[24] research deals with impact of urbanization on the Agarwal family in the Delhi region. Bottomore writes:

> But what is lacking is detailed study of how the contemporary joint family functions, and of the kind of relationships which exist in practice between its members, especially in urban areas. In the absence of such studies it is impossible to analyze precisely the processes of change, and the problem is often obscured by ideological battles between traditionalists and partisans of change.[25]

Srinivas's "Marriage and Family in Mysore" gives an ethnographic account of marriage and family among some caste groups of the southern part of Mysore state. Desai's "Life and Living in Rural Karnatak" is a socioeconomic survey of a particular region of northern part of Mysore State. These studies, however, do not provide us with an empirical account of the impact of

---

20 Dube, 1955; Srinivas, 1955; Dumont, 1957 a; Lewis, O. 1958; Marriot, M. 1955; Madan, 1965.
21 Kapadia, 1959.
22 Desai, I. P. SB. vol. 5. no. 2. 1956.
23 Ross, A. D. 1961.
24 Gore, M. S. 1968. See, Owens, 1971.
25 Bottomore, T. B. 1962, p. 169.

modernization on the family and kinship of specific communities. If for no other reason, the present study is justified in its attempt merely by the paucity of research on modernization and kinship in India.

As expressed in "Contributions to Indian Sociology":

> In the present state of knowledge, to write a book on kinship in India is a daring venture. One would think that, for a general picture to be attempted, a number of intensive studies should first be written, and, apart from tribal monographs, we have very few of them indeed... The elucidation of Indian kinship cannot be the work of one single scholar, however gifted he may be, it will be the work of a number of students whose individual efforts will be intended as a contribution, resting on the contributions of others, towards that common enterprise.[26]

The foregoing review of literature has been an inducement in undertaking this study. The value of such a study perhaps lies in the fact that due to various modern forces the family and kinship values and behaviour in India have not been affected in precisely the same way, as have been the values and behaviour of kinship in certain Western countries under the impact of more or less similar forces.

Theoretical Orientation

Some social theorists[27] argue that modernization not only leads to the isolation and atomization of the nuclear family system through the attenuation of extrafamilial kin network but also that the nuclear family is ideally suited to the patterns of occupational and geographical mobility so characteristic of modern industrial urban society. Research findings of the 1950's and 1960's in the cities of America, Canada, Britain and Western Europe,[28] however, show that the extended family instead of disintegrating is becoming more important to the individual because of the difficulty in developing satisfying primary relationships outside of the family in an urban environment. Furthermore, visiting, getting-together, joint recreational activities, mutual aid and exchange of services, and presents among extended kin outrank similar interaction patterns among friends, neighbours or co-workers. Litwak's[29] research points out that the modified extended kin family does not require geographical propinquity and that since occupational mobility does not hinder its activities it exists in modern urban society as the most functional type.

Nimkoff,[30] summarizing world trends of family change, stated that while societies with differing cultural histories will differ in their response to industrialization, the general direction but not the pace of change is generally the same. The trend, under the impetus of industrialized urbanization, is toward

26   Dumont & Pocock, 1957, p. 43, pp. 63–64.
27   Refer Parsons, T., 1953, 1958, 1959, 1961; Sorokin, P. A. 1957; Zimmerman, C. 1947.
28   Refer note 3.
29   Litwak, E. 1960, 1960a.
30   Nimkoff, M. 1965, p. 346.

more emphasis on marriage and less on kinship. William Goode[31] indicates that the major family systems have not remained static for centuries, nor did they begin to change only with industrialization. At the present time, a somewhat similar set of influences is affecting all world cultures and all of them are moving toward industrialization, although at varying speeds and from different points. Their family systems are also approaching some variant of the conjugal system. Even though all systems are more or less under the impact of industrializing and urbanizing forces, it is pertinent to note that Goode has not assumed that the amount of change is a simple function of one or the other or even of combinations of both. He insists on the independent power of ideological variables and contends that everywhere the ideology of the conjugal family is spreading. According to him the conjugal family system is not equivalent to a "nuclear family" composed only of parents and children, and has shown on both empirical and theoretical grounds that the conjugal family has more kinship ties and correlatively is under far more kinship control than is some times supposed by Western observers or non-Western analysts. After a careful survey of family changes in the Western and non-Western societies Goode concludes that the corporate kindred or lineage may lose most of its functions under urbanization and industrialization, but extensions of kin ties continue to remain alive and important in social control through reciprocal gifts and exchanges, visits and continual contacts and that it is impossible to eliminate such extended kin ties without disrupting the nuclear family itself. He further cautions not to commit the error of *minimizing* the extension of kin in a conjugal family system and also avoid *exaggerating* the ties of the extended family which preceded the modern conjugal family.

In the light of the foregoing empirical data and theoretical formulations it is relevant to examine the hypothesis that the family in urban Indian society is a relatively isolated unit and with increasing modernization the extrafamilial kin network tends to be attenuated. The theoretical position in this study is that there exists in modern urban centres of developing nations, particularly in Indian society, an extended kin family system, organically fused within a network of wider kinship relationships composed of primary, secondary and tertiary kin belonging to different generations. The validity of this theoretical stance is established by the accumulation of empirical evidence on the structure and functioning of urban kin networks based upon research in a middle-sized Indian city.

We shall also be concerned with the examination of the patterns of urbanization and effects of urbanization on family and kinship. There is a common assumption that the effects of urbanization in developing nations follow the same or almost similar lines as in Western nations. For instance, in the context of the family Stephens[32] writes:

---

31   Goode, W., 1963, p. 368 ff.
32   Stephens, 1967, p. 543.

As industrial development accelerates in other countries, it should bring urbanization, geographic mobility, rapid culture change and protracted schooling for the masses— which, in turn, may be expected to lead towards American style family customs: a progressive "isolation" of the nuclear family from the larger kin group; a blurring of cultural guide lines for family roles; love matches in lieu of arranged marriage; greater egalitarianism within the family, loss of the family's economic functions; and—with mass education and urbanization—the emergence of adolescence.

The fact that modernization is the process of change toward those types of social, economic and political systems that have developed in Western Europe and North America from the seventeenth to the nineteenth centuries and which have then spread to other developing countries in the nineteenth and twentieth centuries has led to the notion that the effects of modernization in developing societies will be similar. This assumption implies that the source for change necessarily comes from the Western nations. Changes in any society may be due to exogenous and/or endogenous factors. The very fact that currently modernizing societies have a wide variety of traditional social structures should bring differential impact. In this context the present study attempts to examine the differing nature and rate of modernization and its impact on kin network of two caste groups in an Indian city.

The fact that patterns of modernization in the developing nations have not followed the Western lines and are not likely to do so in the future is due, in large measure, to the difference between present economic, political, social and technological conditions and those that prevailed when Western nations were first experiencing industrial and urban transformation. Unlike the industrialization of Western nations which had required the creation of a new technology from crude beginnings, the developing countries now trying to modernize their economies can acquire ready-made modern technology from the highly industrialized countries. Though there may be problems of adapting that technology to conditions in developing societies, at least the time and effort devoted to experimentation and trial and error can be saved or avoided. Moreover, rapid means of transport and mass communication have broken the relative isolation of developing societies and exposed them to a global mass culture incorporating new norms, values and behaviour patterns. This differing nature of modernization and the differences in subcultures in the developing societies *a priori* should bring a differential impact on the social order.

The next question relating to the process of modernization is that "the transition from pre-urban to urban living *necessarily* (emphasis supplied) involves frictions, which are manifested in social and personal problems."[33] Eisenstadt observes: "The very fact that modernization entails continual changes in all major spheres of a society means of necessity that it involves processes of disorganization and dislocation, with the continual development of social problems, cleavages and conflicts between various groups, and movements of protest, resistance to change. Disorganization and dislocation thus

---

33   Hauser in Hoselitz & Moore (eds.), 1963, p. 209.

constitute a basic part of modernization, and every modern and modernizing society has to cope with them."[34] It is true that by and large the process of modernization in traditional societies has brought about, initially at least, some friction, dislocation and social disorganization. But this does not mean that the process of transformation from the traditional to the modern way of life necessarily involves frictions, conflicts and social problems. It is hypothesized that when the rate of modernization is relatively slow or when we can designate this process as mere transition or transformation and not a rapid change or revolution then there need not necessarily be frictions and socio-cultural maladjustments. Disorganization and dislocation need not constitute a basic part of modernization. This need not imply, however, that frictions and social problems are completely absent. It only means that such frictions and disorganization are kept at as low a level as possible.

Methods of Research

The empirical data presented in this study were obtained primarily from interviews of people in two suburban areas of the city of Dharwar and from observations of their behaviour with members of their families, extrafamilial kin, neighbours and friends. The research was carried out by the author during 1962–63. Initially basic census data of the two suburbs in Dharwar, a middle-sized Indian city in northwestern Mysore state, were collected. This was followed by an intensive interview using interview guide and genealogical method. Two hundred and thirty heads of households, that is, married men and women, widows and widowers, were the respondents. This was supplemented with interviews with resource persons and youths. Resource persons were those who had a special knowledge of the community because of long residence or because of special services they provided, such a priests, teachers, local government officials, caste leaders and the like.

I chose two communities, the Lingayat and the Brahman, which are the major caste groups in this part of India. Census figures on caste are not available because the Census of India (1951 and onwards) does not collect them (except on Scheduled castes). It has been estimated,[35] however, that Lingayats constitute 21 per cent of the population thereby forming the largest single caste in Mysore state. Brahmans form a minority group in the province but play a significant role in cultural, educational and administrative activities of the province. In the Dharwar region of Mysore state these two caste groups are well organized and influential in educational, economic, political and other spheres of society. They are rivals in Dharwar and the neighbouring districts and have been constantly competing in education and employment, in social and cultural activities. The leaders of these two castes zealously try to safeguard their group interests.

---

34 Eisenstadt, S. N., 1964 passim as quoted in Eisenstadt, 1966, p. 20.
35 Refer Srinivas, M. N., 1962. India Government, 1956b.

Separate educational institutions are organized predominantly by these groups and even the daily newspapers and magazines are run in a similar fashion. The modern mass media like the radio, and centres of cultural activities such as literary and women's associations reflect the regional caste colour although they are formally secular and national in character.

Most Lingayats are agriculturists even though some of them are engaged in trade and industry and some as government officials, teachers, lawyers, doctors, engineers, etc. However, this study is concerned mainly with Lingayat agriculturists who reside in an urban setting. The spatial distribution of these people is very limited as they are tied down to the land. Caste customs and traditions, illiteracy and ignorance of languages other than their own act as barriers to spatial mobility.

The Brahmans form the apex of the social pyramid in the traditional Hindu social system, representing the elite. An overwhelming majority of them are educated and constitute the non-agricultural group. They are absorbed mostly in the public services as clerks, teachers, administrative officers and the like. Also among them are lawyers, doctors, engineers and technicians, etc. Even if they own land they themselves are never cultivators. As most Brahmans are in urban and industrial occupations they reside mainly in towns and cities. Among them spatial and social mobility is high.

Dharwar was chosen for two reasons. Firstly, it is fairly representative of the fifteen cities of Mysore state which have a population of more than fifty thousand each. Secondly, the Lingayats and Brahmans are socially and numerically important when compared to other castes in this city. These caste groups in Dharwar, as in other parts of India, are localized. Their community consciousness and territorial integrity can be observed.

Dharwar is the administrative headquarters of the district and is an educational centre, with a growing University. It has been undergoing modernization slowly and steadily during the last hundred years, but especially since 1947 when India became independent.

The pseudonym of the suburb of Dharwar inhabited by Lingayats is *Kalyan* and that for Brahmans is *Gokul*. In these suburbs respectively, the Lingayats and Brahmans constitute 82.55 per cent and 79.08 per cent. Two hundred and thirty households ,that is, one hundred and fifteen households from Kalyan, and one hundred and fifteen households from Gokul, provide material for the present study.

The age structure of respondents was as follows:

The age of the respondents varies from 21 to 85. Of the 230 respondents from both suburbs the majority of them (i.e. 174) fall within the age groups of 35 and 64. For the purpose of this study twenty-nine persons in the age group 21–34 are considered as the younger generation. Those between the ages of (roughly) 35 and 54 constitute the middle age group. Persons in the age group 55–64 are in the pre-retirement period of their life. Respondents who are 65 and above in age are retired senior citizens.

Table 1

Age of Respondents

Age Groups	Kalyan Respondents	Gokul Respondents	Total
21–34	16	13	29
35–44	30	26	56
45-54	27	40	67
55–64	24	27	51
65–74	8	6	14
75 and above	10	3	13
Total	115	115	230

Of the 230 households of Kalyan and Gokul our respondents included 112 men and 73 women; and in 45 households both husband and wife were interviewed. Of the total respondents 196 were married, twenty-two were widows, and eight widowers. Only four respondents were unmarried.

Besides recording the basic census data of each household, a detailed enquiry of their genealogy was made. Ego narrated his or her genealogy with the assistance of other members of the family. This was followed by the elaborate informal interview which lasted from a minimum of two hours at a stretch to a maximum of six hours in different sessions. In several cases, both husband and wife in the same household were interviewed, but at different times. All the interviews took place in the informants' households.

An additional source of information was unmarried male and female adults. In almost every family children also contributed a good deal of information. They directed their parents, assisted them in recalling names of kin and corrected their mistakes. A series of discussions with several key personalities of Kalyan and Gokul such as priests, teachers, caste leaders, elders in the neighbourhood, astrologers, doctors and lawyers were helpful in collecting detailed and valuable information not only about themselves and their families but also about other households.

The schedule devised to record the basic information regarding each household and an interview guide designed to elicit both qualitative and quantitative data during informal talks with informants immensely faciliated field investigations. Unsolicited responses were frequent and they proved valuable. In order to verify the data collected, natural checks and counter-checks were possible as there were many families in the same suburb who were related through descent, marriage or adoption. Practically in every household I noted the duplication of at least a segment of genealogy of another related family residing in the same area. The initial approach to each household was made without any prior intimation. At the beginning of the interview the purpose of the study and my role as a social researcher were made known to the interviewees. I told them that my intention was to study kinship and social life of the Lingayats and Brahmans. This frankness and directness of approach was appreciated by both the communities.

Kalyan is an illiterate, agrarian and traditional community. People are superstitious and conservative. Life in Kalyan goes on at a slow pace in contrast with Gokul which is a literate non-agricultural community where people are more alive and conscious of the modern ways of life. These differences are reflected in the characteristic responses of the interviewees.

Responses and Reactions

Though in both the communities people evinced interest and welcomed me, the people of Kalyan in the beginning were suspicious about my credentials and accepted my bonafides only after I cleared their doubts. With the people of Gokul there was much less difficulty in establishing rapport. The reception in Gokul was warm and pleasant. Despite disclosing my identity and intentions at the beginning of the enquiry, the suspicions that were created in the minds of the people of Kalyan were interesting. Respondents, mostly farmers, believed that the study was sponsored by the Government and I was a Government official. Most of the criticisms against the Government were directed at me. They told me that such studies were of no use, a waste of valuable funds which the Government collects by way of taxation and that it was a device to give jobs to the educated unemployed.

In the course of the investigation other difficulties were encountered. As I set out for field research some fresh administrative measures of the city Corporation had just been put into action. The newly established Corporation for the twin cities of Hubli and Dharwar had imposed extra taxes and the people felt the burden. The Corporation also undertook the programme of broadening the city roads, which involved the acquisition and demolition of several houses, thereby incurring the hostility of the people. A major section of the population of Dharwar organized strikes against the formation of a Corporation and the increased taxes. Under such circumstances some informants mistook me as an official of the Corporation and a volley of criticisms levelled against the Government and the Corporation was directed to me. Likewise, the Communist Chinese aggression on India and the declaration of the Emergency, recruitment for the Indian army, and gold controls by the Government aroused further suspicions. At one time, compulsory anti-smallpox inoculation of children in Kalyan led to pains and fever, with the result that when I approached them, several women abused the Government inoculators profusely and hoped that this inquiry would not lead to similar inoculations in the future. Most of them even today believe that inoculation and modern medicine are unnecessary as diseases can be prevented by indigenous methods. It took me some time to convince them that I was in no way connected with Government or Corporation but was an individual like everybody else in the area. In Gokul, however, people were conscious of the significance of such studies and they rarely entertained such doubts.

Genealogical Method

Genealogies of a hundred and fifteen Lingayat households and the same number of Brahman households have yielded valuable information about knowledge of kin, thereby providing the kinship framework of individual households. Difficulties similar to those experienced by Firth, Garigue and Piddington[36] were encountered. Knowing well the impracticability of isolating the informant in order to acquire the individual's knowledge of kin, voluntary enquiries addressed by the informant to another member of the family considered to be the genealogical experts of the family were permitted. Attempts were not made to prevent promptings made by children. But no positive attempts were made to induce the informant to make queries among other members of the household about names of kin not known by Ego. However, some informants tried to get additional information from neighbouring related households. This was deliberately stopped as it would have complicated the matter and resulted in the partial mixture of kin knowledge of another household. On the whole, it was possible to obtain genealogies from each household and to ascertain the knowledge of total kin of the members of such households. We should not assume, however, that the kin knowledge of each household presented here speaks for the complete knowledge of all members of the household. Only those family members who were present at the time of interview responded. Therefore, knowledge of kin documented in this study appears to be incomplete.

The knowledge of kin of all members of each household tends to be much wider than what is secured. However, this does not by any means affect seriously the attempt to ascertain the overall kin knowledge of the household. The collection of genealogies was made the main focus for the present investigations. Such a study had several advantages. In the first place it gave a concrete frame of reference with regard to the household's kinship universe. It was also for the first time that the people in these two suburbs of the city experienced the novelty of all their kin being recorded. When they saw their "family tree" in all its ramifications in black and white, it not only erased suspicion but also made them feel proud of their ancestry and the kinship network. Most of them believed that it would be a valuable document for successors. Informants often asked for a copy of it. Such data were frequently checked and cross-checked as most households had related families in the neighbourhood and the information was found correct.

The Lingayats are more conscious of the existence of their numerous relatives. The majority of the people, men and especially women, evinced great interest in narrating the genealogy. Often during the enquiry male respondents asked their wives to tell them the names of kin. The following typical remarks indicate the respondents' attitudes towards their kin.

---

36 Firth, R. 1956, p. 26. Garigue, *AA*, vol. 58, 1956, p. 1090; Piddington, *IJCS*, vol. 2. no. 1. 1961, p. 7.

"Our relatives number more than the hair on our head."

"Our kin group is like a beehive, how can we remember the names of all kin?"

"Our circle of relatives is like a herd of elephants. They come and go in bands."

Some respondents refused to divulge the names of some of their kin. Such refusals also gave insight into the understanding of their conception about kinship and threw light on significant sociological aspects. Most of them were willing to give the names of their immediate kin—primary and secondary— mostly consanguines. Sometimes they hesitated to reveal the names of their in-laws. Recording of genealogy spontaneously brought to light some kin conflicts.

It was a common experience of the researcher that male informants could rarely name or otherwise remember female kin on the wife's or mother's side. Voluntarily they do not give the names of dead kin in Ego's own generation or previous or succeeding generations. In their opinion only the living kin should be recorded. However, in response to a deliberate question they mentioned the names of dead kin and along with them the memories, feelings and sentiments attached to the deceased were also manifested.

Women were the genealogical experts. Especially when there were cousin marriages and when Ego (female) was related to the husband's parental family prior to her marriage, then she knew more of her husband's kin than her husband himself. The housewife proudly and enthusiatically narrates the names of married daughters, their spouses, children and their lineage.

The general tone was one of enthusiasm, anxiety, pride and pleasure in having numerous kin. The following remarks illustrate the point:

"Do you have enough ink in your fountain pen? It is an endless story".

"We hope you have enough paper to trace our family tree. It is like the growing tail of the monkey God".

Age and sex of the informant are two important factors in understanding the variations in kin knowledge. With the increase in age both males and females possessed more knowledge of kin. "Pivotal kin are those relatives who act as linking points in the kinship structure by their interest in, and knowledge of, genealogical ramifications."[37] The pivotal kin, namely, the eldest female in the household, is the treasurer of genealogical knowledge and they could contribute much of the information when the necessity arose. By and large the genealogies collected centre around Ego, formally at least, but in fact Ego's spouse, children and pivotal kin assisted invariably in the processes. Isolation of the informant for purposes of assessing individual's knowledge of kin was neither practicable nor sociologically fruitful. It should be conceded for all practical purposes that the respondent's range of kin knowledge is not merely the total number of relatives known to him at any one moment. Reasonably enough it also includes the kin he might probably expect to come into contact

---

37   Firth, R. 1956, p. 39.

with or know about in various future situations, possibly through other members of the household or other kin with whom he is in constant touch. Informants narrated several such experiences.

Tracing the genealogical lore has been cultivated as an art among the Brahmans. They manifest overt pride of their kin verbally at least, and are much more anxious to narrate the names of kin they know. In some cases they made every effort to give precise facts of genealogy and related information by referring to diaries, horoscopes, genealogies and other documents. Women were the storehouse of kin knowledge and were articulate in narrating genealogy. In some instances, Ego (male) to his surprise came to know for the first time through his wife or other female member in the family about the larger number of children of cousin A or affine B and the names of some relatives.

Women in Gokul, as in Kalyan, serve as pivotal kin in the kinship network of the household. Usually the oldest woman in each household can be considered as the mobile encyclopaedia of kin knowledge. In one instance a housewife remarked that I need a week's time to have a complete record of her family genealogy. There were practically no refusals to narrate genealogy from the mother's or wife's side even though they were quite conscious of the fact that they did not belong to their patrilineage.

As in Kalyan, in Gokul too, aged men and women possessed more knowledge of their kin. With the given age women excelled in the quantity and quality of kin knowledge. A woman married to a kinsman knew more of her husband's kin than the husband himself. Preferential kin marriage increases the knowledge of husband's kin on the part of the housewife. Both males and females voluntarily recalled kin in different branches of their genealogy and omissions were pointed out and ultimately a ramified genealogy emerged in each household. The enthusiasm, pleasure and pride in narrating genealogy was more visible in their overt behaviour among the Brahmans than among the Lingayats.

In assessing the range of kin knowledge it is relevant to take into account the demographic configuration of kin of each household. It was observed that the informants in some households had very few relatives and it was a biological fact over which Ego himself or herself had no control. The demographic variations of the kin group of each household present problems in comparing the range of kin knowledge of different households in the universe of study. During the entire period of collection of field data formal and informal visits were made to practically all the members in the two suburbs. This helped in establishing a wide range of contacts in Kalyan and Gokul. I could easily observe their household activities and interpersonal relationships among family members and extended kin.

Furthermore, my use of kinship terms in addressing them according to the sex and age of the respondents as required by the cultural milieu evoked more confidence in them in accepting me in their fictitious kin group which gradually led to the spontaneous narration of their experiences, pleasant and unpleasant.

Since our language was common I could feel the depth of their feelings for their kin while they were narrating their experiences. Often their intonation, emphasis and style of language carried rich meaning. The fact that there are some differences in the kinship terms, intonation and style of language of the people of Kalyan and Gokul could also easily be observed. Though they belong to the same cultural tradition they are in some respects different worlds in themselves.

The Plan of the Book

The chapter following on the milieu presents a brief historical background of the city, its geographical aspects, demography and social structure. It also outlines characteristics of the two suburbs under investigation. This chapter is to serve as a prelude not only to an understanding of the unique features of Dharwar but also of the kinship system delineated in the chapters that follow.

Chapters III through VII deal with kin knowledge, behaviour patterns, marriage, class and social mobility, law and welfare respectively. Since this is a comparative study of two caste groups, in each of these chapters the first part is concerned with the Lingayats of Kalyan suburb, and the second part is devoted to the Brahmans of Gokul. In the concluding chapter the major findings are summarized and a comparative review of some other family and kinship studies is made. In light of empirical data the questions raised at the beginning of the study were examined and tentative conclusions arrived at in order to provide a model of urban kin network in a modernizing society, and to prepare a basis for further rigorous research.

CHAPTER TWO

The Milieu

DHARWAR, a quiet little city in the north-west of Mysore state, India, is situated (15°29'N, 75°5'E) in a transitional belt where the Sahyadrian hilly landscape in the west merges with the undulating plain of black soil in the east. Within a few miles west of Dharwar, forests dominate the landscape. On account of its surroundings and its salubrious climate, Dharwar, built on several hillocks (average altitude 2,580 feet), is aptly known as a "little hill station". Apart from a few buildings visible at the top of the hillocks, much of Dharwar looks like a green grove with little immediate indication of its eighty thousand people.

Historical Background

Dharwar is the anglicised version of the original name of the town, "Daravada" or the "Gateway town". This name appropriately refers to its natural position as a gateway between the region of the hills and forest at one end and of plains at the other. The origin and early development of Dharwar are unknown. However, an inscription at the Durga temple in the Fort area of Dharwar refers to the later Chalukya monarch, Tribhuvanamalla-Vikramaditya VI. and is dated 1117 A.D. Other inscriptions from the twelfth century A.D. discovered in the neighbouring villages also mention the name of this town. They show that Dharwar formed a part of the province of Palasige. Archaeologists and historians also point out that as the earliest allusions to the geographical units of Palasige date approximately from the seventh century, "Daravada" probably originated in that century, if not earlier.[1]

In the past, Dharwar was an important fort because a commanding view of eastern plains could be obtained from the adjoining knoll. It is known for certain that in 1573, when the fifth Vijayapur King, Ali Adil Shah, marched on Dharwar, it was one of the strongest forts in Karnatak held by an officer of Ram Raja of Vijayanagar. After a siege of six months the fort of Dharwar and the surrounding country was annexed to the Vijayapur Kingdom. During subsequent centuries Dharwar and its surrounding areas became part of the territory of various Muslim, Moghul and Maratha rulers, and in 1817 passed on to the British from the Peshwa Kings of Poona.[2] The strategic position and the temperate climate of Dharwar led the British to select it as a station for British garrisons as well as the district headquarters of civil administration, and

---

1 Desai, P. B. *KHR*, vol. VIII, Nos. 1–2, 1957.
2 Gazetteer, 1959. pp. 80–100.

over the years its population and area steadily increased. Dharwar today reflects some of the traits of its stormy past, and its urban landscape is a product of its past and present functions.

Functional Zones

Geomorphologically, the city can be broadly demarcated into six functional zones: (i) the Old Town, (ii) the Fort, (iii) the commercial zone, (iv) the Civil Station, (v) the constellation of satellite villages, and (vi) the new suburbs.

The Old Town is situated to the east of Moti tank and displays an architecture dating back two centuries and more. The residential buildings have stone and mud walls covered with local tiles. Houses are crowded, sanitation is inadequate, streets are narrow, and the drainage system is far from satisfactory. There are temples and mosques with their imposing structures. Being a densely populated part of the city one can observe the concentration of different communities in different segments of the old town, which gives it a distinctive appearance.

The north-west of Old Town and Moti tank is now only a remnant of the Fort, said to have been built in 1403 A.D. It covers an area of 76 acres with an outside diameter of about 800 yards. The massive wooden doors of the granite-and-cement gateways still stand but cannot be shut.

The walls of the Fort reveal Hindu architecture but the gates are Islamic. The garrison buildings in the centre of the Fort are now part of the Civil hospital, the main government agency for public health service in the city. Near the Fort there are Hindu temples, a mosque, schools, and residential buildings which display British and indigenous influences mingling in a haphazard fashion and indicating the complexity of Dharwar's culture-history. Even today the fort retains its identity through the dilapidated walls, impressive gateways and a circular pattern of houses around the hillock.

The commercial zone lies in the west of the Old Town and is delimited by the Old Town, the Fort, and the Civil Station. The main market dominates this zone; commission agents and general merchants and dealers in cloth, stationery, foodgrains are found here. In addition, the vegetable, fruit and flower market, restaurants, drug stores, banks and book stores, publishing and tailoring firms, shoemarts and cinema theatres, the police station and bus station make this zone the scene of intense activity throughout the year.

An area with numerous trees and open spaces, formerly known as the European Civil Station, lies to the west of the commercial zone and is characterized by bungalows with designs of British origin, usually large buildings centrally situated in large compounds. During the period, 1818–1870, when the town was mainly a British military Cantonment, some of the oldest buildings in this area, like the Civil Judge's Court, Collectors' Offices and residence, the Basel Mission Church, the Mental Hospital, the Jail, the Borstal School and in due course, the Forest Offices, came into existence.

Between 1870–1914 there was a westward expansion of the city. The railway buildings, Training College, Dharwar Gymkhana and residential cottage were built. This period is believed to have probably been the climax of European influence on the Dharwar landscape. The "Anglicised" landscape of the city has been changing since 1914, and indigenous influences have been creeping in. Relocation of the railway offices, which coincided with the development of educational institutions, led to the opening of the first college in this area. Migration of the European population from Dharwar after Independence in August 1947 led to the transfer of their poperty to Indians. "Indianization" of the European Civil Station has resulted in construction of smaller houses, and its large compounds seem destined to disappear.

Besides schools and colleges of arts and science, the All-India Radio Broadcasting Station and also colleges of law and education have recently been established in the area of the former European civil station. Indeed, most educational and cultural activities of the city are centered in this area. Although the crowded Old Town now seems to be pressing into this hitherto "excluded territory", there are still large open spaces covered with many trees; usually, they are part and parcel of the administrative offices and are "parks" acting as "lungs" to preserve the public health of the city.

About seven furlongs north and north-west of the Old Town, there is a group of six satellite villages, separated from the Fort in the Old Town by open space. Eighty years ago the District Gazetteer recorded that in these villages:

...except about ten with tiles the houses are small and flat roofed. These villages were chiefly peopled by the Lingayat and Maratha husbandmen and labourers. There were ten or twelve houses of carpenters and as many more of blacksmiths and earthen-pot makers and though there were four or five retail-shops there was no large wholesale shop. However, a little trade in cotton was carried on in these villages.[3]

On the western fringe of the Civil Station there are two villages. But with the growth of the Civil Station these villages have lost their identity to a great extent. All these villages on the northern and western fringe form the suburbs of the city of Dharwar for purposes of corporation administration. However, the same rural setting persists.

In contrast to these suburbs with rural features, there are the "new suburbs", like Malmaddi, which came into being near the railway station in 1908, and is composed of a typical "middle class" population, mostly government officials. Northeast of the railway station is Saraswatpur, a colony of the Saraswat Community which sponsored cooperative housing estate. In these two suburbs, physical planning is relatively orderly and architecture is of the bungalow type, on a smaller scale. Unfortunately, Malmaddi's growth has been overwhelmed by buildings, big and small, and the suburb has lost its former symmetry and neatness, and the hope and promise of its earliest builders have nearly vanished.

South-east of the Old Town is Vidyagiri, another nucleus of educational

---

3 Gazetteer, 1884, p. 668.

institutions which has been developing over the last two decades. Colleges of arts, science, and law, the Institute of Engineering, the Institute of Economic Research, and Handicrafts Centre, are located in this area.

At the extreme south-west of the city, beyond the railway lines, is the fast developing university campus. On a series of hillocks, university buildings have been emerging year after year, and the past decade or so has altered the entire face of the campus. About two hundred million rupees have been spent so far on the construction of buildings in the university campus. For the Fourth Five Year Plan (1967–1971), it has development schemes requiring a total outlay of more than one million rupees. With its various massive and imposing buildings, the university campus attracts the attention of every visitor to the city and is the only suburb of Dharwar City that is planned, modern in design and appearance, and possesses most of the modern amenities.

South of the railway station a miniature industrial belt has been developed. Near the railway station is the plywood factory employing four hundred workers and close by is the wire manufacturing factory. There is a clock and watch manufacturing factory near the university. Plans for the installation of a paper mill are also in progress. Apart from the industrial establishments, Dharwar city has very little modern industry. It gives the appearance of a large village rather than a city, despite the fact that the pace of industrialization in recent years has been increasing.

The foregoing account of the geomorphology of Dharwar, viewed as a whole, presents a loosely woven structure. The Old Town, located on the east, has a closely knit rectangular pattern. The Fort area of the city still retains a circular pattern. Everywhere else, the city manifests a predominance of linear patterns which indicate the growth of the city along roads. Large open spaces in between the suburbs is an outstanding feature of the Dharwar landscape. Although the city promises to grow, it is unfortunate that in its plan and in its functions, Dharwar lacks a basic unity, and seems a collection of "period" pieces.[4]

Dharwar is located in an inland district surrounded by seven other districts. It is connected with all parts of India through modern means of transport and communications. A national highway passes through the city and the railway links it with numerous towns and cities all over the country. The aerodrome is within a distance of fifty miles north of Dharwar. Goa, the nearest seaport, is about a hundred miles west of the city. The Radio Broadcasting station at Dharwar beams its programmes to the people of this region.

As for entertainment, there are four cinema houses which screen Indian films every day, with weekends reserved for English films. Occasionally touring theatres and cultural organizations present drama, dance and music. Because of its educational and cultural activities, Dharwar has its own distinct personality. Estate holders and retired government officials, poets and professionals have established their homes in this city, not only because it is a centre of education

---

4   Prabhu, V. R., *BGM*, vol. 1. No. 1, 1953.

and administration but also because it is a place with sylvan settings and quiet surroundings.

Dharwar, the cultural nucleus of the region, is a city of curious contrasts.[5] Its Old Town, its medieval Fort, the newly developed western part of the city much influenced by British administration, its satellite villages in the northern and southern fringes, and its new suburbs make Dharwar a quaint city, old and modern, administrative and educational, stagnant and growing: an instance of both change and continuity.

Demography

According to the census of 1872, the population of Dharwar was 27,136: 19,836 Hindus, 6,707 Muslims, 493 Christians and ten others. The 1881 census showed a population of 27,191: 19,709 Hindus, 6,545 Muslims, 618 Christians, 271 Jains, 24 Parsis and 24 others. In 1881 in the entire district of Dharwar there were 28,395 Brahmans, that is, 3.46 percent of the Hindu population, and 300,000 Lingayats, that is, 38.47 percent of the Hindus. Since recent census reports do not provide caste-wise population figures it is extremely difficult to know the population size of each caste.

The table below shows the rate at which the population increased in Dharwar during the last one hundred years.

Table 2

Population of Dharwar

Census Year	Total Population	Population Increase
1872	27,136	
1881	27,191	
1901	31,279	
1941	47,992	
1951	66,571	+ 18,579
1961	77,163	+ 10,592
1971	129,996	+ 52,833

During 1881–1951, that is, within a period of seventy years, the population of the city increased by 39,380. This growth in population was evidently due to an increase in the number of district administrative offices and educational institutions. The economic activities of the city, such as trade and non--agricultural production, seem to be the by-product of consumer demand of a typically non-industrial urban centre. The average density in Dharwar is now already twice as great as in many cities of comparable population. According to the 1961 Census, out of the fifteen cities in Mysore State with a population of more

---

5 Gazetteer, 1959.

than 50,000, there were six cities with a population of more than 100,000. Out of the nine cities in the State whose population ranges from 50,000 to less than 100,000, Dharwar city occupied the fourth place. But with the formation of a single Corporation on 1st March, 1962 for the twin cities of Dharwar and Hubli, the latter being a commercial and industrial city at a distance of ten miles, the total population of the mono-city Corporation was 248,489.

During 1941–51 the city population increased by 18,579, mainly due to postwar and post-independence development. During the decade, 1951–1961, the population of the city increased by 10,592. The biggest increase in population was during 1961–1971 decade. Expansion of educational institutions, government offices and industries, inclusion of nearby villages within city corporation limits, and migration of population from rural areas are some of the major forces contributing to rapid population growth.

The Social Map

Hindus, Muslims and Christians form the major religious groups in Dharwar. Hindus, who are in an overwhelming majority, are divided into twenty caste groups, each of them being further divided into 10 to 15 subcastes.[6] Social life in Dharwar is based on the caste system. Of the several castes in the city, numerically the two most prominent ones, namely Brahmans and Lingayats, hold key positions in economic, political, educational and cultural activities.

Brahmans follow the traditional Brahmanic culture of Hinduism in its major elements, whereas Lingayats practise an offshoot of Shaivism, which differs from Hinduism in theory, at least, in certain religious and social aspects. Both have been responding to "modernism". As it emerged in the twelfth century A.D., Lingayatism (also known as Veerashaivism) influenced numerous heterogeneous lower caste groups which later embraced its practices.[7] This is evident in the prevalence of some non-Brahmanic cultural characteristics in the contemporary Lingayat community.

The membership of each of these two castes is normally decided by birth. Both are endogamous and both are segmented into several subcastes which are, again, endogamous by themselves. Among the Lingayats of Kalyan, there are ten subcastes which are hierarchically arranged amongst themselves, and each of these subcastes still continue to be endogamous with very few exceptions of intersubcaste marriages. The Brahmans of Gokul are divided into three subcastes which are hierarchically arranged. The Brahman subcastes are traditionally endogamous, but today there is a faint tendency favouring intersubcaste marriages.

Traditionally, Brahmans are priests and teachers; Lingayats are farmers and traders in the main, though each subcaste among Lingayats is further

---

6   Census figures of castes are unavailable. Census of India collects figures on religion and scheduled castes only. For the list of subcastes in the two suburbs under study please refer to Appendix ii.

7   Chekki, D. A., *JUB*, 1958.

associated with an occupation of its own. For instance, there are subcastes of traders, washermen, weavers, tailors, oilpressers and barbers among Lingayats.

Brahmans occupy the highest position in the caste hierarchy. Lingayats claim equality with Brahmans although they were once classified by British courts as Shudras. Lingayats and Brahmans have different sets of ritual norms. Relations between these two castes are governed, among other things, by the norms of purity and pollution, and the maximum commensality occurs within each caste. Lingayats and Brahmans, who are localized in certain regions of Mysore State, show nuances in their dress and diet, customs and manners, fasts and festivals, language and values.

Although Brahmans and Lingayats are both "castes", anthropologists, Indologists, sociologists and some conservative Lingayat scholars consider Lingayats variably as a sect, a caste and a religious group. Enthoven[8] recorded that the Lingayats of today present the curious and interesting spectacle of a religious sect broken in the course of centuries into social fragments, of which the older sections remain essentially sectarian and the more recent in origin possess the typical attributes of ordinary Hindu castes. Bhandarkar and others consider Lingayats a sect. Max Weber[9] and Hutton[10] expressed the view that Lingayats are the example par excellence of a religious group becoming a caste.

Hindu law, which is applicable to Lingayats with regard to marriage, inheritance and adoption, does not clearly distinguish between caste and sect. Courts of law during the British period in India recognized all Lingayats as members of a single caste. Even after Independence, the codified Hindu law considers Lingayats as Hindus—obviously as one of the many castes that form "Hinduism". McCormack[11] considers Lingayats in an "interactional framework" of caste relations, thus a caste. Irrespective of Lingayat ideologies, the Lingayat group, as it exists in contemporary Indian society, bears the main features of caste.

Each Lingayat subcaste, which for all practical purposes is endogamous, is subdivided into various exogamous groups, known as *bedagu* or *bagi* which in turn may be further subdivided into several *vamsha* (lineages). Endogamous subcastes among Brahmans are subdivided into exogamous *gotra*. The chief function of these exogamous groups is to regulate marital relationships. Lingayats and Brahmans prohibit marriages between persons of the same exogamous group and patrilineage.

Each exogamous group bears a distinct name which either indicates a sage of the ancient times or is totemic in character and functions as an exogamous clan. All persons who belong to the same exogamous group have the belief

---

8   Enthoven, "Lingayats" in Encyclopaedia of Religion & Ethics, (ed.), Hastings vol. 8. pp. 69–75.
9   Weber, Max, 1958, p. 21.
10   Hutton, 1946, p. 103.
11   McCormack, W. *JRAI*, vol. 93, pt. I, Jan.-Jun. 1963, p. 29.

that they are the descendants of the same ancestor and hence avoid marital alliances.

Despite their divisions into subcastes, Lingayats and Brahmans are considered by others as distinct groups based on their respective castes rather than subcastes. Caste members consciously share certain common values which they do not share with non-members and become aware of this when they come into contact with members of castes other than their own. Common beliefs, attitudes, and strong community sentiment that prevail among Lingayats and Brahmans, separate them into two distinct communities and help them maintain social distance with other neighbouring caste groups as well. By and large, Lingayats and Brahmans, have closer associations and deeper sympathies with members of their own community. Their sentiments, friendship and visiting relationships, etc., function along caste lines despite social interaction and interdependence of different caste groups.

Dharwar is an educational center, and the following table indicates the different types of educational institutions in the city in 1962.

Table 3

Schools Primary	Secondary	Colleges	Institutes	University	Total
36	12	12	4	1	65

Students and teachers form a recognizable portion of the population of Dharwar. The growth of the city can be attributed partly to the development of educational institutions. Since the establishment of the University in 1949, Dharwar has become the nerve-centre of educational activities of the surrounding region.

According to the 1961 Census[12] out of the total population of 77,163, the total working population is 22,017, Of the working population, 3,620 are engaged in agriculture as cultivators, agricultural labourers or in other allied activities. Another 10,106 are engaged in non-agricultural occupations such as household industries, manufacturing, construction, trade and commerce, transport and communications and the like, whereas 8,291 are engaged in other services mainly in government service and private enterprise. It is quite evident that a majority of the workers are associated with non-agricultural occupations, while nearly half are in government offices, educational institutions and in the professions like law and medicine. With the expansion of governmental welfare activities since Independence the number of persons engaged in government services has increased. The number of persons following the professions like law, medicine and education has also increased to a great extent. Detailed figures of 1971 Census (1973) are still unavailable.

---

12   Census of India, 1961, Paper No. 1 of 1962. p. 216.

Kalyan

Kalyan, a suburb on the northern fringe of Dharwar, is sandwiched between two neighbourhoods in the east and west. The settlement presents the pattern of closely built small houses of sundried bricks or stones, with small windows and narrow streets where only one-way traffic is possible. Inadequate drainage contributes to the pollution of soil and air. Civic amenities such as running water and electricity, though made available, are not within the reach of many people in Kalyan.

Kalyan has a primary school, three temples, two small tea-shops and two grocery stores where a few things needed for daily consumption are available. There is a Cooperative Credit Society and also a post-box. Its population is mainly engaged in or supported by agriculture. Kalyan's rural look may be more apparent than real because the inhabitants here have taken up urban employment. There is also intensification of farming in response to the heavy demand of city dwellers for fresh vegetables, fruits, and milk. Hence, Kalyan is primarily a peasant community with a settled agricultural population.

Kalyan, the tradition-bound peasant community, while retaining the old ways of life, is integrating new traits into its relatively stable cultural pattern. Exposed to urban influences it forms a part of the larger political unit of state and nation.

Gokul

Gokul, a suburb in the old town of Dharwar and adjacent to the commercial zone of the city is inhabited predominently by Brahmans. Close to the hub of city life Gokul has easy access to the main shopping centre.

Built of stones and mortar, houses in Gokul stand close in almost parallel rows and are larger than those in Kalyan. Roads are wider and run almost in a straight line. Although at first sight houses in Gokul look alike, they have a considerable variety in design, whitewash and upkeep. For instance, some of them with distinct types of doors, windows and balconies remind us of the dwelling patterns which were prevalent in 19th Century Dharwar.

As a stronghold of Brahmans, Gokul has four temples and a *math* (religious establishment). Most of the religious activities of Brahmans are centered in this area. There are three primary schools, a post office, and three dispensaries. There are a few shops and restaurants, and most of the customers are local inhabitants. Many residents of Gokul, however, patronize the nearby "big" stores and restaurants in Dharwar.

The physical and social structure of this urban community still manifests traditional forms. There are the same old buildings inhabited by Brahmans. The occupations of the people, however, are non-traditional because they are characteristically urban. In contrast to Kalyan, Gokul's population is wholly non-agricultural.

Although Gokul is densely populated, its roads are normally not crowded and indeed a casual observer may find it rather desolate. However, closer observation reveals that the place is full of people and activities in which old values mingle with the new. With centuries of distinct physical and social heritage Gokul appears to be a symbol of the past, the mirror of the present, and may serve as a radar indicating the future of the Dharwar region. The following analysis deals with the size of the household, the composition and the type of family, education and occupation of respondents in Kalyan and Gokul.

Table 4

Size of Household

Number of Persons	Kalyan	Percent	Gokul	Percent
1	1	0.87	2	1.74
2–4	31	26.96	31	26.96
5–7	53	46.00	53	46.00
8–10	20	17.30	19	16.52
11–13	7	6.00	5	4.35
14–16	1	0.87	3	2.61
17–19	1	0.87	2	1.74
20 and over	1	0.87	—	—
Total	115	100.00	115	100.00

The highest percentage of households ranges between five and seven persons, followed by 2–4, and by households of 8–10 persons. Since the majority of the households are composed of five to seven persons such a household can be considered as the average size of the family in Dharwar.

Households can be classified as a nuclear family or a non-nuclear family.

Table 5

Family Types

Household Types	Kalyan	Gokul
Nuclear Family	49	43
Non-nuclear	66	72
Total	115	115

The nuclear family is composed of a man and his wife and their unmarried children. In this sense there are more nuclear families in Kalyan than in Gokul. The non-nuclear family is composed of members other than and in addition to the members of the nuclear family. The category non-nuclear family includes extended families and broken families.

Therefore it would be meaningful to classify non-nuclear families into extended family and broken family. The extended family may be extended vertically consisting of 3 or more generations or extended horizontally.

In the extended family Ego stays with members other than and in addition to the members of his or her elementary family, whereas a broken family, for the purpose of the study, is one where Ego is a widower or widow or divorcee or even on reaching menopause has no child or lacks a male child.

Table 6

Non-nuclear Family Types

Suburbs	Extended	Broken
Kalyan	42	24
Gokul	53	19

There are more non-nuclear families in Gokul than in Kalyan. Extended families are more prominent in Gokul than in Kalyan, whereas there are more broken families in Kalyan than in Gokul.

The following table indicates the composition of non-nuclear families.

Table 7

Composition of Families

Ego staying with	Kalyan	Gokul
Married Brothers	12	10
Married Sons	24	12
Widowed Mothers	19	15
Widowed Sisters	4	5
Widowed Daughters	2	2
Parents	2	5
Other relatives	3	23
Total Households	66	72

In the case of 24 households in Kalyan, Ego is staying with married sons. Here boys marry at the average age of 20 and stay with parents to help in agricultural activities. In Gokul men marry at the average age of 25 and by that time economic exigencies usually lead to spatial mobility. Hence in 12 cases Ego stays with married sons in Gokul. The number of cases where Ego stays with married brother and with mother, sister or daughter who are widows is as indicated in Table 7 is not significantly different in both suburbs. In Kalyan, the number of households where Ego is staying with married sons tops the list followed by households with widowed mothers and married brothers respectively. In Gokul, however, the maximum number of households are those where Ego stays with "other relatives".

The literacy and education of the respondents of Kalyan and Gokul is compared in the following table.

Table 8

Literacy and Education of Respondents

Levels of Education	Kalyan	Percent	Gokul	Percent
Illiterate	60	52.17	1	.87
Primary	40	34.78	23	20.00
Secondary	11	9.57	60	52.17
College	4	3.48	28	24.35
University	—	——	3	2.61
Total	115	100.00	115	100.00

52.17 percent of the people of Kalyan are illiterate. But there was only one old widow of 85 years who was illiterate among primary respondents in Gokul. As primarily a peasant community the people of Kalyan do not feel the necessity of formal education. However, with the increasing influence of modernism 34.78 percent have received primary education and 9.57 per cent secondary education. Hardly 3.48 percent have received college education.

In Gokul, however, there is universal literacy. Of these, 52.17% have received secondary education, 24.35% have received college education, and 2.61%, university education. Such striking differences in literacy and education between Kalyan and Gokul are no doubt reflected in their way of life, outlook and attitudes of the people.

Occupations

Just as there is a wide gulf in the educational attainments of the people in both suburbs there are also differences in occupational structure.

Table 9

Occupation of Respondents

| | Kalyan | | Gokul | |
	Respondents	Percent	Respondents	Percent
I. Agricultural				
Rent Receiver	2	1.74	10	8.70
Owner Cultivator	50	43.47	—	——
Tenant	4	3.48	—	——
Labourer	14	12.17	—	——
II. Non-Agricultural				
Trade and Professions	12	10.44	24	20.88
Clerks	4	3.48	30	26.08
Other Services				
(Govt. & Non-Govt.)	4	3.48	15	23.04
Blue-collar workers	15	13.04	—	——
Retired	10	8.70	17	14.78
Miscellaneous	—	——	19	16.22
Total	115	100.00	115	100.00

In Kalyan, of the 60.86% who pursue agriculture 43.47% are owner-cultivators and 12.17% are agricultural labourers. 13.04% are employed in the urban establishments especially in the lower cadres as janitors and manual labourers. Those in Government and private service, and those working as teachers and clerks are relatively few in number. 6.70% of them are engaged in trade and there is none in professions like law and medicine. However about 30% of the respondents are employed in urban occupations.

In Gokul, however, 8.70% of them are agricultural rent receivers or land-lords. The majority of respondents (49.12%) are in clerical and other government and private services. Of those, 20.88% are in the category of trades and professions, 9.57% constitute teachers of the secondary schools, and 11.31% are in various modern professions such as law, medicine, and engineering. It is evident that more than 90% of the respondents in Gokul are actively engaged in the non-agricultural urban occupations.

The two hundred and thirty households may be classified into three social classes on the basis of annual income, education and occupational prestige. The lower class consists of families earning less than 3000 rupees per annum, the head of the household having primary education and an occupation having lower prestige ranking in the community. The middle class includes families with an income ranging from 3000 to 7,999 rupees, the head of the household having secondary and in some cases, a few years of college education. Men in the middle class pursue occupations which generally possess higher prestige than the lower class occupations but less prestige when compared to the upper class occupations. The annual income of the upper class families range from 8,000 rupees to 15,000 and over. Generally the heads of households had college and university education and their occupation commanded higher prestige than the middle class occupations. Though income levels are not necessarily class levels they can be rough indicators of social class. As a rule the higher the income the higher the occupational prestige tends to be. But this correlation is by no means perfect since there are a few exceptions. Differences in occupational prestige, life-styles, and life-chances seem to be crucial.

Table 10

Households and Class

Classes	Kalyan	Percent	Gokul	Percent	Both Suburbs	Percent
Upper class	12	10.43	23	20.00	35	30.43
Middle class	74	64.35	72	62.61	146	126.96
Lower class	29	25.22	20	17.39	49	42.61
Total	115	100.00	115	100.00	230	200.00

Table 10 indicates that in each suburb an overwhelming majority of households, that is, more than 62% belong to the middle class. Of the households 20% in Gokul and 10.43% in Kalyan belong to the upper class. There are more lower class households in Kalyan (25.22%) than in Gokul (17.39%). The present study, based on a large majority of middle class households, tends to reflect middle class values, norms, and behaviour. However, the upper and lower classes have also been represented in our investigation.

Kalyan is mainly a cluster of twelve patrilineages. Several families of the same lineage usually form a neighbourhood, and some streets are named after the patrilineages. People are very conscious of their patrilineage and kin group. In Gokul there are four lineages with relatively limited ramifications in the same locality. Though the lineage members are scattered spatially, there appears to be a feeling of closeness.

The family in Kalyan occupies a traditional type of single-storied house without any front or backyard, the main entrance almost touching the road and the sidewalls always serving as common walls to adjacent houses. In most of the houses there is on the right side a raised platform normally used for storage of grains, and on another side the shed for livestock and agricultural implements. Floors are plastered with cow dung and walls whitewashed. Pictures of gods and goddesses are usually hung on the walls. Rarely one finds photographs of family members and relatives. Sometimes the front portion serves also as a parlour where a cradle and articles of embroidery are found. Inside the parlour is the living room which is also used as bedroom or there is sometimes a separate bedroom-cum-storeroom. Often the kitchen and bathroom are together. But there is always a separate place of worship. Earthen vessels, a few brass utensils, cups and saucers constitute their kitchen equipment.

In Gokul, though the family occupies a traditional type of single storied house, double storied houses are not rare. Some houses have a small front or backyard. In contrast to those in Kalyan, residential quarters in Gokul do not possess a livestock shed. The interior of the house is relatively neat and clean. In the parlour there are usually two or three chairs, a table, a bench, easy chairs, a cupboard, and a bookshelf. Adjacent to it is the bedroom and close to it is a storeroom. There is another room or hall used for dining and kitchen. The bathroom and place of worship are separate. Sacred verses in praise of god are written in bold letters at the main entrance, and pictures of gods and goddesses and national leaders are hung on the walls together with a number of individual and group photographs of family members and relatives. Articles of embroidery are also artistically displayed, reflecting in the interior decoration the aesthetic sense of the people of Gokul. Brass and copper vessels are kept clean and shining.

About 4% of the households in Kalyan get daily newspapers. 43.47% of the households in Gokul subscribe to daily newspapers as well as monthly or weekly periodicals. In Kalyan only 8.70% of the households possess radio sets but in Gokul 34.78% of the households have radios. Possession of a radio in Kalyan is in itself a symbolic display of one's wealth and social status whereas in Gokul it is not.

The people of Kalyan seem to have a relatively higher degree of community sentiment. They know one another better and constitute an effective social group. The sense of communal unity is manifested in times of marriages, festivals and funerals. In Gokul the sense of belonging and community feeling are expressed on various religious and social ceremonies. Most of the activities revolve around hearth and home, and men and women meet freely in sacred and secular matters almost every evening, on Sundays and on religious festivals. While the women folk actively participate in religious and social events, exchanging news and views on domestic and community affairs, men meet and talk more about the economic, social and political problems of wider ramifications. The foregoing description and analysis of the life of these communities sets the stage for a better understanding of the kinship system.

CHAPTER THREE

Structure of Kin Knowledge

THE PURPOSE of this chapter is to analyze the structure of kin knowledge among the Lingayats of Kalyan and the Brahmans of Gokul. We are concerned with questions such as these: How many and what sorts of kin are known? What is the quality of kin knowledge? The description and analysis of kin knowledge is a prelude to an understanding of the dynamics of social relations based on consanguinity and affinity. However before we present the structure of kin knowledge a brief introduction to the concept of kinship and kinship terminology is in order.

The Lingayats often use the term *Kallu(Karul)balli* for kinship which literally means "creeper of love" and the Brahmans use the term *Bandhu-Balaga* or only *Balaga* meaning "brothers and relatives" or only "relative" for the same referant, "kin", which includes both consanguines and affines. Both castes do distinguish affines from consanguines with the term *Beegaru*, which refers to affines exclusively. Since both castes practise bilateral cross-cousin marriage and uncle-niece marriages, it is difficult to distinguish the consanguines and affines. The difference between relationships is blurred, and they frequently merge. Preferential mating is reflected in the kinship system by the fact that there are no separate terms for affines. A detailed list of kinship terms appears in Appendix (i); at this point only a few important kinship terms will be presented.

Relatives younger than Ego are usually addressed by name and those who are older by appropriate kinship terms. Siblings are classified by their age relative to the speaker as *Anna* (elder brother) and *Tamma* (younger brother) and *Akka* (elder sister) and *tangi* (younger sister). Likewise, parents' siblings are classified as *Doddappa* (big father) and *Chikkappa* (little father), *Doddavva* (big mother) and *Chikkavva* (little mother). There is no generic term for brother or sister.

The kinship terms not only suggest cross-cousin marriages but a dual system so that the term *Atte* for the wife of MoBr is the same as that for FaSi and WiMo. So also MoBr, FaSiHu, wife's or husband's father are grouped together as *Mava*, although the first two are distinguished as *Sodar-mava*. Similarly, FaSi and MoBrWi are distinguished as *Sodar-atte* while WiMo is called only *Atte*.

Separate sets of terms are found for each of the three generations ascending from Ego but not beyond that. The terms for grandfather *Ajja* or grandmother *Amma* or *Ajji* are the same whether they are father's parents or mother's parents. There are no grand-uncles and grand-aunts. *Bhava* (if elder) and *Maiduna* (if younger) are used for male and female cross-cousins respectively. Terms like *Aliya* (nephew) and *Sose* (niece) are also used for cross-nephews and sons-in-law, and cross-nieces and daughters-in-law respectively. *Maga* (son) and *Magalu* (daughter) are terms used both for one's own children, BrChi, WiSiChi (man speaking), and SiChi and HuBrChi (woman speaking).

Kalyan

Professional genealogists (*Helava*) visit all Lingayat households in Kalyan once a year or at least once in two years. They recite the names of ancestors of each household. Only four Lingayat households studied here record their genealogies themselves; others depend on professional genealogists. The records usually contain genealogical tables, dates of births, deaths, marriages of members of the household, horoscopes, purchases of movable and immovable property, names of family gods and the names of a chain of priests associated with the family, and other details. Only details about agnates, i.e. patrilineage, are recorded and even in the father's line females are discarded. In one exceptional case among the four households mentioned above, up to the eighth ascending generation from Ego (Diagram 1), but in the third and fourth ascending generations, only two males in each of these generations were mentioned. The rest of the three households preserved genealogy up to the third ascending generation. None of these showed female kin in the purely agnatic line and none maintained genealogies from the wife's side, mother's side and married daughter's side. These crucial aspects of genealogical records give us an idea of the importance of patrilineage.

Among all the Lingayat households studied, the greatest depth in an exceptional example was found with eleven generations in all, eight ascending generations and two descending generations plus Ego's own generation. Normally the depth is six generations in all, that is, usually three generations ascendant and two generations descendant from Ego.

There is differentiation in the intensity of kin awareness. The average adult does not know the names of all his kin. Even if all the persons are known to be kin, contacts are not maintained in the same way or it may be that they are not treated with the same intimacy and affection. Sometimes an individual may not know the names of children of a relative residing at a distant place, but their sex may be known. Sometimes even the sex is not known, although they may be recognised as kin. These kin whose name is currently not known may in future enter into a more effective and active relationship and then may be known by name and intimacy may develop. The category "recognised kin" as indicated by Firth[1] is made up of all persons who are recognised by the informant as related to him by consanguinity or affinity, whether known by name or not.

Recognised kin is composed of two categories: named and unnamed kin.

---

1 Firth, R., 1956, p. 42.

Named kin may be further divided into effective and non-effective kin. Effective kin are those with whom social contact is maintained by visits, services, attendance at family social and religious ceremonies, exchange of gifts or correspondence. Non-effective kin are those kin who are recognized to be geneologically related, but with whom no contact of any kind is maintained, though contact may be initiated or revived in future. In the category of effective kin it is possible to distinguish "intimate kin" and "non-intimate" or "peripheral" kin. Intimate kin are those with whom contact tends to be purposeful, close and frequent. Non-intimate or peripheral kin are those with whom contact tends to be casual or accidental, distant and sporadic.[2]

The total number of recognized kin, named and unnamed kin in the fourteen genealogies of Kalyan, used for detailed analysis in this study, are given in the following table.

Table 11

Genealogy	Recognized kin	Named kin	Unnamed kin	Depth of Generations
I	226	191	35	5
II	140	88	52	5
III	266	174	92	6
IV	183	136	47	5
V	314	216	98	6
VI	140	119	21	6
VII	253	139	114	6
VIII	397	266	131	6
IX	261	217	44	8
X	141	129	12	11
XI	170	146	24	5
XII	324	228	96	6
XIII	260	154	106	6
XIV	186	142	44	6
Total	3,261	2,345	916	

The total kin recognised in the 14 genealogies range from a minimum of 140 to a maximum of 397. The number of unnamed kin ranges between 12 and 131, the average unnamed kin being 65.43 where the average depth of generations is six. In the genealogies VII, VIII and XIII, where the number of unnamed kin is more than 100, old age and loss of memory of Ego, loss of kin contacts, wider spatial distribution of kin, a great number of newborn children, were responsible for the narrow span of memory. By and large, the number of unnamed kin implies kin with whom one has no contact and they are non-effective at the time. When Ego is male he does not normally remember the names of females and children who are secondary and tertiary relatives even though there is close kin relationship. All named kin may not be in effective

---

2 Firth, R. et al, 1970, pp. 155–156.

contact with Ego's family. Out of a total of 2,502 living kin in 14 genealogies taken up for detailed study, 28.09% kin are unnamed.

Analysis of genealogies of 14 households revealed knowledge of ascendants' names as given in the following table.

Table 12

Knowledge of Ancestors (Kalyan)

Ego's Patrilineage		Ego's matrilineage		Ego's spouse's patrilineage	
FaFa	14 Cases	MoFa	11 Cases	Spouse's Fa	13 Cases
FaMo	12 Cases	MoMo	10 Cases	Spouse's Mo	13 Cases
FaFaFa	7 Cases	MoFaFa	1 Case	Spouse's FaFa	2 Cases
FaFaMo	3 Cases	MoFaMo	1 Case	Spouse's FaMo	2 Cases

It should be stressed that names of relatives are not remembered in isolation. Ego's knowledge of names of kin is closely interlinked with kinship status and roles that go along with each relative known to him or her. More often than not, within one's own kin network names of persons are remembered not as individuals *per se* but as kin with specific rights and obligations. Though knowledge of names is generally not the same as knowledge of kin in so far as Ego's kin knowledge is concerned, kinship status is more significant and meaningful than just names of persons. However, if one does not know the name of a kin it may suggest Ego's lack of contact with or lack of interest in that unnamed kin.

The knowledge of ascendant's names in the second and third generation is greater in the patrilineage. This is due to the fact that patrikin form territorial, descent and inheritance groups in Kalyan. Next in line is the knowledge of names of ascendants of spouse which can be reasonably expected because of the greater knowledge of kin of the housewife as regards her own patrilineage. These data present a strong paternal orientation followed closely by the knowledge of affines. The relative lack of knowledge of maternal ascendants may be due to an absence of territorial contiguity of residence, early death and lack of contacts with mother's kin or because of the fact that the mother's property is not inherited. Nevertheless, the kinship system of Lingayats is matral in action and in sentiment. That is, Ego and siblings are in intimate contact more with MoFa, MoBr, MoSi and their children, than with father's parents and siblings.

In agreement with a three generation depth from the informant, the limit of the consanguineal kin range is normally Ego's third cousin. The study of genealogies reveals that 7 out of 14 knew the name of their FaFaFa but only 2 knew the name of their FaFaMo. All 14 informants knew the name of their FaFa but 2 of them could not remember the name of their FaMo. In the maternal line of ascendants, 3 did not know the names of MoFa, 4 did not know the names of MoMo, only one knew the name of MoFaFa and one the name of MoFaMo. On the affinal side, interestingly enough, one informant did not know the name of his WiFa and another that of his WiMo because of child marriage and early death of parents-in-law. Only two informants knew the name of their WiFaFa and WiFaMo. Exceptional as these cases were it was mostly due to a series of cousin marriages generation after generation and also because of the special interest of the informants. The foregoing discussion brings out clearly the fact that knowledge of paternal kin is greater than maternal kin and it decreases sharply in the case of affines.

The people of Kalyan are aware of the lateral categories of kin. In most cases Ego is aware of the third cousin and, in rare instances, even of the fourth cousin in the paternal line. Whereas in the case of maternal kin and affinals the knowledge reaches up to two degrees removed.

Kinship knowledge extends laterally to the greatest extent within one's own generation provided the informant is relatively young. But ten of the 14 informants are in the age group of 50–85. Hence the knowledge of kin for the generation below, that is the first descending line, is deeper. This reflects greater interest of the Ego in his immediate descendants. Knowledge of kin decreases in the second and the third descending line as they comprise a majority of children, whose numbers are still increasing with new births; it also diminishes for the generation above, because its numbers are decreasing through death and lack of contact. Women especially possess vast kin knowledge of ascendants and of descendants because of their interest and participation in the events such as births, marriages and deaths.

Not only the generation depth and the lateral extension of kin knowledge but also the actual number of recognised kin are important. The total number of recognised kin in the kin universe of any household is usually more than a hundred and forty. In those 14 households the range of kin knowledge varied between 140 and 397, with an average figure of 232.93. These figures are

Table 13

Depth of Generations and Lateral Distribution-Kalyan

Households Generations	I	II	III	IV	V	VI	VII	VIII	IX	X	XI	XII	XIII	XIV
8th Ascending										1				
7th Ascending										1				
6th Ascending										1				
5th Ascending										1				
4th Ascending	—	—	—	—	—	—	—	—	—	2	—	—	—	—
3rd Ascending	—	2	2	—	—	2	2	4	4	2	—	2	—	—
2nd Ascending	2	5	6	6	6	4	34	12	13	6	6	20	4	4
1st Ascending	40	20	34	30	30	24	76	79	32	19	21	64	29	19
Ego	98	64	53	53	57	51	88	138	52	37	47	135	84	23
1st Descending	81	49	91	62	105	56	51	151	85	48	81	97	89	56
2nd Descending	5	—	80	32	99	1	2	13	53	29	15	6	47	72
3rd Descending	—	—	—	—	17	—	—	—	20	—	—	—	7	12
4th Descending	—	—	—	—	—	—	—	—	2	—	—	—	—	—
Total	266	140	268	183	314	140	253	397	261	147	170	324	260	186

merely indicators of their knowledge of kin. Table 13 presents the depth of generations and lateral distribution of kin.

In the four instances in which the knowledge of kin is most extensive in Ego's own generation, as in household I, II, VII, XII, it can be explained as being due either to the fact that Ego is relatively young in age or where Ego's own generation members predominate without enough progeny or Ego has lost contact with the descending generation. Often it is a biological phenomenon reflected in the genealogy. When the consanguinal and affinal kin lived in the same city or in nearby villages, Ego and other household members remembered more number of kin than when they were residing relatively far off.

The inclusion of dead kin among those mentioned in the genealogy has several functions. Firth remarks that "Memory of the dead kin is part of the social personality of an informant, the dead serve as a focus for sentiment; they are links of justification for active social ties with other kin."[3] Although the genealogical material collected contains some reference to dead kin, most of the informants were rather hesitant to revive the memories of dear ones especially in Ego's own and in the descending generation. Mainly because of the premature deaths of some of their kin, respondents felt unhappy to mention names, especially of their own children. Of the 3,261 kin mentioned in a set of genealogies from 14 households, 759 or approximately 23% were dead kin. Most of the dead kin mentioned were in the ascending generations, mostly consanguines; others were in Ego's own generation who had active social relations with Ego's family. The majority of the dead were of the "link" or "channel" type, and they were remembered for reasons relevant at least apparently to utilitarian aspects of maintaining social relations. The percentage of such kin was considerably higher in the families with the largest number of kin.

We should consider these figures of dead kin as socially significant rather than genealogically accurate. It is evident here that just as biological paternity is less important than social paternity, so also is biological death less important than social death.[4]

Pivotal Kin

In Kalyan women, both young and old, showed intimate knowledge of the wider kinship universe of the household and their latest events. The women may be described as the pivotal kin and they knew both consanguines and affines of the husband's family besides being the sole expert on the genealogy of their parental families. Increased number of cross-cousin marriages and SiDa-MoBr marriages made women main representatives from two different kin groups.

The patrinominal principle of kin grouping wherein a wife takes the sur-

---

3 Firth, R., 1956, p. 38.
4 Ibid, p. 39.

name of her husband and the children take the surname of their father gives a frame of reference to the formation of distinct kin groups. Rights, privileges, laws and regulations, customs and conventions go with a particular surname, in regard to marriage, maintenance, succession, and applications of various laws to individuals.

Such a kinship grouping has special reference to the decisive role of the mother in the functioning of kinship. She acts as a bridge between her conjugal family of procreation and her parental family of orientation on the one hand and her conjugal family and her daughter's conjugal family on the other.

Traditionally legal rights of inheritance of property and rules of descent are associated with partilineage. There has been a major emphasis on jural aspects of relationships among patrikin. However, in the kinship system of Kalyan with the mother as key figure, the strong emotional ties, social contacts and mutual help is manifested between mother and children. So long as there is the mother, all married daughters often cluster. When the mother, who acts as the central planet, dies the kin constellation disintegrates. Then we may call the kinship system of Lingayats dominantly "matri-centered" or "matral" in action, and in sentiment.

The genealogical material indicates the tendency toward more knowledge of paternal kin than maternal kin, but there is greater intimacy and sentimental attachment with maternal kin. When children go to their mother's parental family they are geneologically merged with the mother's father's kin group. They are known and referred to collectively by the surname of MoFa and recognized as his grandchildren. Such kin "aggregates" or the naming of kinship "sets", as Firth puts it, may change according to social purpose and place of a gathering.

It is natural that no two members of the same household have the same knowledge of their kin because of difference in upbringing, kin contacts and personal affiliations. The frequency of inter-kin marriages is another influencing factor in the knowledge of kin. Inter-kin marriages to a greater extent reduce the distinctions between patrilineal and matrilineal kin.

To summarize, the people of Kalyan possess knowledge of kin with an average depth of six generations with a greater lateral range of recognition. Knowledge of the average number of recognized kin, named kin and ancestors in the patrilineage is great. Knowledge of paternal kin is greater than that of maternal kin, and knowledge of affines is less than that of maternal kin. The majority of dead kin mentioned were of the "link" type. Women have more kin knowledge than men. Residential nearness of relatives increases kin knowledge whereas geographical distance normally reduces the range of kin knowledge. The higher the social contracts among kin and greater the frequency of inter-kin marriages the greater is the kin knowledge and vice versa. In other words, the age and sex of Ego, the propinquity of kin, frequency of contacts and preferential marriage among kin are some of the major influencing factors in determining the range of kin knowledge.

Gokul

When we turn our attention from Kalyan to Gokul it appears that kin knowledge among Brahmans is influenced by caste customs and rituals. *Sraddha*, a ceremony to propitiate ancestors, is one of them. For ritual purposes, during *Sraddha*, Brahmans are required to know the names of ascendants for three generations in father's, mother's and wife's lines.

The professional genealogists are conspicuously absent among Brahmans. Of the 115 Brahman households, 43.48% maintained genealogies. The study of several genealogies reveals significant facts about their conception of kin. The relatives represented on the genealogy are related wholly through males (agnates), that is, the patrikin. Ego's father, FaFa and FaFaFa, and their spouses' names are recorded. In the father's line if any ancestors are recorded in the 4th or 5th or 6th generations, it is only the male ancestors. Only the male collaterals and their male children in the different ascending line are represented. In the descending line also it is the male children and their male children who are prominent (Diagram 2).

Four households had printed genealogical books. Such printed genealogical books contain (Diagram 3) mostly agnatic kin and make hardly any reference to the matrilineage or to relatives from wife's side.

Table 14 indicates the different facets of the range of kin knowledge as recorded in the fourteen households.

Table 14

Genealogy	Recognised Kin	Named Kin	Unnamed Kin	Depth of Generations
I	199	149	50	6
II	308	220	88	6
III	338	197	141	6
IV	140	72	68	5
V	176	117	59	7
VI	184	112	72	7
VII	228	186	42	10
VIII	238	200	38	8
IX	210	154	56	8
X	266	186	80	6
XI	150	96	52	6
XII	208	125	73	7
XIII	172	124	48	8
XIV	371	287	84	7
Total	3,188	2,227	951	

The total number of kin recognised in the kin universe of a Brahman household is normally more than 240. In 14 households the range of kin knowledge varied between 140 and 371, with an average figure of 227.71. While the minimum number of kin kowledge of both the Lingayat and Brahman households is almost the same, the maximum number of kin knowledge among the Brahman households is a little less compared to the Lingayats. The number of unnamed kin range between 31 and 141, the average unnamed kin being 67.93 where the average depth of generations is seven. In the genealogy of household III the number of unnamed kin is greatest because of the wider spatial distribution of Ego's kin and thus less contact with kin. In household VIII, however, Ego (male) is 32 years of age and the number of unnamed kin is minimum. In household IV the total kin recognized is minimum, that is, 140; the depth of generations is five, the smallest of the 14 households. In this case Ego's (male) limited kin universe is due to widespread spatial distribution of kin. In household VII the genealogical depth of generations is exceptional (10); also a large number of dead kin was mentioned because Ego referred to a printed genealogical book on his clan. In household X, the least number of dead kin was mentioned by Ego (Female). She had keen interest in and constant contact with her kin.

The detailed study of genealogies of 14 households reveals that out of 3,186 total kin recognized in all these households, only 951, that is, 29.83%, were not named, and of them 645 were dead, so that ultimately 306 living kin were not named. Even if one supposes that unnamed kin are non-effective and distant kin lack contact with Ego's family at the time of response, it is quite reasonable to expect that in future unnamed kin may become effective kin because of vicinity, matrimonial relationship, mutual help and such other factors. It does not necessarily mean, however, that all those named kin are effective kin of Ego's family. This kind of differentiation between recognized kin, named and unnamed kin is useful for analytic purposes.

The knowledge of ascendants' names as found in the genealogies of 14 Brahman households is represented in Table 15.

Table 15

Knowledge of Ancestors (Gokul)

Ego's patrilineage		Ego's matrilineage		Ego's spouse's patrilineage	
FaFa	14 Cases	MoFa	13 Cases	Spouse's Fa	14 Cases
FaMo	12 Cases	MoMo	12 Cases	Spouses's Mo	13 Cases
FaFaFa	13 Cases	MoFaFa	9 Cases	Spouse's FaFa	12 Cases
FaFaMo	9 Cases	MoFaMo	6 Cases	Spouse's FaMo	5 Cases
FaFaFaFa	8 Cases	MoFaFaFa	7 Cases	Spouse's FaFaFa	5 Cases
FaFaFaMo	2 Cases	MoFaFaMo	6 Cases	Spouse's FaFaMo	2 Cases

The predominant knowledge of ancestors in the patrilineage among Brahmans is not due to patrikin being a territorial group, but because of the fact that patrilineage is a descent and inheritance group. Moreover, every Brahman householder is enjoined by religion to perform *Sraddha*—the worship of ancestors, wherein patrilineal ancestors receive precedence even though matrilineal ancestors and ancestors of the spouse are also worshipped. In the maximum number of cases Ego's knowledge of ancestors in the patrilineage even in the fourth ascendant generation is quite strong. Especially in the third and fourth ascendant generations the collaterals of grandparents and great-grandparents are not remembered. So the genealogy in the ascending generation looks like a steep pyramid. The knowledge of ancestors in Ego's matrilineage is somewhat less than knowledge of ancestors in the Ego's patrilineage. Ego's matrilineage has also four generations depth in ascendant line as is Ego's patrilineage. However, Ego's spouse's patrilineage ascendant line normally indicates only three generations depth.

It is evident that knowledge of ancestors of the Brahmans in generation depth exceeds that of the Lingayats by one generation (vide, Tables 14, 17). Although the Lingayats worship ancestors once a year, ancestors include only deceased parents and grandparents of Ego (male), and normally do not refer to Ego's ancestors in the matrilineage or spouse's patrilineage. The pattern of lateral distribution of kin and the depth of generations as revealed in the genealogy of fourteen Brahman households is presented in Table 16.

Table 16

Depth of Generations and Lateral Distribution-Gokul

Households Generations	I	II	III	IV	V	VI	VII	VIII	IX	X	XI	XII	XIII	XIV
7th Ascending	—	—	—	—	—	—	1	—	—	—	—	—	—	—
6th Ascending	—	—	—	—	—	—	1	—	—	—	—	—	—	—
5th Ascending	—	—	—	—	—	—	8	—	2	—	—	—	—	—
4th Ascending	2	—	—	—	4	2	9	2	4	2	—	2	4	2
3rd Ascending	12	10	4	6	15	4	12	4	8	4	2	4	4	4
2nd Ascending	16	28	6	12	18	12	14	6	17	12	6	8	8	8
1st Ascending	26	64	16	22	28	31	30	32	31	34	22	37	27	28
Ego	63	93	95	38	56	65	75	80	61	128	43	61	62	80
1st Descending	75	66	133	46	48	47	71	74	62	86	49	57	35	137
2nd Descending	5	40	84	16	7	23	7	33	25	—	28	37	28	112
3rd Descending	—	—	—	—	—	—	—	7	—	—	—	2	4	—
Total	199	208	338	140	176	134	228	238	210	266	150	208	172	371

A Brahman's knowledge of kin is most extensive in Ego's own generation. However, in the households I, II, IV, IX, XI and XIV the lateral distribution of kin is greater in the first descending generation of Ego. This is due to the advanced age of the informant and death of kin belonging to his own generation or loss of contact with his own generation or the presence of many children, own and that of siblings and other collaterals. In household IX the lateral distribution of kin in Ego's own generation and in the first descending generation is generally equal. In household V the difference in the lateral distribution of kin between Ego's own and in the first descending generation is not significant. Therefore in the majority of these 14 Brahman households it is Ego's own generation which manifests the greater lateral distribution of kin in contrast to the Lingayat households, where lateral distribution of kin is most extensive in the first descending generation of Ego. Moreover, the average depth of generations among the Brahmans is seven which is one generation more than the average depth of generations among Lingayats. Naming habits, such as a grandson receiving the name of grandfather, facilitates the remembrance of names of ancestors through generations. Such repetition of names over six generations was found in four instances.

Sometimes Ego and members of the household remembered only the surname of the affinal kin as it is the only easy device to differentiate kin groups patrinominally. Often, when Brahmans do not remember names of kin—secondary, tertiary or distant—they recognize their kin by their profession or occupation. Unnamed kin were recognized in the Brahman households as teachers, engineers, and lawyers. Those kin in the service of Indian railways, posts and telegraphs and Air Lines were also recognized and stressed with pride even though proper names of such persons were not known.

It is also characteristic of the Brahman males that they do not remember the names of females and children of their kinship network even though they reside in the same or nearby city or town. For instance, one male respondent did not know his MoBrSoWi even though there were frequent contacts with the informant's family. Another respondent did recognize the number of children of his secondary and tertiary relatives but could not remember the names of children except for that of the eldest one or of two children.

In ten cases, Ego did not know the number and the sex of children of those kin who had migrated to distant places. This was due to lack of contact for a long time. The knowledge of paternal kin on the whole is more extensive than that of maternal or affinal kin. When, due to wife's death, Ego's affinal (male) kin marries a woman from another kin group, Ego and other members of the household lose contact with and interest in that affinal kin and do not remember the name of the second wife or the children of this marriage. Also a childless young widow who returns and stays for life with her parental family loses contact with the deceased husband's siblings, spouses and children. All this suggests that mutal recognition and rememberance of names of kin reflects to a greater extent the degree of contact and intimacy among kin.

Contrary to the normal patterns of dominance of patrikin knowledge, in one exceptional case Ego, a thirty-five year old lawyer, remembered his wife's parental genealogy up to the sixth ascending line. This was due to the fact that the sixth male ascendant was a famous leader who revolted against the British regime in 1857 in the first war of Indian independence. Such exceptional generation depth of wife's parental or matrilineal line is the result of some significant event, close relationship due to mutual help and/or interkin marriages.

The study of genealogies of 14 Brahman households reveals the nature and extent of the inclusion of the dead kin. Out of the 3,189 total kin recognized in all the 14 households, 645, or nearly 20.23%, were dead kin. Out of dead kin mentioned almost 80% belonged to Ego's ascending generations nearly 15% to Ego's own generation and only 5% in the descending generations. Most of these dead kin were remembered because Ego and the household members maintained some relationship with the descendants of the dead kin. The dead kin in Ego's descending line were cited mostly due to sentimental attachment and nearness of kinship relationship with the descendants of the dead kin. The dead kin mentioned were usually in the paternal line rather than in the maternal line or in the wife's paternal line. Among Brahmans a large percentage of dead kin mentioned were of "link" or "channel" type and were found more often in families with a large number of kin. In these genealogies the figures of the dead kin may not be genealogically exact. Nevertheless the figures of dead kin are socially significant.

The eldest female member in each household was the "pivotal kin". She was the storehouse of kin knowledge. Ego often consulted her while narrating genealogy. Usually Ego's mother was the sole expert on her paternal line besides providing information on her husbands' kin. So far as Ego's wife's paternal line was concerned, Ego's wife naturally knew much more about her own paternal line than anybody else in the family and her knowledge of affines also increased if there were inter-kin marriages.

The importance of the patrinominal principle of kin grouping is vividly demonstrated in the fact that informants remembered some kin not by their proper names but by their surnames, which is a basis for kin group formation. Surname serves as the main frame of reference to distinguish between consanguines and affines. Among Brahmans the patrilineal and patrinominal principle is more important than among the Lingayats for purposes of performing "Sraddha", succession and marriage regulations. Rights and obligations are associated with the paternal line of kin and jural relationships are also established accordingly.

In the entire fabric of kinship of each household it is the mother who is the prominent figure, and a strong link between consanguines and affines. She is the embodiment of sentimental ties with her children, both married and unmarried. When the mother dies it is the sibling-bond that may hold the members of the wider family together. That is why the kinship system of the Brahmans though predominantly patri-centred in theory is matri-centred in sentiment and action. Once the mother dies, even the sibling network becomes uncertain at times.

The main features of the Brahman kinship system, such as dominance of the knowledge of patrilineage, presence of pivotal kin, matral orientation in sentiment and in action, patrinominal principle of kin differentation, total number of kin recognized, the number of living kin and the number of unnamed kin mentioned by Ego, are more or less similar to those of the kinship system of the Lingayats. However, there are other features which are peculiar to Brahmans. For instance, the total number of named kin and dead kin cited by the Brahmans is less than those cited by the Lingayats. Yet there is a greater depth of genealogy, and a greater lateral range of recognition. Greater emphasis on the ritual aspects of ancestor worship, rigid clan exogamy, presence of genealogical records, lesser number of cousin marriages, and wider geographical distribution of kin, are other distinctive characteristics of the Brahman kinship. The Brahman cultural complex keeps every Brahman more alive to his kin. Practically every one is articulate and aware of one's own kinship universe and it is perceived as an organic whole. Ego is verbally proud of his kin group.

"In any society, genealogical tie by itself is no basis for social relations. It is a conceptualization of this tie in terms of a social bond, often with moral force, which gives it its significance".[5] Therefore, it may be said that in these two suburbs of Dharwar the genealogical tie is the basis for the understanding of a certain set of social relationships among kin which from the subject of study in the next chapter.

---

5   Ibid, p. 29.

CHAPTER FOUR

Patterns of Interaction

IN THE PREVIOUS CHAPTER we examined the structure of kin knowledge in almost all its ramifications: recognized kin, both living and dead, effective and non-effective kin, intimate as well as non-intimate kin. Let us now consider those kin with whom our respondents have active social relationships. These effective kin are not just recognized to be geneologically related but the recognition of the kinship relationship has some effect, however minimal, on the life of the respondent. For the purpose of our analysis, as the simple indicator of effect, we have taken into account contact of any kind with the kin, whether through visiting, exchange of services or gifts, attendance at family gatherings, or correspondence, naming and counselling.[1] In all these aspects some kind of social interaction can be observed. We shall examine the quantitative as well as qualitative aspects of behaviour among effective kin and the recent changes in such behaviour patterns. In what follows we shall begin with an analysis of visiting as one form of contact among kin, and follow it up with a discussion of forms of contact other than visiting.

Visiting

Patterns of kinship behaviour among Lingayats of Kalyan can be discerned by examining their day to day interactions with, and attitudes toward, their kin. The effects of the range of kin recognition on behaviour of kin can be observed. One of the important indices of kin contacts is frequency of mutual visits. The affectionate feelings and emotional ties amongst kin need to be constantly reinforced by contacts, personal or otherwise. Otherwise they gradually weaken and die. Moreover, when a person visits a relative at regular intervals accidentally or purposefully at the latter's home, he or she naturally comes into contact with several other kin living in that relative's household.

Mutual visits among kin serve as an indicator of the effective and non-effective kin. However, absence of visits, unnamed kin and non-effective kin are nevertheless socially significant as they may in due course become effective kin because of marital relations, migration and physical proximity, mutual help and the like.

Social interaction among kin as manifested through visits reveals partly the nature and extent of intimacy, affection, help and cooperation, roles and expectations. The data regarding the frequency of visits can be a pointer to mutual

---

1 Firth, R., et al, 1970, p. 195.

Table 17

Kalyan

Relatives visit Ego	Ego visits Relatives	
Kin on the side of	%*	%*
Spouse	40.87	31.30
Sister	38.26	38.26
Daughter	33.91	32.17
Mother	20.00	20.00
Father	13.91	13.91

* These percentages represent the average number of visits.

ties though the number of contacts is less important than their content. However, such quantitative measures proclaim the significance of several relationships amongst relatives.

The pattern of who visits whom among the Lingayats is quite significant. Ego was asked to rate his kin in order of importance, based on who has been frequently visiting his or her household during the last five years, and also to rate in order of importance kin whom Ego has been visiting during the last five years. The responses indicate an impressive array of patterns of mutual visits. The maximum number of visits to Ego's household are made by Ego's relatives on the spouse's side. Ego, however, visits relatives on the spouse's side less often.

Such frequent visits to Ego's household by the spouse's kin is due to physical proximity. Of the 303 marriages in 150 cases, parents of the spouse resided in Kalyan and in 16 more cases parental families of spouse lived in other suburbs of Dharwar. The people had regular daily visits or met at least twice a week. Next in frequency, kin on the sister's side visit Ego's household and in turn Ego visits them exactly the same number of times. The reciprocity of relationships between Ego and elder sister is greatest. This is probably because Ego (male) has the preference of marrying his sister's daughter and likewise the sister may even bring pressure to give her daughter as spouse to her brother or her brother's son. Such marriages in fact have reinforced kinship relationships among the Lingayats.

A married daughter visits Ego's household even less than the number of times a sister visits Ego. Ego also visits his or her daughter almost the same number of times as daughter visits Ego. What matters most here is the fact that Ego visits and is visited more by the kin on the sister's side than on the daughter's side. The frequency of mutual visits of Ego and relatives on son's side and brother's side is considerably less than 15 percent. The interesting fact here is that between kin on the father's side and that on the mother's, Ego seems to be more attached to and sentimental towards relatives on the mother's side.

However, this general pattern of visits among kin seems to be affected by the economic factor. A housewife remarked that the rich have more relatives but they neglect their kin who are poor. In some cases Ego pointed out that visits were more frequent among kin in the past when Ego's household had a better economic status. Now due to loss of property and income, relatives do not visit the household of Ego.

Within the range of named kin there are effective kin—those with whom some kind of social contact is maintained, through occasional visits, or attendance at family rituals and ceremonies, mutual help, correspondence and the like. This is in contrast with non-effective kin with whom such contact is not maintained. With the intimate kin social contact is purposeful, close and frequent whereas with peripheral kin social contact is distant, accidental or sporadic.[2]

Intimate kin

Respondents, by and large, consider parents, spouse, siblings and children as their most intimate kin. The following responses to the query "With whom do you have more contact (other than visiting) among your relatives?" gave a clue to the understanding of the degree of contact, affection and intimacy of Ego with a certain set of relatives.

Table 18

Ego's contact with relatives on the side of	Percentage* (represent average frequency of contacts of any kind)	Kin other than those living in the house whom Ego considers as intimate kin	Percentage
Fa	12.17	Fa	7.83
Mo	30.43	Mo	29.57
Br	9.57	Br	11.30
Si	18.26	Si	26.70
Wi/Hu	32.17	Wi/Hu	17.39
So	6.09	So	12.70
Da	17.39	Da	24.35
All kin equal	13.04	Undecided	6.96

* Totals do not add up to 100 percent because many respondents have contact with more than one relative.

The Ego is more in contact with relatives on the side of spouse than with any other set of kin. In the majority of cases the Ego (male) maintains close contact with and is emotionally attached to relatives on wife's side, especially with wife's parents and wife's siblings. Next in order of importance Ego maintains close and affectionate relations with relatives on the mother's side rather than with relatives on the father's side. Relatives on the mother's side include mother's brothers and sisters and mother's parents in the main. His contact and affection with kin on the side of sister and daughter closely approximate.

2 Firth, R., 1956, p. 45.

But it is surprising that the sibling solidarity that prevails before marriage and the close brother-sister tie manifested even after marriage cannot be found, especially, amongst brothers after their marriage. Brothers tend to become rivals with regard to the sharing of parental property or due to conflicts amongst wives of brothers. Although paternal relatives are a territorial kin group and live in close spatial proximity in Kalyan, the close ties between brother-sister instead of brother-brother appear to be really significant.

It is significant to note that Ego maintains a considerable amount of contact with parents. Even among children, Ego maintains more contract with kin on the married daughter's side than with kin on the married son's side. Among several kin other than those living in the house of Ego, he or she feels closest with kin on the side of mother, sister, daughter and spouse respectively in order of closeness of contact and intensity of affection. These relationships of the Lingayats are oriented more towards their female kin than their male kin.

Though the kinship of Lingayats is patrinominal and they possess more knowledge of paternal kin than of maternal kin, their emotional ties tend to be more matrilateral than patrilateral. Kin groups in some situations are matral-patrinominal, rather than simple patrinominal. When a woman with her husband and children goes to attend a family ritual or ceremony or to spend her holidays at her parental home they are usually merged into a group known collectively as the Y's—the surname of her father and even individually they are referred to as daughter or son-in-law or grand-children of so and so namely that of the father of the concerned woman. Several such instances were brought to the notice of the researcher during investigations. In many households married daughters with their children were staying with their parents for a considerable period for confinement, festivals or holidays.

Daughters marry relatively early in life and beget children sooner than sons. In some households Ego and his wife acted as foster-parents to their daughter's children. Such grand-children (that is, daughter's children) were commonly included matrinominally in virtue of the sentimental attachment of their mother to her parental family. But the naming of such kinship sets is altered according to the main social interest and the place and purpose of assemblage of kin. Such inclusion of daughter's children matrinominally can be noticed only on limited occasions and for limited purposes, as during weddings and other family rituals and festivals. For all practical purposes, children are known patrinominally. So, the patrinominally extended family is only a partially operative social unit and not a completely regular one.

For all such matrilateral kin contacts and congregations, it is the mother who is the main focus, the central figure linking two patrinominal kin groups. Such kinship sets cannot be traced exclusively through women over generations with continuity. For purposes of naming, marital relations, succession of property and the like, the group is usually remembered, recorded and distinguished by her husband's surname.

Exchange of Services

The frequency of services performed between relatives is closely related to the frequency of contacts. Those kin who meet each other most frequently and those who are held by close bonds of kinship help each other most frequently. The nature and extent of social interaction between kin can be measured through an examination of the exchange of services among them. In the Lingayat kinship system the exchange of services between members of different closely related households in the city and outside is most important.

All members of 95% of the households in Kalyan are crossrelated by patrilateral, matri-lateral or affinal ties, and acquire their major roles in the social life of the suburb through kinship affiliations. The significance of extrafamilial kin ties in the Lingayat community lies primarily in the positive social contacts in visiting, in exchange of services, in attendance on ceremonial occasions and at crises of life, in exchange of news, consultation and advice.

Everyday exchange of services among kin include the giving or receiving on loan of articles needed for domestic use and consumption such as a cup of sugar or food grains, flour, edible oil, and utensils. If they are in need of such things, the members of the related household in the vicinity, rather than the non-kin neighbours, are the people to be approached first. If the things loaned are not returned, it will be excused because the people involved are kin. Related womenfolk in the suburb help each other in such tasks as baby sitting, preparation of food, whitewashing the house and shopping, especially on occasions of family rituals and festivals. All respondents reported that they had received such services during almost every month.

In this kin-oriented community, people were unwilling to move to another suburb or town where they had no relatives. One informant stated that the problems of looking after children was minimized because of the help and services of relatives such as a grandmother or aunt of the children. Another reported that life would have been very miserable for him and his family members if his relatives had not helped him when he was unemployed for six months.

Traditionally, women go to their parental home to give birth to their first child and also the second. The expectant mothers stay at their parental home, the confinement period extending over three months and more. It is the responsibility of the brother to come to her conjugal family and escort her to her family of orientation. Her mother and brother's wife or elder sister act as midwives besides the professional midwife. The mother-daughter relationship is very close and affectionate even after the daughter's marriage and is reinforced by this prolonged stay during and after confinement. The mother is the embodiment of experience and knowledge. She is the person to decide and advise the daughter on movements, food, health and habits, child-care and upbringing. The frequent directions and naggings of the mother directed at her daughter are quite common. All complex situations, doubts, fears and desires of the daughters are discussed invariably with her mother or grandmother.

In spite of the establishment of maternity hospitals by the government, the family at times of a child-birth usually receives the support it needs from kin. It appears that the public health agencies have not in any way displaced the role of relatives. It is also true to a certain extent that during other emergencies such as illness, the relatives have the moral obligation to look after the patient even though the patient may be admitted to a hospital.

The Role of the Mother's Brother

On the occasion of the first child birth, the child's mother's brother plays an important role. He is the person who carries the happy news to the family of the sister's husband. The mother's brother will be honoured with presents at the child's father's family. The quantity and quality of gifts increase if the child is a male, presents including gold ring, silk turban, shirts and *dhotis*. In case of birth of a female child he may not get a gold ring or even other things.

When the period of confinement is over it is customary for the brother to accompany her to her husband's family. At this time he carries the traditional gifts made to his sister and her child, such as a cradle, a silver cup for the baby, a cow, ornaments, clothing for the baby and the mother. The mother's brother in return receives gifts in the form of clothes, ornaments and cash. Exchange of gifts is on a smaller scale in subsequent births. Today even on first births, rituals and gifts are becoming nominal and symbolic due to increasing high cost of living.

Esprit de Corps

Mutual aid, cooperation and active participation of kin can be observed in various *rites de passage* such as that of first pregnancy rites, child births, naming ceremonies, puberty rites, mate selection and betrothal ceremonies, weddings, religious rites, and festivals, etc. As marriages are arranged by parents and other intimate kin, they take active interest and responsibility in choosing a bride or groom according to their tastes and values. It is the task of one's wider kin group to find a "best" partner and to investigate their family background and to decide the suitability of the new alliance. The team spirit, the *esprit de corps* of the kin group, is overtly manifested on such various occasions. Even now the intimate kin group functions as a marriage guidance bureau.

For the wedding ceremony, preparations begin weeks and even months in advance. Intimate kin congregate much before the actual wedding day. The pivotal kin and other key figures in the kin group play an important role and help in purchasing ornaments, clothes and other goods. The intimate kin and especially persons who were instrumental for the alliance will identify themselves with the whole marriage affair, and even after the wedding such kin should be ready at any time to mediate disputes between spouses and kin groups.

Gifts in cash and kind come form several kin to the bride and groom at the wedding ceremony. All such gifts have to be returned to the respective kin when similar occasion arises in their family. Such help and cooperation and giving of gifts at the wedding by relatives suggest kin solidarity and tends to strengthen kin ties. Kin both on the father's side and mother's side attend Ego's (male) marriage. But there is a larger attendance of kin from mother' side.

In response to invitations it is obligatory for the intimate kin to attend weddings and give presents while it may be optional for the peripheral kin. In practice, most of the peripheral kin attend the wedding or at least send presents.

Attendance at funerals is equally obligatory for intimate kin. The attendance depends on several factors—the sex and age of the deceased, the socio-economic status, the degree of intimacy, personal attributes and the degree of geneological ties. An event of grief such as death in a family needs sympathy, consolation and help from relatives. In the kinship network of the deceased, at least one representative from each related family or lineage is expected to attend the funeral. If these kinship expectations are not fulfilled by an individual, he is ostracised by his intimate kin.

It was rather difficult to record the precise number of kin and the degree of relationship of kin who attended marriages, funerals or any other family rituals and ceremonies, as the respondents themselves did not remember such things distinctly. However, it was possible to work out a rough rank order of different categories of kin who attended various rituals and ceremonies of the household. In emergencies ranging from everyday needs, child birth, marriages to that of illness and funerals it is the kin related through the spouse (mostly kin on wife's side when Ego is male) who help most, i.e. 38.26%. Next in rank of those who have extended their help are relatives from the mothers' side, i.e. 27.83%, and kin on the sister's side, 12.17%. Although the Lingayat society is patrilineal and patrilocal it is rather interesting to observe that kin on the father's side help to the extent of 7.83% and kin on brother's side only 5.22%.

An overwhelming majority (79.13%) of the Lingayats do not give or receive monetary help. It is almost a taboo to demand or give money as loan among kin, especially between consanguines and affines. Informants indicate that financial transactions among relatives spoil kinship bonds and affection. So, borrowing and lending among kin is not generally favoured. Further enquiries, however, revealed that Ego had received financial help from kin on mother's side (4.35%), brother's side (4.35%), wife's side (3.48%) and sister's side (2.61%). But the majority of them had received financial aid from non-kin, that is, from friends and neighbours. Borrowing and lending of money is a delicate private affair. There was a general reluctance to discuss such monetary affairs. It is evident that kinship relationships include visits, help and cooperation on various normal and difficult times but ideally it does not include financial help.

In Kalyan mutual aid and cooperation among kin in farming operations can be observed.

Table 19

Mutual Aid among Kin in Farming Operations

Relatives on the side of	Percentage of help and cooperation
Fa	6.09
Mo	2.61
Wi/Hu	6.96
Br	14.78
Si	6.09
So	3.48
Da	2.61
No Help	41.74

Though a maximum percentage of them do not receive help from kin in agricultural activities the help is frequently forthcoming from kin on the brother's side. As patrilateral kin are a territorial group the reciprocity of kin relationships are more pronounced in their economic activities rather than in social activities. Wife's paternal kin also help probably because most of them reside in the same suburb or neighbouring villages. In this community borrowing and lending of agricultural implements and bullocks is inevitable because most of them have limited resources. Sowing especially is an operation performed by all farmers during a particular period of time. Mutual aid is greatest on these days. Kin help each other in ploughing and harvesting, in the transportation of manure and fodder, and storage of grains. This kind of cooperation in economic life reinforces kinship solidarity.

Ancestor Worship

Observance of ancestor worship is one of the main functions of the family and the practice implies the belief that the ancestors are endowed with supernatural powers and continue to live and participate in life activities of the worshippers. It is believed that those who propitiate their ancestors receive blessings and help for prosperity and happiness of all living descendants. The ritual requires that a brass pot full of water together with a new *dhoti* and a new *saree*, decorated with ornaments, is kept in the place of worship. A special feast in honour of the dead marks the day. The intimate kin in the neighbourhood join the celebrations. This annual ancestor worship, known as *Hiriyara-Habba*, emphasizes the importance of elders, both dead and living. This tends to reinforce the authority of the eldest male member of the family. The mental image of ancestors is handed down from one generation to another by such rites. Thereby it serves to keep family and kin group solidarity alive.

Communication

The letters mailed and received by the members of a household broadly suggest the range of effective kin. However, it should be noted that since 52.17%

of the primary respondents are illiterate and most of their kin are in Dharwar and neighbouring villages within a five to eight mile radius, writing letters among kin is neither possible nor necessary. Because of the narrow spatial distribution of kin, personal visits are common and news is communicated by word of mouth. The largest single majority of the respondents (33.04%) have not so far posted letters to their kin or received any from them.

Further enquiries, however, revealed that contact through correspondence is maintained with kin staying relatively far away. Ego receives most of the letters (18.25%) from kin on daughter's side, following from kin on spouse's side (14.78%). Relatives on the sister's and mother's side also write letters to Ego who maintains reciprocal contacts through correspondence. Letter-writing among kin is an activity confined only to the communication of "important" news such as births, marriages and deaths.

The majority of invitations sent and received were between the members of the wider kin group. Responses indicated that 86.96% of the invitations were either sent or received by kin on occasions such as naming ceremony, marriage celebrations, fairs and festivals, and hardly 13.04% of the invitations were exchanged with persons who were not related. This suggests a strong kin orientation as regards exchange of invitations.

In Kalyan the habit of getting themselves and their kin photographed, and the preservation and display of photographs of kin are not so widespread. In almost every household one can observe various pictures of gods and goddesses displayed on the walls. But one rarely sees photos of family members and other kin. In 46.96% of the cases Ego did not possess photographs of parents; in 24.35% of the cases he possessed father's photo, and mother's photo in 8.70% of the cases. The number of photographs of Ego's children exceed that of Ego's own and Ego's parental generation. There has been a visible change in the desire to have photographs of the members of the family and intimate kin through the generations. As photographs preserve for posterity the memories of the near and dear ones, people often repented for not having the photographs of their ancestors. The habit of having themselves photographed with kin and displaying photographs has been growing slowly. In most of the households Ego's children would like to have photographs. What is striking is the fact that photos of Ego's siblings and photos of kin on the side of the spouse are extremely few. There are fewer photos of kin in company with non-kin. These various indices of kin contacts and communications in person or by some material token among the Lingayats illustrate their kinship orientation.

Naming Habits

In most of the communities it is common to name the newborn after their ancestors. The practice of naming children symbolizes the close ties between the youngest generation and the kin of previous generations. As one grows up, numerous social ties and various significant experiences and ideas become associated with one's personal name. The name is a means of displaying egoistic feelings and self-esteem, but one has no say in the choice of one's own name. As McDougall rightly points out, "one's name" becomes a handle by aid of which he gets hold of himself as an agent, a striver, a desirer, a refuser."

The naming habits reflect the cultural values and norms of the community. Names indicate ingroup feelings, group consciousness as well as pride and solidarity of family and kingroup. Moreover, personal names, by and large, indicate the caste or religious group to which one belongs. Among Lingayats it has been customary to name the first born male child after the father's father of the child. The first female born is named after the child's father's mother. The rest of the children are named after closely related ancestors of the kin group. Children are also given the names of gods and goddesses, saints of Lingayats in particular, and Shaivites in general; most of these names happen to be identical with names of kin. The practice of naming children after their ascendant kin is so crystallized and persistent that it is common to find almost all persons living in the suburb with exactly the same names as those found in the previous generations.

Table 20

Traditional Naming Patterns

Pattern I		Pattern II	
Males	*Females*	*Males*	*Females*
Basappa	Basavva	Adiveppa	Adivevva
Gurupadappa	Gangavva	Channappa	Dyamavva
Mahadevappa	Nilavva	Honappa	Kallavva
Sivappa	Shankaravva	Madivalappa	Ningavva
		Veerappa	Siddavva

Table 21

Pattern III	
Males	*Females*
Bharamappa	Ambavva
Goolappa	Nondavva
Mudakappa	Kontevva
Sakreppa	Sakrevva
Tippanna	Settevva

Of the genealogies collected from 115 Lingayat households, those of 14 households were taken up for detailed analysis. These genealogies reveal the traditional naming patterns as represented in Tables 20 and 21. The names in Patterns I and II account for about 80% of the names that appear in the gene-alogies of all the households investigated. Names in Pattern I are names more or less unique to the Lingayats and represent their gods, goddesses and saints or indicate their significant philosophy. The names of Pattern I and II are often repeated in five or six generations. Names of Pattern I are more common and more often repeated in genealogies of the Lingayats than those found in Pattern II. Names in Pattern II, however, are not unique to Lingayats since they are also found among non-Lingayats (except Brahmans). Names of Pattern III are not common and appear in about 12% of the 14 genealogies under detailed investigation.

In 43.48% of the cases names of first and second children were suggested by the mother of the child and 8.70% of the names were suggested by kin on the mother's side, namely, mother's mother, mother's father, mother's brother and the like. Also, it has been customary that child's father's sister should name the child during the naming ritual. In 34.78% of the cases it was the father's sister who performed this ritual role and received a gift in return. The naming ceremony usually takes place on the fifth day or 13th day after the birth of the child. Relatives, neighbours and friends congregate and present gifts to the baby and the mother. The priest is invited to consult the position of stars, and on his advice and that of elders a name is selected.

The child's father and relatives on the father's side also have a controlling voice in naming affairs. In 29.57% of the cases, children were given names as suggested by the father and 11.30% as suggested by kin on fathers' side, mostly father's father and father's mother. Name giving is usually the activity of women folk. Names of patrilateral kin are preferred to the names of matrilateral kin. However, names of matrilateral kin also occur frequently in case of female children.

Even now these traditional naming patterns serve as a frame of reference for the overwhelming majority of the Lingayats. Why do these people name their children after their ancestors? There are several motives as the respondents themselves express:

"Our children will also lead a good life and live long as our forefathers."

"It is a means to preserve the earlier seeds. It is a means to continue the family torch."

"We can remember our ancestors often by giving the same names to our kids."

"We are so much indebted to our ancestors that we should pass on their names to posterity and we shouldn't at any cost erase their names."

"Our deceased parents and grand-parents take rebirth as our children."

Such statements are not uncommon and suggest that Lingayats see the image of the dead in the names of their ancestors and consider these names as vital instruments in the continuation of the lineage. Names express filial piety, respect and obedience, deep debt of gratitude and the warmth of feelings towards their deceased relatives. The fact that 89.57% of the respondents are strongly in favour of naming their children after deceased elders illustrates the intensity of kinship sentiments and the close link that cements generations—past, present and future. Such traditional naming patterns indicate a strong kin orientation among Lingayats.

However, slowly and steadily, new ideas and values of urban life have been infiltrating. Modern means of communication, education, and the increasing influence of modern values have been responsible for new ideals and aspirations among Lingayats. Table 22 represents a gradual change that has been taking place in the habits of naming children among a few of the upper class in the suburb.

Table 22

Pattern IV

Males	Females
Ashok	Kamala (kshi)
Babu	Leela
Kumar	Prema
Satish	Shobha
Suresh	Usha

These names, according to the respondents, are modern and fashionable, adopted mostly from the movies. However, hardly 8% of such modern names are found in all the genealogies of Ego's children's and grand-children's generations. Names in Pattern IV are modern in contrast to those in the traditional naming Patterns I, II and III in the sense that they are secular and do not indicate the caste to which one belongs. Modern names mostly indicate abstract qualities, physical and mental attributes, or objects of nature, and not necessarily the names of gods and goddesses.

In Kalyan 7.83% favour the practice of naming children according to modern ideals. They are a few educated young men who consider traditional names too orthodox and primitive. A young housewife said, "In the modern fashionable world 'old names' do not seem nice; it is better to have names for our children from those of filmstars." Another respondent remarked that "Repetition of the same old names in the same family leads to calling two individuals as 'Big Basappa' and 'Little Basappa' and we need some variety in names."

However, 2.61% are in favour of both old and new names. People rationalize and say that old names are good. They think modern names are a little better since they indicate the cherished values. Some people adopt a compromise in that they name the first born after parents and grand-parents and the rest, especially the younger ones, are given modern names. As they say: "We have to adjust ourselves to the modern environment and accept new names as they are in vogue." Nevertheless, it is evident from the foregoing analysis that Lingayat tradition weighs heavily in favour of naming children after their ancestors, thereby manifesting a kin-oriented culture.

Authority and Counselling

Traditionally, the eldest male, whether grandfather or father or father's eldest brother, is recognised as the head of the household. Although theoretically the eldest male is the head of the household, in fact, the main male bread-winner exercises considerable authority as he holds the strings of the family purse. Nevertheless, if the titular (*de jure*) and effective (*de facto*) head are not the same, the latter consults the former on various important occasions, such as purchasing movable or immovable property, matrimonial affairs, land cultivation and other family and kin activities. The experience, wisdom and counsel of the titular head are often respected and obeyed not only by members of the household but also by members of the wider kin group.

The mother or the eldest female member wields considerable influence within the domestic family and intimate kin group. In various family rituals and ceremonies, in visiting kin or extending invitations to kin, women have the leading role. In almost all internal affairs of family and kin, husbands consult wives in making important decisions affecting family members. However, the final decision rests with the male head of the household. Usually, the father, representing the family, participates in social, religious and other activities of the community. The housewife also attends such activities either with the husband or in the company of her kin and neighbours.

In 25.22% of the cases Ego was consulted by other members of the family and kin group. In making important decisions Ego consulted father in 21.74% of the cases, eldest brother in 20% of the cases and son, usually the eldest, in 4.35% of the cases. Besides these paternal kin, Ego also consulted the mother's kin in 17.39% of cases and the kin on the spouse's side in 17.30% of cases. In 10.44% of the cases Ego consulted relatives on the side of the married sister and daughter. This demonstrates the role of matrilateral kin and affines, in matters of the authority structure, counselling and decision-making.

Despite rivalry among brothers, which is usually expressed in the sharing of parental property, sibling bonds of affection continue even after marriage unless seriously punctured by jealous wives. When Ego has a personal problem, he or she would prefer to talk it over with brother in 20.87% of the cases, with father in 15.65%, and in 7.83% of the cases with a son. Here again, 13.91% prefer to discuss their personal problems with mother and mother's kin, and 13.91% with spouse and spouse's kin. Approximately 7% also narrate and resolve problems with kin on the side of a married sister and daughter. So the individual and nuclear family are not single units by themselves but are deeply embedded in the larger kinship network.

When children are in trouble, 43.48% of them approach the mother, 33.91% the father, 24.34% both father and mother, and 8.70% other members of the household. The mother seems to be the most affectionate figure for children in the family. But, at the same time, when children do wrong, it is the mother in 43.48% of the cases who punishes them corporally or otherwise, and it is only in 14.78% of the cases that the father does so. It is both mother and father who punish in 34.78% of the cases, and in 8.70% other members of the household are punishers. So the mother also controls the conduct of children through reward and punishment and thereby plays a dominant role in the socialization process of the child.

Within the household mother is considered a goddess. A respondent remarked, "One is not an orphan when father dies but certainly when one loses mother the unfortunate one becomes a real orphan." The people of Kalyan are conscious of the importance of kin. One housewife succinctly summarized the role of kin: "We can live without money but indeed it is difficult to live without kin."

Substitution of Kin and Distance

Some of the main functions of kinship are to provide replacements for intimate and non-intimate kin lost by death or migration and to compensate for the absence of parents, children, grandchildren or siblings by providing substitutes. In Kalyan, in the absence of intimate kin the process of substitution is at work. Replacement for dead kin and compensation for the absence of certain kin are quick and inevitable. In case the father dies it is usually either his brother or the mother's brother or grandfather or even his elder brother who becomes the guardian. Likewise, in case of the death of the mother, it is her sister's or the father's brother's wife or elder sister or grandmother who acts as a surrogate. In the absence of a male child a person in his old age adopts one of his intimate kin. Whenever Ego's kinship universe is biologically restricted and when one has no siblings or children, one leans heavily on neighbours and friends. In several cases Ego acted as foster parent to his sister's children. Children are often looked after by maternal grand-parents.

Geographical distance influences interaction among kin. As observed earlier, the kin in Kalyan are territorial groups. Parents and other relatives not only reside in the same city but also in the same suburb, and are likely to meet quite frequently.

"My parents live just in the adjacent street. We visit almost every day" said a housewife.

"I see my uncles and aunts at least twice a day since they reside at the other end of the same street," remarked another respondent.

"Oh! it is like staying in a big joint family even though all of us (brothers) live in adjacent houses," mentioned another enthusiastic youth.

Relatives on the side of the wife, mother, sister and daughter visited weekly or monthly because they reside in the neighbouring villages. Distance is given as the reason when they could not maintain contacts with a certain set of kin. On the whole, however, distance is no barrier to close contacts among intimate kin.

Filial Piety

Respect and obedience is due to parents and other kin who are older in age than the Ego. Such an expectation is traditionally the norm. As viewed by the informants aged fifty and above, there has been a change in filial piety, respect and obedience towards elders:

"We as youngsters paid respects and obeyed our elders unhesitatingly."

"We respected our parents as Gods. If at all we were on the wrong elders used to cut off our noses and squeeze our ears. Nowadays, youngsters show superficial or token respect to the old."

According to aged repondents deviation from the traditional norms on the part of youngsters is due to modern ideals of individual liberty and democracy, modern education, movies, economic independence and lack of religious and moral discipline. Aged men and women say that "Now immediately after marriage sons neglect and ignore their parents."

The following representative selection of verbal responses indicates the attitudes of youth as regards their relationships with the old people. "The world is fast changing. Our old people are reluctant to adjust to the new environment. It may result in a clash of ideas as long as they stick to the same old ideas, beliefs and practices. Elders are expected to change their outlook and adjust to the modern conditions."

Gokul: The ritual of Sraddha

The Brahman cultural complex embodying the ethos of Hindu sacred scriptures symbolises distinct kinship values and behaviour patterns. What distinguishes the Brahman kinship from Lingayat kinship is *Sraddha*, an institution of great religious significance. It is also an occasion for the kin to gather. Of the respondents, 86.96% mentioned *Sraddha* ceremony as a unique occasion to meet relatives. For centuries ancestor worship has been crystallised into a religious ritual. Propitiation of deceased ascendants reflects their posthumous glory, real or supposed.

When Brahmans offer oblations to their ancestors filial sentiments are expressed, though one may not have had any personal contact with them. Thus the *Sraddha* ceremony facilitates feelings of belonging to a family and lineage. The members of the patrilineage internalize norms of responsibility to preserve, enhance and perpetuate the prestige and traditions of the family and lineage.

Brahmans emphasize bilateral counting of kinship in the *Sraddha* ceremony. Acceptance of the mother's ancestors as deities of the *Sraddha* has religious sanction, and the mother's kin who are recognized for all social relationships are relatives within three generations.[3] Besides worshipping matrilateral ancestors, Ego's wife's patrilateral ancestors within three generations are significant at least for purposes of *Sraddha*.

On the day of the *Sraddha* ceremony Ego's (male) brothers and other kin meet together. It is on such occasions that relatives enquire of each other's well being, the prospects of marriage, education and employment of youngsters, etc. These kin gatherings help to strengthen bonds of kinship.

During times of serious illness, intimate kin immediately offer their services. It is an occasion of kin congregation for 63.48% respondents. The emotional

---

3 Kapadia, K. M., 1947, p. 310.

security, confidence and help during hospitalization and convalescence are provided for the kin. For 48.70%, festivals such as *Deepavali, Dasara, Nagapan-chami*, and the like are the occasions, especially for the women folk, for making trips to their natal home. The kin group gathers for initiation ceremonies, religious worship and fasting. It is the kin group which organizes journeys to holy places and to places of their lineage god or goddess.

Among Brahmans, 41.74% spend holidays with their relatives. Their holidays need to be pre-planned because children accompany adults. Holiday trips have to be made without disturbing children's school attendance and studies. Proper timing in visiting kin is necessary because of the Brahmans' greater reliance on employment for their livelihood.

Patterns of Visits

The Table below indicates the pattern of mutual visits among kin.

Table 23

Gokul

Relatives visit Ego	Ego visits relatives	
Kin on the side of	%*	%*
Spouse	45.22	18.26
Brother	42.61	29.57
Sister	34.78	27.83
Mother	32.00	27.00

*   These percentages represent the average number of visits.

It is clear from the data that the greatest percentage of visits to Ego's household are made by Ego's spouse's kin. This indicates that Ego's affines visit more often and maintain frequent, intimate contacts. However, Ego visits its spouse's kin with less average frequency. When Ego is male he cannot often visit affines because of job requirements. But Ego's wife's kin who visit him are mostly composed of women and children; and in 30 cases parent of the spouse and other relatives lived in Gokul. Mutual visits once or twice a week are common among kin who reside in the city.

Next in the frequency of visits are brothers and kin on brothers' side who visit Ego's household. This suggests partly close and cordial relationships between brother-brother among the Brahmans.

The quantitative and qualitative data of visits among siblings suggest that the brother-sister tie is equally important because the brother is considered as protector of his sister throughout life. At marriage, illness and during widowhood of the sister, it is the brother who takes the responsibility of looking after her welfare. Moreover, the practice of uncle-niece marriage brings them closer (see next chapter). Mutual visits are slightly more frequent among kin on the mother's side than on the father's side.

Owing to wider spatial distribution of kin among the Brahmans, sons and daughters visit Ego once or twice a year. On the average, the number of visits among kin varies with geographical distance. Those living in the same suburb visit once or twice a week. Relatives residing in other parts of the city meet once a fortnight and those living in the neighbouring villages and towns gather monthly or quarterly. But those kin living far away visit once a year or once every two or three years. Although this is the normal frequency of visits differing with spatial distribution of kin there are no definite set patterns of mutual visits according to respondents. The frequency of visits among a particular category of kin, however, depends on the degree of genealogical relationships, needs, capabilities and motives of kin, and geographical distance measured in terms of time and money spent in travel rather than the actual distance in mileage.

Among the effective kin, intimate kin of Ego are few in number. Table 24 indicates kin of Ego with whom Ego's social contact is reported to be close, purposeful and frequent.

Table 24

Ego's contact with Relatives on the side of	Percentage (represent average frequency of contacts of any kind)	Kin other than those living in the house whom Ego considers as intimate kin	Percentage*
Fa	19.13	Fa	19.91
Mo	33.04	Mo	27.83
Br	20.00	Br	7.83
Si	12.17	Si	16.52
Wi/Hu	15.65	Wi/Hu	11.30
So	3.48	So	3.48
Da	2.61	Da	6.96
All kin equal	17.39		

* Totals do not add up to 100% because many respondents have contact with more than one relative.

Evidently kin on the mother's side have more contact with Ego than any other category of relatives and the greatest percentage of intimate kin who live outside Ego's household are mother's kin. Social contacts, help and cooperation with mother's kin are reported to be close and intimate. Intimacy and degree of relationships with relatives on the side of brother and father follow. Respondents mention kin on the side of a spouse and sister in less than 17% of the cases. More than 17% of the respondents consider all kin equal in terms of intimacy, affection and contacts.

The brother-brother tie is most pronounced only next to mother-children tie among Brahmans. The economic rivalry for earning a livelihood is considerably less among the brothers in Gokul than among the brothers in Kalyan which in part leads to cordial relationships amongst brothers in Gokul. Such a strong tie between male siblings is significant because patrikin are not so much a territorial group in Gokul as it is in Kalyan. It seems spatial distance avoids friction.

The Ego maintains more contact with parents than with one's children. Amongst those kin living outside the household Ego feels closest, next to mother, to sister. Such emotional emphasis and leaning of Ego on the mother's and sister's kin is really striking within the matrix of the patrilineal kinship system.

Children's close attachment towards mother's natal family is manifested in the behavior patterns of Ego. Children's relationship with matrilateral grand-parents is more frequent and affectionate than with patrilateral grand-parents. Whereas father's brother is an authoritarian figure, the mother's brother is an affectionate figure. One can maintain joking relationships with the mother's brother. He plays a key role on all ceremonial occasions pertaining to his sister's children. Emphasis on matrilateral kin and mother as the main focus of the kinship network is pronounced among Brahmans. 81.74% said that since their childhood the mother was kinder and more affectionate than anybody else in the kinship constellation. Whereas in 56.52% of the cases it was father who was most kind and affectionate and only 4.35% responded that elder brother was most affectionate and tended Ego in case of early death of parents.

The Ego's responsibility for socialization and formal schooling of the children of one's sister, daughter and brother can be observed in the Brahman kinship system. Cordial relations amongst brothers in Gokul is in sharp contrast to the often strained relationships between male siblings in Kalyan. Among Brahmans unmarried younger brothers live with their married elder brother. Even after marriage it is noticed that a good deal of mutual help and coopera-tion prevail, and in several cases Ego helped his brother's son in schooling and in getting a job.

Aid and Cooperation

In times of crisis Ego receives help in 45.22% of the cases from kin on the mother's side. Next in order of frequency of services offered is by relatives on the side of spouse and sister. Those who do not receive financial help from kin are in a majority (53.04%). Amongst those kin who help them financially are one's brothers (17.39%). Such sibling solidarity as manifested in times of financial crises is a unique phenomenon. But generally speaking Lingayats and Brahmans do not ask for financial help as it is believed to have adverse effects on kinship relationships.

Members of 45% of the households in Gokul are inter-related with various ties of kinship and nearly 82% of the households in Gokul have bonds of kinship with members living in the city. In Gokul as in Kalyan social roles of individuals are influenced by kinship rights and obligations. In Gokul extrafamilial kin ties can be observed in overt behaviour such as mutual contacts through visits and correspondence, help and cooperation in normal and in difficult times, exchange of news and views, counselling, exchange of gifts, and attendance at initiation, marriage, funerals, *sraddha*, etc.

Besides everyday borrowing and lending of goods and services, what matters most is the help extended to relatives at times of births, initiation, marriage, illness, schooling, and in getting jobs. It is customary for Brahman women to return to their parental home to give birth to their first child. The daughter's delivery, confinement and her safe return to her conjugal family are the responsibility of her mother, brother and father. A married daughter and mother are close and daughter's confinement at the parental home often tends to reinforce their relationships. A daughter respects and obeys her mother's wisdom regarding her health and that of her child.

Nowadays the daughter is more educated and modernized than her mother. Slowly and steadily young women are resorting to the maternity hospital and the trained midwife rather than the services of the natal home for reasons of safety and because modern health services are easily available in the vicinity. Even when women choose to have their babies in hospitals, in 92% of such cases relatives were by far the most important source of help in looking after the home and making preparations for the care of the new baby. Therefore, on occasions of birth and illness the role of relatives has not diminished significantly and the modern public health agencies have not been completely substituted for the functions of kinship.

Brahmans prefer their kin to non-kin in matters of help and advice. In one instance a lawyer reported that when his relatives, both consanguineal and affinal, approached him for legal advice he charged no fee. In another case a physician offered free professional services to his relatives. Specific family problems such as selection of mates or education and employment of children were referred more to relatives than to non-kin. This does not, however, mean that all advice and help were obtained through relatives only. But it does mean that there is a certain degree of social reciprocity holding the kin group together.

Mother's Brother

In the Brahman kinship system the mother's brother has a distinct role to play on various ceremonial occasions and especially during *rites de passage* of his sister's children. Joking relationships prevail between the mother's brother and her children. They are allowed or rather expected to speak and behave in ways that would be insulting and offensive between persons not so related. Radcliffe-Brown regarded such a "joking" relationship in its reciprocal form as a kind of friendliness expressed by a show of hostility. When one's behaviour is not in conformity with the norms of the community the mother's brother is privileged to admonish her son in the language and tone which appears to be friendly. This seems to operate as a social device to rectify deviant behaviour.

Normally the mother's brother is not the person to exercise authority over his sister's son. Only when one's father is dead does the mother's brother exercise authority and assume responsiblities of the father. Otherwise the mother's brother is expected to show affectionate interest in his nephew and give him aid when he needs it. Next to mother, mother's brother seems to be a most close and affectionate figure in the kinship network. During interviews, respondents showed considerable interest towards their mother's brother. Informants often said that "Even if one's mother is dead, let there be one's mother's brother." This remark stresses the important role of mother's brother in the entire kinship constellation.

The mother's brother should give presents to his sister's children in the form of clothes, ornaments, etc., on their naming, initiation, wedding ceremonies and the like. The first ritual tonsure of Ego will be made by the mother's brother at a sacred place. During the initiation ceremony the mother's brother puts the "sacred thread" on her son. In these respects the role and status of mother's brother is not comparable with that of any other kin. In recent decades the increasing spatial and social mobility, education and the process of modernization have altered the kind and degree of relationship of mother's brother and her children.

Communication among Kin

Since almost all the Brahmans are literate and have high school or college education, contact among them through letters is more frequent than among Lingayats. Moreover, the wider spatial distribution of kin among Brahmans necessitates correspondence. While 33.04% of the Lingayats had never written to or received letters from their kin, all the Brahmans had done so. Ego's frequency of communication through letters was maximum with his brother and brother's relatives (34.78%), followed next by kin on spouse's side (26.96%) and then with relatives on the sister's side (19.18%), mother's side (15.65%), father's side (12.17%) and both son's and daughter's side (11.30%). It is not possible to ascertain the effective kin through knowledge of the frequency of correspondence with a particular set of relatives, because in addition to the degree of kin relationship other factors such as spatial distance, the purpose and urgency of communication, personal selectivity, age and sex of kin, operate simultaneously. However, such analysis shows the role played by communication through letters which keeps residentially separated kin in touch and helps to maintain kin ties between periodic visits.

The majority of invitations sent and received were between the kin (62.62%). In 37.39% of the cases they exchanged invitations with nonkin on various occasions such as naming, initiation ceremonies, weddings, fairs and festivals, etc.

In Gokul the practice of getting themselves photographed, the preservation and display of the photographs of kin are quite widespread. Along with pictures of gods and goddesses one can often see a series of photos of the members of the family and kin group. All the households possessed photographs of Ego's children. 58.26% of the households had photos of Ego's father and 29.57% possessed photos of Ego's mother and 17.39% of the households had photos of kin on the side of spouse and 17.39% possessed photos of Ego and his or her siblings. In several houses enlarged photos of Ego's parents were displayed.

Photos of weddings, initiation ceremony, and photos of household members with their kin indicate the Brahman's interest in the preservation of photos of kin, thereby increasing kin consciousness and orientation toward kin in such material tokens.

Naming and Kinship Cohesiveness

Williams points out, "... analysis of names is of great significance since they provide detailed documentation of kinship values that are otherwise difficult to analyse."[4] The names that appear in the genealogies reflect Brahmanic culture and unfold a vista of the Hindu epics of *Ramayana* and *Mahabharata*, recalling various legends and mythologies. It has been customary to name the first born male child after the father's father and the first female child after her father's mother. The remaining children bear the names of other closely related ancestors of the patrikin or they are named after the gods, goddesses and saints of the Brahmans or the names of sacred rivers. It is evident from the genealogies that such traditional naming patterns were common and persistent through generations. Exactly the same names have been repeated in every alternate generation of almost all the genealogies.

Table 25

Traditional Naming Patterns

Pattern I		Pattern II	
Males	*Females*	*Males*	*Females*
Anant	Bhagirathi	Bindu	Arundhati
Chidambar	Janaki	Martand	Damayanti
Gopal	Laxmi	Shyama	Kaushalya
Krishna	Rukmini	Vasudev	Subhadra
Narayan	Yamuna	Vishnu	Yashoda

Table 26

Pattern III	
Males	*Females*
Achyuta	Bayabai
Atmaram	Gundabai
Damodar	Hanuma
Gundu	Mahina
Janaradana	Thakubai

Brahman women receive new names after marriage. This custom initially created some difficulty in recording genealogies and in ascertaining kin mar-

---

4 Williams, W. M. 1956, p. 82.

riages. The names of males usually end with suffixes such as *Rao*, *Bhatta*, *Acharya*, *Shastri*, etc., and that of females with *Bai*, or *Amma*. In Gokul there is a variety of pet names, names on record and in daily use for the same individual.

Genealogies of the 14 Brahman households indicate the traditional naming patterns as shown in three different models above. The names in Pattern I and II amount to nearly 71% of the names recorded in the genealogies of all the Brahman households. While names in pattern I are fossilized in the Brahman community, some names in pattern II have diffused to other communities as well. But names in pattern III are less common (13%) among the Brahmans of Gokul.

Who suggests a name for the newborn baby? In 50.64% of the cases it is the mother of the child and child's kin on the mother's side who take the lead in giving a name to the offspring. In 40.86% of the cases it was the child's father and relatives on the father's side such as father's father and father's mother, who gave a name to the baby. Naming is controlled by the mother's kin rather than that of the father. However, they all prefer names from patrilateral ancestors.

By and large such traditional naming habits continue to exert influence among the Brahmans. 77.39% of them are still in favour of naming children after their ancestors:

"This is in accordance with the tradition that we cherish. In that way we respect and remember elders."

"Our traditional culture is embedded in the names of gods, goddesses and ancestors. If our children are named after gods and elders we believe that they will grow strong, live long and imbibe virtues of our fore-fathers."

It is their belief that the deceased father is re-born as son. Moreover, "names of our ancestors should not sink. Continuation of the names of elders is made possible by such a custom of naming."

"Children are born by the grace of our elders and we attain religious merit (*punya*) by naming children after them."

Such remarks express high regards, warm sentiments and deep reverence for ancestors. Respect for the deceased elders as expressed in the naming

Table 27

Modern Naming Patterns

Pattern IV	
Males	*Females*
Anil	Baby
Arun	Chhaya
Deepak	Maya
Suhas	Rekha
Vinod	Sandhya
Ranjan	Sadhana
	Vaijayantimala

patterns act as a great force in the solidarity of kin through generations.

New values and new desires, modern urban environment, education, secular ideologies, press, movies and other media of mass communications, and the exigencies of modern times have been responsible for changing naming patterns.

Emerging out of the genealogies of 14 Brahman households (pattern IV) are new habits of naming children which deviate from the kin-oriented traditional naming habits. These names are "modern" as opposed to the traditional kin-oriented names, and the "new" names are imitated from filmstars and are inspired by motives of prestige. These modern names are secular and have no caste reference. To name the children in this manner is considered fashionable and to that extent modernized. Nearly 16% of the names recorded in the genealogies of all the Brahman households are modern names that appear mostly in Ego's children's and grand-children's generations.

The increasing number of modern names which are secular, and devoid of sentimental ties with ancestors, seem to indicate that people of Gokul are becoming more prestige-bound than bound by sentimental attachments of kinship. A young housewife said, "The repetition of the same old names of ancestors like Rama and Krishna is monotonous. Modern names are not only better for a change but are also best suited for the modern environment." Another educated young man pointed out, "Modern names do not indicate caste and hence promote a casteless society." Those in favour of giving modern names to their children represent 17.39%, while 5.22% wish to have both "old" and "new" names for their children. Compared with Lingayats, the greater percentage and variety of modern names among Brahmans illustrate their assimilation of modern values to a greater degree.

Therefore, relatively speaking, the custom of naming children after their deceased relatives is less prevalent now than it was formerly. Nevertheless, the majority are at least verbally in favour of naming children after ancestors; and many of them try to give a modern look to the "old" names or try to interpret the "new" names as representing gods and ancestors. It is evident that both communities still by and large follow the traditional patterns of naming.

Authority and Decision-making

The authority pattern among Brahmans is similar to that among Lingayats. In Gokul women are quite conscious of their role inside the family and kin group. Egalitarian views have been emerging and Brahman women seem to be more assertive and vocal. The father makes decisions of far-reaching importance in consultation with the mother and even the eldest adult son. Parents control the life of children till they get adequate education and a "good" job. After marriage, children become economically independent. Thereupon, the authority of parents begins to wane. There are greater chances for the parents in their old age to depend upon the resources of their earning son.

On important matters and on personal problems Ego consults the kin on mother's side in 27.83% of the cases, the kin on brother's side 20.87%, father's side 15.65%, on spouse's side 15.65%, and on sister's side 9.57%. In approximately 7% of the cases the Ego consults married son, daughter and daughter's husband. Such responses illustrate the importance of extrafamilial kinship in the life of the individual and his family.

When children are in trouble 34.78% of them approach the mother for help and sympathy, 31.30% of them approach the father and 31.30% of them go to both father and mother. The father and mother both punish children in 41.74% of the cases, mother alone in 34.78% of the cases, and in 19.13% of the cases father alone punishes children. Other relatives punish only in 4.35% of the cases. Corporal punishment continues till the children reach 12 or 14 years of age. Thereafter non-corporal forms of punishment such as ridicule and denial of treats continue to operate.

Of the parent as many as 90.24% give tuition and other instruction in the school studies of children at home. The breakdown shows that in 45.22% of the cases it was the father who tutored children, in 20% of the cases it was the mother, and both the father and mother in 9.57% of the cases; other relatives in 15.65% of the cases and, in the rest of the cases, children did not receive tuition from any of the relatives. Brahmans, being aware of the values of education, take keen interest in their children's study.

It is the father in 41.74% of the cases who gives pocket money to children, the mother in 19.13% of the cases, and both the father and mother in 6.96%; other relatives give pocket money to children only in 5.22% of the cases. Although the mother is affectionate the strings of the family purse are held by the father.

Sibling Solidarity

Though the structure of interpersonal relationships among kin in Gokul broadly resembles that of Kalyan kinship system, there are some differences. Conflicts among brothers are rare. Education and employment makes them spatially and socially mobile. Brothers establish their new families in different places. This spatial distribution of brothers could probably account, at least in part, for the absence of quarrels, bickerings and jealousies amongst brother's wives. Likewise, conflicts regarding the partition of family property are generally infrequent since most of the Brahmans depend on non-agricultural occupations for their livelihood. In Gokul bonds of kinship amongst brothers, even after marriage, were strong and the relationships were seldom strained.

The existence of relative harmony between Brahman brothers and relative disharmony among Lingayat brothers at the dissolution of the extended family is a matter that needs further investigation. It appears that the patrilineal extended family rather than the lineage is more important to the Lingayat, and the reverse seems true for the Brahman. The greater degree of modernization of Brahman values and occupations also accounts for the differences. One possible explanation may be that Brahmans are more educated and with education it is possible to clearly state options in a family crisis situation. This is likely to bring them to a rational decision point where no hard feelings result.

In these urban communities it appears that "kinship is the rod on which one leans throughout life" (R. Lowie). In the absence of a certain set of kin, replacement and substitution takes place automatically as it is necessary for even the smallest kin group to function in a state of equilibrium. The substitution of kin and foster parentage in Gokul follows the same pattern as that already delineated for the people of Kalyan.

The nature of social contacts and mutual visits in Gokul is rather different from that in Kalyan since the inhabitants of Gokul are not territorial kin groups. Unlike the lingayats who see their kin almost daily or weekly, the Brahmans meet their relatives in Dharwar once a fortnight or monthly. The frequency of visits is much less among Brahmans due to wider spatial distribution of kin. Distance, pressure of time and high cost of transport limit the number of visits. However, in some cases it was noticed that these factors were no hindrance for "kinminded" people who liked to meet their dear ones.

Respect and Obedience

Filial piety is one of the most treasured virtues. Now, as the elders indicate, social frictions between generations are on the increase. Elderly respondents pointed out that now the younger generation gives less respect to the elders. Traditional ideas tend to conflict with new ideas and ideals in case of the mother-in-law and daughter-in-law.

In the opinion of the informants ages 65 and over, the uncontrolled behaviour of youngsters is due to modern ideas of individual liberty and democracy, new education, economic independence, separate residential patterns of living, government policies and legislation such as that of removal of untouchability and restrictions on intercaste marriages, and modern civilization have corrupted the entire fabric of society. Lack of religious and moral education, and greater social mobility of younger generation have led to clash of ideologies between the old and the young.

On the other hand youngsters complain that most of the misunderstanding and conflict between generations is due to a wide gap in ideologies, the adherence to the same old traditional norms by the aged and their disinclination to make adjustments to changing circumstances. Ross observed:

"It is only when conditions change, and parents find themselves helpless to handle disobedient children that tensions, frictions and conflicts ensue and parents must reconsider their methods of promoting obedience. In the period of transition parents are unsure of their authority, and both they and their children feel resentment towards each other.

"The extent to which training in obedience is carried over into adult life can be seen both in the extent to which adult men and women are still willing to follow their elders' wishes and in the degree to which they feel guilty if they transgress them, that is, to the extent to which these patterns are internalized and become part of the person's conscience."[5]

The behaviour of kin in mutual aid and cooperation, and other values of kinship have undergone some change. Such change was felt by the aged respondents of Gokul in their own life span.

"There was a time in our younger days when the eldest of the kingroup helped almost all of us even sacrificing his own comforts. Now there is no solidarity among kin. To help relatives is a heavy burden," said an old man of sixty-eight.

"It is difficult to make both ends meet to maintain one's wife and children. To help my younger brothers is a pressure on my budget. We should not expect help from our relatives since each has his own difficulties. In these days only non-monetary help, blessings, mutual visits and small gifts among kin are the only possibilities," said a young man of thirty-two.

Aged respondents complained that after marriage sons forget their parents and are more inclined towards kin on wife's side than on their siblings or parents. There is a consensus of opinion that high cost of living, rapid growth of population, new aspirations, avarice, selfishness, economic independence and social mobility have conspired to bring about diminishing rate of actual help among kin. Despite these verbal responses observations of inter-kin relationships show that the traditional kinship values, attitudes and behaviour still persist. The foregoing analysis of kin behaviour among the Lingayats and Brahmans suggests that in the process of modernization, though there has been some change in the attitudes and behaviour patterns of kin towards each other, the kinship values in its essentials have remained practically the same. To provide additional evidence for the continuity of traditional kinship norms, we shall devote the next chapter to an analysis of marital ties.

---

5   Ross, A.D., 1961, p. 133.

CHAPTER FIVE

Bonds of Marriage

AN UNDERSTANDING of the marriage system, which is one of the most important sources for kinship links, is essential to any understanding of Indian kinship systems. Both the Lingayats and Brahmans consider marriage as a prerequisite for the normal state of life for every adult of marriageable age. So the proverb "sooner or later a man must have a wife and a woman a husband" is followed in practice. The aim of this chapter is to discuss some aspects of marriage, namely, mate selection, age of marriage, propinquity, interkin marriage, wedding customs and rituals. We shall examine the attitudes toward dowry, intercaste marriage, divorce and widow remarriage. We wish to show how, along with some attitudinal and behavioural changes, traditional norms and behaviour regarding marriage still persist.

Mate Selection

For the selections of a mate, the real unit of endogamy is not the caste but the subcaste. Traditionally the individual is restricted to selecting his or her partner within his or her own subcaste. Even within one's own subcaste, while selecting a mate, factors such as socioeconomic status of the potential spouse's family and kingroup, language, region, occupation, customs and manners exert their influence.

Rules of exogamy prevent marriages among members of the same patrilineage or clan. The exogamous group called *bedagu* among the Lingayats and the *gotra* among the Brahmans is in most cases composed of persons who are, or who consider themselves to be, related by "blood." Members belonging to the same *bedagu* or same *gotra (sagotra)* cannot intermarry.

Although marriage of parallel cousins is prohibited, a man prefers or is expected to marry his own or classificatory mother's brother's daughter or father's sister's daughter (uncle-niece marriage). Marriages among other preferential kin are allowed except between those persons related either actually or by analogy as parent and child, or as brother and sister. Such intermarriages among kin are characteristic features among the Lingayats and Brahmans.

Arranged Marriages

Among the Lingayats marriages of children are arranged by parents and other elders of the kin group. In this respect the intimate kin group functions as a Marriage Guidance Bureau. Marriage is considered as a union of two families and kin groups rather than merely as a link between two individuals.

The bride should adjust to the groom's household and his kin group instead of satisfying the interests and tastes of the husband only. So the interests of the parties who enter into the marital union will be subordinated to the ends of the family and kin group. In such cases love between future spouses does not precede marriage, but it is supposed to develop after it.

In the selection of a bride, the first consideration is the social status and economic condition of the bride's family. Besides the traditions of the family, her character, age, health and her possible capacity for adjusting to the new household are of prime importance. In the selection of a bridegroom, the social and economic status of the groom's family, and the health and earning level of the boy are usually the factors that matter. The astrologer is consulted. He screens the horoscopes and gives his verdict as regards the compatibility of stars. Thereafter, the engagement ceremony takes place at the bride's residence.

The early age at which the children are married necessitates initiative by parents in arranging marriages. Among men 60% have never even cast a glance at their fiancees prior to the wedding ceremony. When 40% of marriages took place in childhood, the question of mutual likes and consent of parties to the union never arose. 67% of the respondents feel that the elders should take the responsibility for the marriage of children.

Those influenced by modern values (33%), however, believe that personal choice of mate is essential. The consensus is that, in matters of marital alliance, the parents should approve the family of the bride and the boy should approve the girl. This idea itself seems to be a radical one. More radical would be the idea of a girl's need to approve the boy.

Age of marriage

The age of marriage is closely related to the patterns of arranged marriages. The age of first marriage of girls and boys has been varying in time and space and it differs with caste, class, customs and language. In traditional India it has been customary to arrange the marriage of the girl before she attains puberty. The main considerations for early marriages have been the high regard for the chastity of the woman, easy transfer of the bride from the domination of her father to that of her husband and the greater possibilities of better adjustments with her husband and in-laws, endogamy, hypergamy and the social prestige attached to such unions. Though the girl is usually married before puberty, she remains in her natal home till she attains puberty.

Analysis of 303 marriages in Kalyan indicates that in 80.53% of the females age at first marriage was below 15 years and in 19.47% of the females age at first marriage was 15 years and above. Hence the overwhelming majority of girls marry at an early age in contravention of the provisions of the Hindu Marriage Act, 1955, which fixes 15 as the minimum age of marriage for girls. The age at first marriage in the case of 81.52% of the males was 18 years and above, and in only 18.48% of the cases were males below 18 years of age at their first marriage.

A study of the age at first marriage of 257 females (Table 28) gives a glimpse of the changing age at first marriage in different age groups.

Table 28

Age at First Marriage of Females

Present Age of Females	Below 13	13–15	16–20	Total
35 and above	53	23	10	86
23–34	43	20	20	83
14–23	33	20	24	77
Below 14	11	—	—	11
Total	140	63	54	257*

* Data regarding age at first marriage were available for 257 women only.

These figures indicate that among all age groups the number of marriages is largest for females who marry before 13 years of age. This phenomenon is closely interrelated with a high frequency (40%) of preferential kin marriages. There has been a slow and steady trend toward the postponement of the girl's age at marriage. It is significant that the incidence of pre-puberty marriage is greatest for women who are now 35 years and over. This slow rise in the age of marriage is not because of female education but because of the practical difficulty of finding a suitable bridegroom within the subcaste: "For it very often happens that a bridegroom is not available within a small endogamous group. People cannot shed their endogamous habits and so they look for a bridegroom, and imperceptibly and unwillingly the girl grows up. This is the situation prevailing in the Hindu community today and it is bound to worsen."[1]

Table 29

Average Age at First Marriage of Females

Present Age of Females	Average Age
35 and above	11.2
24–34	12.1
14–23	13.0
Below 14	9.0
Overall average	12.0

But the social situation among the Lingayats has not worsened with regard to the selection of grooms. Out of 303 marriages analyzed, in 80.53% of the cases girls married when they were below 15 years. The very fact that practically all these marriages took place within subcastes indicates that even

---

1 Kapadia, K. M. 1959, p. 159.

now finding a partner for the girl in the same subcaste is not difficult.

The average age at first marriage of females for all age groups is 12.0 years. Within each of the groups, however, the average age at first marriage of females has been slowly increasing.

In contrast, the average age at first marriage of males has been 20.0 years consistently in the different age groups. This suggests that men have been marrying almost at the same age for the last two or three generations.

Difference in Age between Spouses

"Not only the age at which men and women marry, but also the *difference in age* between husband and wife is important in determining their relationship. The traditional attitude that the wife is completely subordinate to the husband and must look up to him as a god is more likely to fit in with a large difference in age than equal age. If the age difference changes and at the same time women became more equally educated to men, then the traditional attitude between husband and wife is likely to break down into one of more equal authority and more companionship."[2]

In Kalyan the average difference in age between husband and wife at first marriage for all age groups is 8.0 years. But within each age group the average difference in age between husband and wife has been gradually decreasing.

Table 30

Difference in Age between Husband and Wife at First Marriage

Present Age of Females	Average Age
35 and above	8.2
24–34	8.3
14–23	7.8
Below 14	7.0
Overall average	8.0

Taking into account the averages of actual age at marriage and the age difference between husband and wife at first marriage, one can analyze the respondents' opinions about the ideal age for marriage of females and males.

Table 31

Ideal Age for Marriage of Females and Males

Respondent's Age	Average Ideal Age for Females	Average Ideal Age for Males
35 and above	14.0	21.0
24–34	15.0	23.0
19–23	14.0	22.0

---

2   Ross, A. D. 1961, p. 249.

Although the people of Kalyan think that the ideal age for marriage of girls and boys should be 14 and 22 respectively, the data at our disposal make it clear that in reality they marry two years before they reach the ideal age of marriage. Interestingly, though the average ideal age difference in the youngest generation is slightly more than in the oldest generation, the average ideal age difference between husband and wife for all age groups coincides with the actual age difference (i.e. eight years) between spouses.

Since the average age at first marriage of females is 12.0 years, one might expect attendant social, economic and psychological stresses and strains. Early marriage prevents the exercise of free will by the parties and results in early consummation, early maternity and birth of sickly children, a high incidence of infant and maternal mortality, debility and disease, too many children, and poverty. Further, early marriage deprives the wife of opportunities of education and contributes to inter-personal tensions and conflicts. Despite these evil consequences the Lingayats of Kalyan, being mainly a peasant community, have found early marriages socially more suitable, economically advantageous, and psychologically easy on the relations between spouses and the kin groups. Thus the consensus of opinion among the Lingayats is that early marriages, that is, marriages between 14–15, are preferable because of their normality and inherent strengths.

Propinquity and Marital Ties

In matrimonial relationships, the manifestation of narrow geographical distance is a remarkable feature of the Kalyan community. Analysis of 303 marriages presents an interesting pattern of spatial distribution of affinal links.

Table 32

Geographical Distribution of Marital Ties
According to Administrative Units

No. of Marriages	Kalyan	Dharwar City	Dharwar Taluk & District	Outside District	Outside State
303	120	49	85	48	1
100%	39.61%	16.17%	28.05%	15.84%	.33%

Since there is no village or territorial exogamy, more than half of the marriages have been contracted with spouses coming from the same suburb or the same city. The next largest frequency is that of marriages having partners from within Dharwar *Taluk* and district within a radius of five to fifteen miles.

The absence of territorial exogamy, easy availability of mates from the same physical proximity, knowledge of the other's family background the possibility of personal visits and mutual aid among kin, the preference for interkin marriages and suspicion and fear of conflicts in having marital links with unknown people of differing socio-economic backgrounds living in far off places have accounted for selection of mates within a short distance.

However, girls whose natal home is in Kalyan are given in marriage to men from different places. In 87 such recorded marriages, the largest number of marriages are within a radius of 15 miles, followed next by the marriages which have taken place in Dharwar itself.

Table 33

Patterns of Wife Giving

| No. of marriages | Dharwar | Radius (Distance in miles) | | | |
		15	30	60	120
87	24	41	19	2	1
Girls go as wives from = 100% Kalyan	27.59%	47.15%	21.83%	2.29%	1.14%

Significantly, marriages within a radius of 60 to 120 miles are very few indeed. While some girls of Kalyan, married in the same city, others went as wives to 50 different villages, towns and cities, the average distance being 22.6 miles.

The same order of frequency can be observed in 166 marriages wherein girls come as wives from 64 different villages, towns and cities, besides coming from Dharwar itself.

Table 34

Patterns of Wife Receiving

| No. of Matches | Dharwar | Radius (Distance in miles) | | | |
		15	30	60	120
166	56	64	26	16	4
Girls come as wives to Kalyan = 100%	34.93%	40.61%	12.04%	9.63%	2.79%

The average distance from which girls come as wives to Kalyan is 28.9 miles. There seems to be an appreciable distinction among the people of Kalyan in their wife-giving and wife-receiving activities. The figures show a trend towards giving wives to men from places nearer than the places from which they receive wives. On the average they go approximately six miles farther to bring wives than to give their daughters in marriage. The affinal links of Kalyan stretch out, in most of the cases, from 15 miles to a maximum of 60 miles. This indicates to a certain extent the geographical distribution of subcaste membership within the region.

It is difficult, however, to determine whether the propinquity pattern is connected with the geographical distribution of the subcaste members, since a caste census is not available. All the same, it may be pointed out that, since the majority of the marital links of the Lingayats stretch across the north, east, and south (the directions in which subcaste members happen to be distributed) instead of the west (in which direction the subcaste members are absent), the phenomenon may be said to conform broadly to the geographical distribution of subcaste members.

The greater frequency of inter-kin marriages within the limited territory has an advantage of renewing and strengthening the bonds of kinship, thereby preventing further geographical expansion of marital ties. The foregoing analysis suggests that the traditional mode of mate selection tends to influence the age at marriage. Further, the rules of subcaste endogamy go a long way in determining the territorial limits within which the marital relationships are confined.

Interkin Marriages

It is considered appropriate that a man should prefer to marry his own or classificatory elder sister's daughter or his cross-cousin, matrilateral or patrilateral. Such types of marriages among certain relatives are not merely permitted but are regarded as desirable. Preferential kin marriages among the Lingayats renew and reinforce the existing kinship system, thereby the distinction between relatives by blood and by marriage is often blurred.

Marriages with a man's sister's daughter or with a cross-cousin are preferable to any other. In order of preference a person would like to marry his own SiDa in the first instance or his own MoBrDa. Otherwise he will marry his FaSiDa. Marriages with daughters of classificatory sister, mother's brother or father's sister will follow in the absence of the real ones. However, in the preferential choices again priority was given to the MoBrDa. Likewise, "who else shall give a bride to a crippled boy except his own elder sister?" is the proverb often quoted in this community.

Karve writes that "Among non-Brahman castes (Hindu as well as Lingayat) there is a taboo against a man's marriage with the 'younger' sister's daughter. The rule is that a man marries his elder sister's daughter and never his younger sister's daughter." For Karve even very minute and exhaustive enquiries did not reveal a single exception to this rule.[3] However, in the present investigations the researcher recorded among the Lingayats of Kalyan two cases of a man marrying his younger sister's daughter. Enquires revealed that although there is a general rule that a man can marry his elder sister's daughter and such marriages do occur in greater frequency, there is no rigid taboo against marrying a younger sister's daughter. In reality, however, such marriages are rare because of wide disparity in age between uncle and niece (younger sister's daughter).

In Kalyan cousin marriages are not compulsory. The claims of relationship can be offset by the lack of other desirable qualities, and if either the girl or her

---

3   Karve, I. 1953, p. 188.

parents fail to reach satisfactory standards of conduct and character a wife will be sought somewhere else. Her own people, similarly, may refuse to hand her over to some cousin of whom they disapprove or with whose parents they have quarrelled. And, of course, it happens often enough that no suitable cousin is available. In such cases it is held that a more remote relative should be married if possible, but there is no special category for whom preference is expressed.[4]

Levirate is a taboo. However sororate is practised. When a person's wife is dead or barren, the wife's (younger) sister is always considered by far the most suitable woman to take her place. Being the sister of the deceased wife, she would look after her children as her own, thus creating the least disturbance in the family equilibrium. Recorded genealogies revealed three cases of sororate. This implies that sororate in general is never obligatory. Where the two families were previously related, or if they were on friendly terms, they might agree to substitute another woman for a dead or barren wife, but the wife's people were not bound to provide such a substitute nor the husband to seek one.

Although polygamy is allowed by the traditional Hindu custom, it appears that normally men do not like to have more than one wife at a time. Only four cases of polygamy were recorded out of which three happened to be sororal polygamy. It was under special circumstances that when the first wife was barren or gave birth to female children only that the Ego took to a second wife, preferably his first wife's younger sister, possibly to minimize the tensions and conflicts among cowives. In any case, polygomy is resorted to only in exceptional cases in order to get a male child for the perpetuation of the family line and to attain salvation.

But much more common is the practice of inter-marriage between sets of siblings. The genealogies revealed 16 pairs of unions of two brothers marrying (women related as sisters) two sisters. There were three cases of "exchange marriage" that is, a brother and a sister married a sister and a brother. Obviously such types of marriages help to strengthen kinship ties and in course of time they increase the complexity of kinship network.

Type and Frequency of Interkin Marriage

How far do the Lingayats actually marry relatives and what categories of kin do they prefer? The material upon which the following discussion is based consists of genealogies collected from 115 households of Kalyan and embrace 303 marriages altogether.

A striking feature is the high frequency of uncle-niece marriages followed by matrilateral cross-cousin marriages. Relatively speaking, patrilateral cross-cousin marriages and other types of kin marriages are less in number. The close brother-sister tie in the Lingayat community is the pivotal relationship respon-

---

4   See, Radcliffe-Brown & Forde (eds.), 1950. p. 152.

Table 35

Frequency of Kin Marriages

Total No. of Kin Marriages	SiDa	MoBrDa	FaSiDa	Other types	Kin marriages
118	30	38	25	9	16
%	25.42	32.20	21.19	7.63	13.56

sible for high incidence of uncle-niece marriages. As William McCormack[5] rightly points out: "The bond between siblings, when qualified by the factor of sex difference between them, functions as the axis for cordial relationships among relatives. Brother-sister ties are maintained by festival visits, gifts and mutual assistance, and by marriages... The brother-sister relationship is more particularly renewed and intensified if the brother is himself marrying his sister's daughter or if the marriage is between the children of the brother and sister. A surety exists in these cases that the ideal of mutual assistance between the children of brother and sister is realized in the obligations created by marriage. It would be difficult to over-emphasize the effect of these favoured marriages on preserving the bonds of friendship and cooperation, which are founded on the affection of brother and sister, as it appears that herein lies one of the major functions served by sister's daughter and cross-cousin marriage."

In the case of uncle-niece marriage, husband and wife are not strangers. For him she is his elder sister's daughter and for her he is her mother's brother. Now her mother-in-law and her father-in-law are her mother's mother and her mother's father respectively. For him his own elder sister becomes his mother-in-law and his sister's husband the father-in-law. In spite of change in relationships due to such a marriage it is significant that when a man marries one of his preferred kin his original kinship ties with her family tend to persist. When a man marries his sister's daughter he addresses his wife's mother (mother-in-law) "elder sister" and she refers to him reciprocally as "younger brother" and not as "son-in-law". The wife addresses her parents-in-law as "grand parents" and her children will call her "mother" and their father's sister "grand mother". So, broadly, the former patterns of inter-personal relationships continue to dominate.

As observed by Karve,[6] marriage in this part of the country "is not arranged with a view to seek new alliances, or for widening a kin group but each marriage strengthens already existing bonds and makes doubly near those people who were already very near kin. In this respect marriage is a continuous exchange of daughters between a few families, with the result that marriage merely strengthens already existing bonds, without involving entirely new adjustments to new personalities and new situations."

Uncle-niece and cross-cousin marriages not only renew and strengthen the

---

5   McCormack, W. *MI*, vol. 38. no. 1. 1957, pp. 44–45.
6   Karve, I. 1953, pp. 219–220.

existing kinship ties but they also involve less expenses for the ceremony. As there is a greater degree of informality between members of families already linked by affinal relationships there is no need to put on a big and costly show at the wedding ceremony. In establishing a new alliance altogether it is necessary to perform the wedding ceremony with great pomp and show in order to preserve and enhance family prestige. Moreover, most of the Lingayat families of Kalyan are not economically well-to-do. Hence they tend to marry among preferred kin thereby incurring fewer obligations. A family having alliances with a limited number of families is more likely to reciprocate its obligations, and the chances of tensions and conflict due to omissions and probably commissions also can be reduced considerably.

Furthermore, inter-marriage among kin prevents dispersion of the family property and facilitates concentration, distribution and exchange of family resources within a limited circle of kin. In Kalyan parents wish to find a good wife for their son and they prefer to marry him, if possible, to the daughter of some close relative (preferential mate), with whose conduct and reputation they are themselves well acquainted. Near relatives are likely to be more tolerant of each other than strangers, and because of the pre-existing kinship ties, their kin will take greater interest in the welfare of the marriage and try to ensure its success. Such marriages bind the two families closer and make for increased harmony and cooperation. People favour kin marriages because the industriousness and good character of the girl and family background of the parties are known to each other and also because both parties have a strong interest in smoothing out conflicts that may arise between spouses.

Among the various types of interkin marriages, it is evident that in Kalyan uncle-niece marriages and matrilateral cross-cousin marriage types predominate as against patrilateral cross-cousin marriages and other types of kin marriages. Several factors determine the preference shown by people for marriage with the sister's daughter or mother's brother's daughter. In the first instance there is greater frequency of social interaction and more intensity of affection between a man and his sister and his mother's brother in contrast to his father's sister. Such a behaviour pattern is upheld and approved by the social values and norms. In the second place, which seems more important from the point of view of maintaining social equilibrium in the kinship system, in the uncle-niece and matrilateral cross-cousin marriages, the chances of proverbial mother-in-law and daughter-in-law conflicts are minimized. In the case of uncle-niece marriages the former grand-mother-grand-daughter relationships dominate between the present mother-in-law and daughter-in-law. And in the case of matrilateral cross-cousin marriage, mother-in-law is the father's sister and daughter-in-law is no stranger but her brother's daughter. In both these types of kin marriages, the daughter-in-law is closely related to her mother-in-law by consanguinity. So mother-in-law naturally tends to bestow love and affection on daughter-in-law.

The lesser frequency of patri-lateral cross-cousin marriages can be explained by the fact that the mother-in-law is the mother's brother's wife. However more often a non-kin, a stranger; and daughter-in-law is husband's sister's daughter, again related by affinity and not by consanguinity. Hence, there are many chances for the real mother-in-law and daughter-in-law relationships to prevail, which contribute to tensions and conflicts between them. This seems to be the reason for the lesser percentage of patrilateral cross-cousin marriages. However, as opposed to non-kin marriages, inter-kin marriages of this type still offer certain advantages.

Attitudes toward Interkin Marriage

Although the elder generation feels that the ideal mate for a man is his sister's daughter or a cross-cousin, the younger generation tends to avoid preferential kin marriages. Marriage among preferential kin, the young informants indicated, would lead to a decline in fertility and limitation of kinship and social horizons. However, quantitative responses reveal 54.78% in favour of inter-kin marriage, 39.13% against it, and 6.09% consider both inter-kin and non-kin marriages as desirable and show no preference for one or the other.

These trends in attitudes towards inter-kin marriage throw light on the divergent opinions about inter-marriages among kin and suggest that there are certain forces working against such marriages. Yet the majority (54.78%) of them still favour inter-kin marriages. Besides, the striking fact in Kalyan is that during the last half of a century or so, the percentage of kin marriages has been more or less the same through the generations. Despite the urban environment Kalyan is still largely a peasant community. Subcaste endogamy, traditional values, poverty, and other related social forces have contributed to a relatively greater percentage of kin marriage and its continued practice. However, there are some symptoms suggesting a weakening of parental authority and traditional values. Imbued with modern values of democracy, individual liberty and new aspirations, Lingayat youths would like to have their own choice in the selection of their mates. Such a tendency among the modern youths may lead to a decrease in the percentage of preferential kin marriage in the future.

Gifts

Exchange of gifts among relatives is another characteristic mechanism which reinforces ties of kinship. Among other kin, the mother's brother is the "first and foremost of a series of present-giving relatives." Besides his major role in various marriage rituals of his sister's children, the mother's brother's presents will be singled out in quantity and quality. Traditionally he presents wedding costumes and ornaments to the sister's son or daughter. The mother's brother will in turn be honoured with gifts.

Likewise, both parties of the marriage union exchange gifts. Louis Dumont[7]

---

7 Dumont, L. *RAI*, Occ. papers. No. 12, 1957.

remarks: "The most conspicuous feature of alliance as an enduring marriage institution that defines and links the two kinds of relatives consists in ceremonial gifts and functions. The chain of gifts, or 'prestations' and counter-prestations, symbolizes the alliance tie and is the most important feature of marriage ceremonies from the point of view of the relation between the two families."

The process of establishing a valid marriage involves a whole series of prestations. Traditionally, gifts such as clothes, ornaments, and household utensils are exchanged between the marriage parties. Although such gifts were exchanged in all marriages, in 45.21% of the marriages men did not receive "dowry".

Of the people here, 11.30% are in favour of dowry if it is a voluntary payment. But the overwhelming majority, that is, 88.70% of them, are not in favour of receiving or giving dowry. Presents made voluntarily with affection can be accepted. But it should not be due to compulsion, and marriage should not become a commercial transaction, according to them.

Desertion and Divorce

In extreme cases of conflict between spouses, all the Lingayats (except members of the Jangam and Banajiga subcastes) allow or at least tolerate desertion or divorce. It is not only the man who may desert his wife but also the woman who may desert her husband. The reasons in either case are severe cruelty, adultery, serious disease, early or forced marriage, impotency or barrenness, and other kinds of incompatibility. There were 14 cases of desertions and divorces in Kalyan.

Although marriage is considered a sacred bond that lasts for life, and after death as well, there are certain social forces which lead to the instability of marriage. In such cases the kinship system of the Lingayats provides the mechanism to restore equilibrium in marital life.

Secondary Union-Udaki

"Remarriage" or "secondary union" (*udaki*) is an institution found among all the Lingayats except the "*jangam*" and "*banajiga*" subcastes. "Secondary union" is allowed though not highly approved of by the people. Such union takes place mostly between widows and widowers or between deserted or divorced men and women. There were 14 cases of secondary unions. Parties to such a union do not enjoy the same prestige as others normally married. 35.65% of the respondents favour divorce when it is inevitable in some extreme cases of conflict between spouses. Such disputes, according to them, should be decided by the traditional caste *panchayats* (councils) and not by the courts of law.

The attitudes are highly favourable toward widow remarriage, as 88.70% are in favour of widow remarriage when a woman is widowed young and has no children, and for divorcees.

There were only 4 cases of inter-subcaste marriages and only 8.70% of the respondents were in favour of such marriages. Otherwise a very large majority (91.30%) are against inter-subcaste marriage let alone inter-caste marriage. Inter-subcaste marriages are vehemently discouraged by the people because of social stigma, fear of ex-communication, difficulty of children's marriages, and conflicts that may arise due to differences of subcaste cultures and of difference in occupations.

Subcaste endogamy is still strong and only recently a microscopic minority braved solid opposition and severe criticism to cross the subcaste boundaries.

Gokul

Among the Brahmans, as among the Lingayats, arranged marriages are the rule. Parents and intimate kin, by and large, select mates for their children. The limited opportunities for boys and girls to meet in schools and colleges and other social gatherings allow only superficial contacts. Conservative persons consider "love marriages" (that is, marriage by personal choice) "skin deep" and non-enduring.

Criteria in the Choice of Mates

The Brahmans have both endogamous and exogamous rules restricting the field of mate selection. One is expected to marry within one's own caste and subcaste, and within a subcaste he should select a partner belonging to a *gotra* other than his own. Among other considerations, education and occupation of the bride-groom are of prime importance in choosing a spouse for one's daughter. Likewise, educated young men desire to have educated brides. The bride's beauty and education may reduce the amount of dowry. While in earlier decades it was solely the parents who selected mates for their children, now boys accompany their elders in selecting brides. The boy has greater choice in selecting his partner and the final approval depends upon his parents. In the event of clash of interest between parents and the boy, the wishes of the boy will receive attention. Yet the boy is rather reluctant to displease his parents. Ultimately a balance is struck between the choice of the boy and his parents. The girl on her part is less frequently consulted by her parents.

The youths of Gokul have greater liberty than those of Kalyan and exercise considerable power and discretion in selecting mates because of their relatively later marriage age, their education and economic independence. While selecting a mate for their children, parents in Gokul think in terms of family and kingroup interests rather than the individual's interests and aspirations, personality traits and talents. Youths, however, try to compromise by adjusting their individual interests and aspirations to the needs of the family and kin group. Therefore, they stress the individual qualities of the bride, and the satisfaction of their own interests as well as her suitability and adjustability to their family environment.

Age at marriage

It is significant that even though the sacred scriptures enjoin prepuberty marriage, the Brahmans in Dharwar postpone marriage.

A study of age at marriage reveals that as high as 75.19% of women were married at 15 years and above, and only 24.81% below 15. These figures indicate the high frequency of postpuberty marriages among the Brahmans.

Table 36 represents frequencies of age at first marriage of females belonging to different age groups.

Table 36

Age at First Marriage of Females						
Present Age of Females	Below 13	13–15	16–20	21–25	26–28	Total
35 and above	21	33	48	5	—	107
24–34	—	12	67	23	2	104
14–23	—	—	37	6	—	43
Total	21	45	152	34	2	254

The foregoing data suggest that the people of Gokul marry later than the people in Kalyan. There is no evidence to indicate a correlationship between kin marriages and early age at marriage in Gokul. Among the Lingayats, however, we noticed that the greater the kin marriages, the greater the number of early marriages. In Gokul the average age at first marriage of females for all age groups is 17.3 years. However, the average age at marriage in the younger generation (i.e. below 35 years) had increased by two years when compared to the average age at marriage in the older generation (i.e. 35 and above).

Table 37

Average Age at First Marriage of Females

Present Age of Females	Average Age
35 and above	16.0
24–34	18.0
14–23	18.0
Overall average	17.3

On the average, girls in Gokul marry 5 years later than the girls in Kalyan. What is striking is the fact that comparing the younger generations in both suburbs, a five year difference in the age at first marriage is maintained.

The average age at first marriage of males for the older generation (i.e. 35 and above) was 24.0 years and for the younger generation (i.e. below 35 years) the average age has been 25.0 years. This again shows that the Brahman males marry 4 or 5 years later than the Lingayat males. Desire for more education and economic independence, the institution of dowry, caste endogamy and new aspirations have all been responsible for the postponement of the age at marriage for both males and females. In the contemporary Brahman community the task of finding a bridegroom for the daughter has become almost a full-time one for the parents. The payment of dowry has assumed unusual proportions in all strata of the community. The lower middle and lower class people with more daughters are particularly financially hard hit. At the time of investigation there were thirty-eight girls in Gokul who were not yet married though they had passed the ideal age of marriage. Such a phenomenon is indeed rare in Kalyan.

Difference in Age between Husband and Wife

The difference in age between spouses influences their interpersonal relationships. Among the Brahmans the difference in age between spouses has consistently been 8 years in both older and younger generations.

Table 38

Ideal and Actual Age at Marriage of Females

Respondent's Age	Average ideal age of marriage	Average actual age of marriage
35 and above	17.0	16.0
24–34	19.0	18.0
20–23	20.0	18.0
20–34	19.0	18.0
Overall average	18.0	17.0

The consensus of opinion is that the ideal age at first marriage of females should be 18. In the age group 20–23 there is a difference of two years between the ideal and the actual age. It is highly significant that the age group 20–23 is in favour of females marrying at the ideal age of 20 years even though in reality girls marry two years earlier than the ideal age. Such an ideational change as regards the age of marriage of girls may be a prelude to a behavioural change. Because education has become necessary for a female not only for marriage but for her economic independence, a college education is desired if the female is to be a worthy partner in marriage."[8]

As regards the age at first marriage of males for all age groups the ideal age at marriage is 24.0 years whereas they marry in fact nearly at the age of 25. Probably their prolonged education, economic pressure and new aspirations postpone the age of marriage. In the older generation, however, the ideal and the actual ages at first marriage of males coincide (i.e. 24 years). Likewise, in the younger generation the ideal and actual ages at marriage are the same (i.e. 25.0 years).

---

8 Kapadia, K. M., 1959, p. 165.

What should be the difference in age between husband and wife? According to the responses of the people belonging to all age groups (20–34 and 35 and above) the ideal age difference between spouses should be 6.0 years. Amongst these groups the older generation desired to have an ideal age difference of 7 years between spouses, but the younger generation wishes to have an ideal age difference of 6 years between spouses. But the actual age difference between spouses as found in all age groups is 8 years. Though the younger generation wishes to have a 6 year age difference that is the husband should be 6 years older than wife, in reality, it is difficult to get partners with such age differences. Although single men and women are anxious to reduce the age difference between them and their prospective spouses, when they actually marry they do not succeed in getting mates of the age they desire. In other words, the traditional age difference in marriage still prevails. Further it may be noted that "This may be due to the fact that even young men and women who want to make their own marriage choice find they must still rely on their parents' help. And it may be either difficult to persuade parents to change their ideas about age or difficult for parents to find mates of the 'nontraditional' age difference."[9]

It is not only difficult to find mates with a suitable age difference but it is still more difficult to find a mate at all for girls by the time they attain the ideal age of marriage. Besides 28 unmarried girls between 15–17 years, there were 34 unmarried girls between 18–25 years of age and 4 unmarried girls between the ages of 26–35. To find a suitable bridegroom for the daughter by the time she reaches the ideal age of marriage has become a problem for her parents and intimate kin group. Despite various efforts made by parents and the kin group the girl unwillingly has to remain without marriage even after crossing the ideal age of marriage.

If there are social evils as a result of early marriage in Kalyan, there are certain evils associated with relatively late marriages in Gokul. The emotional and physiological strains experienced by the girl, the social criticism, financial burden and stresses and strains experienced by the parents in arranging the marriage of the daughter have adversely affected a number of families. The various new social forces such as demand for education, changing values of age of marriage, economic pressures and new aspirations and new norms are trying to mitigate the evils of late marriage to a certain extent.

The Brahmans who at one time idealized pre-puberty marriages and set a model for other castes to emulate and who in the old days desired to acquire higher prestige no longer stick to that ideal. The ideational and behavioural changes with regard to postpuberty marriages have become inevitable among the Brahmans because of new social requirements such as better education, nontraditional occupations, desire for higher living standards and other urban values.

As long as the Lingayats of Kalyan remain largely a peasant community

---

9   Ross, A. D. 1961, pp. 250–251.

with practically no radical changes in education, employment, values and aspirations, it could be assumed that the traditional age of marriage is maintained. If new social forces and new social demands impinge on them there is every likelihood of change taking place in their ideals and behaviour patterns as regards age of marriage.

Geography and Marital Alliances

An analysis of 266 marriages of 115 households of the Brahmans reveals a wider geographical distribution of marital relationships.

Table 39

Geographical Distribution of Marital Ties

No. of Marriages	According to Administrative Units				
	Gokul	Dharwar City	Dharwar Taluk & District	Outside District	Outside State
266	9	85	65	85	22
100%	3.88%	31.95%	24.45%	31.95%	8.27%

These figures indicate that the Brahmans like the Lingayats do not have village or territorial exogamy since in 35.83% of the marriages one of the parties comes from the same suburb or the same city. The frequency of marriages in which one of the spouses belongs to an area outside the district in Gokul is greater than the frequency of marriages of the same type in Kalyan. Moreover, the number of marriages where the partner is from outside the state is nearly eight times greater in Gokul than in Kalyan. Unlike the people of Kalyan, the people of Gokul travel far and wide in search of mates. That is mainly because of rigid adherence to the rules of *gotra* exogamy among the Brahmans.

The girls in Gokul have gone as wives to 61 different villages, towns and cities, besides marrying in the same city. Out of 69 marriages more than half involve mates from within a radius of 30 to 60 miles.

Table 40

Girls go as Wives from Gokul

No. of Matches	Radius (Distance in miles)					
	Dharwar	15	30	60	120	240 and over
89	12	11	28	24	2	12

The marriages in Gokul in which case spouses were from Dharwar city are fewer than those in Kalyan. What is striking in Gokul is the fact that 12 girls were given in marriage as far away as 240 miles and farther. Social mobility of the Brahmans leads to wider spatial distribution of kin and hence affinal links stretch wider because of endogamy and exogamy. The average distance of girls going as wives from Gokul is 72.3 miles.

More or less the same pattern is revealed in 161 matches wherein girls came as wives to Gokul from as many as 95 different villages, towns and cities, besides Dharwar.

Table 41

Girls who have come as Wives to Gokul

No. of Matches	Dharwar	Radius (Distance in miles)				
		15	30	60	120	240 and over
161	17	33	28	58	15	10

The average distance from which girls have come as wives to Gokul is 62.6 miles. Evidently this suggests that the people of Gokul give their daughters in marriage to more distant places than the places from where they get their wives. It appears that it is relatively difficult to get bridegrooms for their daughters within the same distance wherein they get brides for their sons. Caste endogamy, prohibition of intra-clan marriages and the difficulty of finding suitable grooms for daughters in the nearby areas makes the Brahmans seek alliances with persons living approximately 9 miles further away on the average. On the whole, the Brahmans have wider affinal links than the Lingayats.

Interkin Marriage

Traditionally the Brahmans practise preferential kin marriages. In Gokul the two subcastes of the Brahmans, namely Vaishnava and Smartha, who constitute 92.17% of the households, allow uncle-niece, cross-cousin and other types of preferential kin marriages. 7.83% of the households studied which belong to a subcaste known as *Konkanastha* have a strict taboo against kin marriages, because such unions are considered incestuous.

Until the first one or two decades of this century, uncle-niece and cross-cousin marriages were preferred and even obligatory. Although interkin marriages are preferred by the older generation this is not in any case obligatory.

Table 42

Frequency of Kin Marriages

Total No. of Kin Marriages	SiDa	MoBrDa	FaSiDa	Other Types	Kin Marriages-exact relationship not traceable
59	26	12	7	5	9
100%	44.08%	20.34%	11.86%	8.47%	15.25%

Among the Brahmans, 36.52% were against preferential kin marriage and 6.96% of the people favoured both kin and non-kin marriages.

The following figures refer to the marriages of persons living in the 106 households, embracing all 266 marriages, and presents the frequency of various categories of kin marriages.

Among the Brahman, 21.18% are kin marriages. The pattern characteristic of them is the high number of uncle-niece marriages. Next in order are the bilateral cross-cousin marriages. Within the bilateral cross-cousin marriages the matrilateral cross-cousin marriages are more numerous than the patrilateral cross-cousin marriages.

Cross-Cousin Marriages: Some Theoretical Considerations

On the basis of the foregoing data the theories of cross-cousin marriage may be examined. These theories generally refer to communities which practise unilateral cross-cousin marriage. Both communities in the present study practise bilateral cross-cousin marriage. The material, however, shows that there is a definite preference for matrilateral cross-cousin marriage as against patrilateral cross-cousin marriage.

William Goode[10] believes that these behaviour patterns are supported by local values, and that some structural elements in India's patrilineal kinship system give it emotional support. First, "the marriage of a mother's brother's daughter to a father's sister's son repeats the relationship of deference and respect which is due from the matriline. The woman's parents are expected to be grateful to the man's family for marrying her, and this harmony is created in the next generation if the daughter moves in the same direction. By contrast, if a daughter from the father's line were to be married to the mother's brother's son, the deference would be reversed and disharmony would be created. More important, however, is the case of social relations between a boy and his mother's brother as contrasted with the patriarchal respect in his relations with the father's brother or the father's line generally. The permissiveness on both sides makes for a closeness and simplicity of social interaction in which a further union of the two lines may come to seem desirable. It does not, however, explain why it would develop as a *preferred* social arrangement, that is, an explicit part of the system."

Karve explains the preference for matrilateral cross-cousin marriage and discouragement (lesser incidence) of patrilateral cross-cousin marriage by a folk-saying "The creeper should not return" (*Balli tirugu baradu*). The creeper is the girl given in marriage. Her daughter must not be brought back as a bride into the house as it would be returning of the creeper back to the place where it started, which would stop the growth of the family and bring it disaster. If a marriage does take place, some expiatory ritual is performed.[11] Srinivas, how-

---

10 Goode, W. 1963. p. 221.
11 Karve, I. *DCB*, vol. X, pt. 1. p. 191.

ever, considers that "the rule that 'the creeper should not return' is a dead letter in practice. It is only used to avoid an unwelcome bride."[12]

It is true that marriage like many important social relationships must have been a system of mutual obligations and returns. If "A" took a girl from B's family he had to compensate B's family in some way. The best compensation always is doing to the others what they have done to you, in this case by exchange of girls, or, through a process of delayed payment, giving to B's family their daughter's daughter in marriage. When a daughter's daughter returns to the family as a bride the original obligation is cancelled. On this principle a man marrying his father's sister's daughter fulfils the obligation in the second generation. The same principle is at work when a man marries his elder sister's daughter.

In a society based on mutuality of social relationships this marriage procedure appears to be the most natural. Wherever there is an exchange of daughters, naturally the father's sister's daughter is identical with the mother's brother's daughter, but the stress is on the first relationship and not on the second.

Karve further argues that matrilateral cross-cousin marriage is preferred to patrilateral cross-cousin marriage because there is a feeling of social superiority arising out of cultural contact and dominance of one class over another and because of the practice of hypergamy. "The creeper cannot return in such a society. A man's mother may belong to an inferior family, he can choose a bride from her family and by preference the choice falls upon the mother's brother's daughter. His father's sister on the other hand must have married into a family of equal status or preferably into a family of higher status; she can therefore not give her daughter back into a brother's family."[13]

Levi-Strauss advanced the hypothesis that matrilateral cross-cousin marriage for a man occurs more frequently than patrilateral cross-cousin marriage because it leads to generalized exchange of women and produces greater solidarity in the society. He holds that generalized exchange is better than restricted exchange from the point of view of the organic solidarity of a society, and argues that, from the same point of view, MoBrDa marriage (generalized exchange) is better than FaSiDa marriage and so more societies follow the former than the latter rule.

Homans and Schneider[14] concentrated their attention on a study of unilateral cross-cousin marriage and considered Levi-Strauss's theory to be a final cause theory and therefore unsatisfactory. Thus, they sought an efficient cause theory. Their theory was that the matrilateral form would be found in societies possessing patrilineal kin groups, while the patrilateral form would be found in societies possessing matrilineal kin groups. This hypothesis arose from a more general theory presented by Homans that "a man seeks affectionate relationships where authority does not lie."

12　Srinivas, M. N. 1942. p. 42.
13　Karve, I. *DCB*, vol. X. pt. 1.
14　Homans & Schneider, 1955, pp. 21, 28–29.

The proposition was tested in various societies and the new formulation stated that "Societies in which marriage is allowed or preferred with the mother's brother's daughter but forbidden or disapproved with the father's sister's daughter will be societies in which jural authority over ego male, before marriage, is vested in his father or father's lineage, and societies in which marriage is allowed or preferred with the father's sister's daughter but forbidden or disapproved with the mother's brother's daughter will be societies in which jural authority over ego male, before marriage, is vested in his mother's brother or mother's brother's lineage."

Homans and Schneider consider that mother's brother's daughter marriage may be particularly common in patrilineal societies because of the close nature of the tie between Ego and mother's brother in these societies. They found, in the structure of interpersonal relations, the individual motivations, or efficient cause, for the adoption of a particular form of unilateral cross-cousin marriage. It is further observed that "As he visits mother's brother often, Ego will see a great deal of the daughter; contact will be established. As he is fond of mother's brother and his daughter in the patrilineal complex, the Oedipus Complex if you will, are themselves particularly close to one another, he will tend to get fond of the daughter. Their marriage will be sentimentally appropriate; it will cement the relationship. Or if women are indeed scarce and valued goods, and Ego is in doubt where he can get one, he will certainly be wise to ask his mother's brother, on whom he already has so strong sentimental claim." Their general theory is that the "form of unilateral cross-cousin marriage will be determined by the system of interpersonal relations precipitated by a social structure, especially by the locus of jural authority over ego."

Considering the foregoing theories it could be stated that FaSiDa marriages are fewer because in the Lingayat and Brahman communities, among the various types of kin marriages, the most preferred are uncle-niece marriage. In this case by the time when Ego (male) wishes to marry it is quite possible that Ego's father might have married his own SiDa. In these circumstances, the Ego's FaSi becomes MoMo and her daughters become Mo or mother's sisters (see Diagram). Hence Ego cannot marry his mother's siblings. Therefore Ego has to look for his MoBrDa. Hence we see a greater frequency of matrilateral cross-cousin marriages than patrilateral ones.

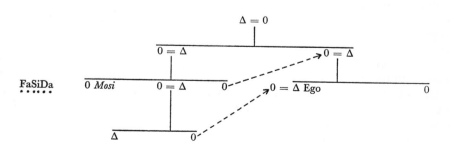

The views expressed by Goode, Karve, Levi-Strauss, Homans and Schneider about cross-cousin marriage explain the various factors responsible for the
greater incidence of matrilateral cross-cousin marriages in patrilineal societies
such as those of the Lingayats and Brahmans. Mutual obligations among kin
and the consequent exchange of girls, hypergamy, interpersonal relations and
organic solidarity, jural authority, and high incidence of uncle-niece marriage
are the social forces significantly correlated with a higher frequency of the
matrilateral form over the patrilateral form of cross-cousin marriage in the
patrilineal Lingayat and Brahman communities. Moreover, the patrilineal
communities such as the Lingayats and Brahmans, practising both bilateral
cross-cousin marriage and uncle-niece marriage, show a definite preference for
uncle-niece marriages over the matrilateral form of cross-cousin marriage.

Table 43

Frequency of Uncle-Niece and Cross-Cousin Marriages

	SiDa	MoBrDa	FaSiDa	Total
Lingayats	111	96	62	269
Brahmans	79	42	13	134
Total	190	138	75	403

It could be stated generally that in societies in which uncle-niece marriage
is allowed along with bilateral cross-cousin marriage, people prefer uncle-niece
marriage in the first instance, followed by matrilateral and patrilateral cross-
cousin marriages.

It is evident from the data that the total number of kin marriages is lower
among the Brahmans than among the Lingayats. The reasons are obvious. In
the first instance people belonging to the *konkanastha* subcaste of Brahmans who
constitute 7.83% in Gokul do not practise kin marriage. A great majority of the
rest of the Brahmans do not favour marriage with preferred relatives, because
they believe that kin marriage is not good *per se* because inbreeding will lead to
lack of issues or defective progeny.

Factors such as higher education, urban industrial occupations, social
mobility, new values and aspirations together with the advantages of non-kin
marriage such as those of better progeny, enlargement of kin circle and wider
social contacts, the desire to have a pretty and educated wife and temptations
of dowry, influence the Brahmans to favour non-kin marriage instead of kin
marriage.

The figures for cousin marriages in both communities in Dharwar show no
marked difference between stated preferences and actual practice. There were
two cases of sororate, one case of exchange marriage and four cases of marriages
of sets of siblings. All such inter-marriages of kin not only renew and strengthen
bonds of kinship but create a complexity of kinship network.

The analysis of the frequency of preferential kin marriage among the

Brahmans indicates a declining trend and with the present increase in the tempo of modernization, kin marriages tend to be exceptions.

The Exchange of Gifts

In strengthening kinship solidarity and in keeping alive the relationships among effective kin, the exchange of gifts (*Aheru-Muyya*) on various ceremonial occasions plays a dominant part. The presents are made at naming and initiation ceremonies. Gift giving and receiving is at its climax during wedding ceremonies. The bride or the groom receives special gifts of considerable value in the form of clothes, ornaments and utensils for the new household. The mother's brother protects the bride from evil spirits and performs a series of religious ceremonies. In the absence of a father, MoBr makes a ritual presentation of the bride to the bridegroom. The mother's brother will receive a gift in return. Every marriage is followed by a series of prestations and counter prestations between the two families firmly establishing the new marital link. The extended kin and friends present gifts to the bride and/or the bridegroom symbolizing cordial relationships.

Problem of Dowry

Dowry is a well-established institution among the Brahmans. Today young men are unwilling to marry without a dowry. Dowry refers primarily to a large sum of money besides customary presents made to the bridegroom in the form of clothes, ornaments and vessels. Of the respondents studied, 50.44% received dowry in cash and/or lands, 26.08% of them did not receive dowry in cash but in kind, and 23.48% of them received customary gifts only.

Among the Brahmans the giving and receiving of dowry seems to have become an accepted pattern of behaviour. Willingly or unwillingly 40.87% of the respondents favour payment of dowry. According to them, payment of dowry should be voluntary, and the sum of money paid should not be exorbitant. They like neither bargaining nor compulsion and exploitation.

The Brahman middle class and working class families with many daughters are hard hit by the dowry system. The social, economic and psychological stresses and strains experienced by parents and daughters on account of dowry have increased. A man of limited means has to incur debts, and may go bankrupt or else a pretty daughter may remain unmarried. Caste and subcaste endogamy, hypergamy and desire to give daughters to highly educated youths has increased the amount of dowry.

As observed by Kapadia, "the amount of dowry is generally regulated by the social and economic status of the bridegroom's father, the social prestige of the bridegroom's family, and the educational qualifications of the bridegroom. A girl's physical beauty or educational qualifications reduce this amount at times, but often this reduction is very meagre. Naturally the girl whose father cannot afford to satisfy the exhorbitant demands of the person whom she would like to marry cannot succeed in securing him as her partner in marriage. On the other hand, a girl may be at times married to an undeserving person when the latter is prepared to marry her with a dowry within the means of her father. Ill-assorted marriages have at times resulted from this practice of dowry."[15] In Gokul educated bridegrooms demand a fabulous amount of dowry ranging from a minimum of Rs. 5,000 to Rs. 25,000. Especially when the bridegroom is a doctor, engineer or an officer in the upper echelons of state or Central Government service, the amount of dowry demanded is high.

It is argued that the dowry system still plays an important function. It has been the means of providing many poor students with enough money to complete their education indirectly. It has been the means of helping to raise the age of marriage, forcing parents to go beyond subcaste and caste barriers to find bridegrooms for their daughters. It has also helped young couples to set up a new house with the gifts and money received at marriage. Yet this system of 'bridegroom-buying', has now become a widespread social disease among the Brahmans. "Economic pressure which has made young men put off marriage till they can stand on their own feet has made most of them more unscrupulous in exacting a dowry."[16] Therefore many girls remain unmarried whose parents' purse does not allow them to pay a high amount of dowry.

The consensus of opinion is that "nowadays bridegrooms demand educated brides and parents have to spend a lot of money on the education of daughters. Moreover, daughters influenced by the Hindu Succession Act of 1956 are gradually asserting their legal right to a share in the parental property thereby leading to strained relationships. Therefore there is no necessity to give dowry. One's companion is wife and not money. Young men should change their attitudes towards claiming and insisting on a high amount of dowry." Of the interviewees, 59.13% are not in favour of the dowry system. Although several unmarried young men reported that either demanding a particular amount of dowry or not demanding it at all depends on the beauty and education of the bride, it appears that the younger generation has not basically changed its attitudes towards receiving dowry. Almost every one advocates, ideally at least, a marriage without dowry. In practice it is quite the contrary. However, the Brahmans feel that the leaders of the community should alleviate the social evil of dowry.

Wedding Ceremonies

A wedding among the Brahmans as in most other communities constitutes one of the important occasions on which relatives can meet, exchange ideas and entertain themselves. Marriage ceremonies revitalize the feelings of kin soli-

---

15   Kapadia, K. M. 1959, p. 137.
16   Kar, "A Solution to the Dowry Problem", *Aryan Path*, Nov. 1954, p. 523, as quoted in Ross, A.D., 1961, p. 262.

darity. This can be seen in the concern of even distant relatives to help their kin and to attend weddings. If the wedding is one of a close relative all the members of the family will attend, but if the wedding is one of a distant relative, one person will represent the family. Assistance to relatives on these occasions takes the form of both financial aid and household work. Usually the members of a joint family will share the expense of religious or marriage ceremonies, but sometimes distant relatives may help in the payment of dowry or the actual financing of the wedding. Presents to the young couple may take the form of a financial gift. The wedding arrangements, including cooking, serving, looking after the guests, etc., will be taken care of by the extended kin.

The Brahmans advocate simplicity in marriage ceremonies and want to cut down elaborate rituals. Often in these days the high cost of transport, lack of time and difficulty in taking a leave of absence from service prevent relatives, near and distant, from attending weddings. Ross observes that the decline in this participation is due to the fact that weddings have become less elaborate, and that relatives, less inclined to attend family ceremonials, may be an important factor in assisting to break up the unity of the large kin group.[17]

Attitudes toward Divorce and Widow Remarriage

For the Brahmans marriage has been a sacrament which is irrevocable. Imbued with traditional ideals the Brahmans do not think of divorce. Though there are tensions and conflicts between spouses, compromise and adjustment is demanded rather than divorce. "Even if the husband is cruel, diseased and a man of vices, he is God and one should die for the sake of husband and divorce is against religious injunctions," said one old widow. There was not a single instance of divorce in Gokul.

The principle of divorce is quite alien to the Brahmanic cultural pattern. A majority of interviewees (77.39) are against divorce under any conditions, and 22.61% of them, mostly educated young men, are in favour of divorce under extreme circumstances such as cruelty, adultery, incurable disease and the like. Even this minority group feels that compromise is best. These are merely indeational changes without any behavioural change. But such ideational change expressed in their verbal responses are suggestive of the future possibility of change in their outlook and behaviour.

Despite more than a century of British rule, and the spread of modern education and democratic values of equality and individual liberty, the attitudes towards widow remarriage remain practically the same. There is still a social ban on widow remarriage. There is not a single case of widow remarriage in Gokul. Of the interviewees 66.96% strongly opposed widow remarriage in principle. A widow's statement reflects the general attitude of the people toward remarriage of widows. "Widows should even starve and die for the

---

17 Ross, A. D. 1961, pp. 83–84.

sake of the deceased husband and must not think of remarrying even if she is young and childless. That is righteousness (*Dharma*)."

However, it seems there is some change in the attitude of the Brahman community towards widows. As many as 33.04% are in favour of remarriage of widows. A few young men recognize remarriage as a right and privilege of a woman on the principle of social justice and most others favour remarriage provided the widow is young, childless, lacks economic support or finds it difficult to remain chaste. It is not only that men are not yet prepared to concede a right of remarriage to widows, but women do not like to remarry. Since the Brahman girl is being brought up to cherish and practice firm devotion and strict fidelity to her husband during her husband's lifetime and even after his death, the prevailing social milieu makes remarriage of widows difficult. However, there has been a change in the last two decades. In several households while mothers opposed widow remarriage their educated unmarried daughters were in favour of such remarriage. In spite of changes in attitudes of the younger generation, they are unable to implement their new attitudes if the occasion arises because of strong opposition by the orthodox majority.

Endogamy

Traditionally, Brahmans marry within their own subcaste. Hypergamous rules allow a man of Vaishnava subcaste to marry a girl of Smartha subcaste. However, a Smartha man cannot marry a Vaishnava bride. Hypergamy, accepted as the social ideal of Brahmanic culture, has, with the growth of the endogamous character of caste and prestige determined by social hierarchy, become a more widely distributed pattern of marriage.[18] Inter-subcaste marriages among the Brahmans show an increasing trend. Rules of hypergamy are being ignored. In Gokul 70.43% are in favour of inter-subcaste marriage. In view of the traditional ideal of hypergamy, it would be possible for the Brahmans to be "traditional" and also favour inter-subcaste marriage. Those who oppose inter-subcaste marriage consider that differences in customs, rituals and gods would lead to social friction.

Intercaste marriages are not accepted by the large majority. Such marriages create problems such as difficulty of getting spouses for siblings and children, and possible conflicts between spouses because of cultural differences. However, less than 4% of the educated young men favour intercaste marriages if mutual love demands it. But in reality one seldom thinks to put it in practice because of oppostion from one's family, kin-group and community.

Although the number of intercaste marriages has been increasing, particularly during the last twenty-five years in bid cities of India,[19] there is at the same time clear evidence of the persistence of not only caste endogamy but also sub-

---

18   Kapadia, K. M. 1959, p. 105.
19   Refer, Kannan, C. T. *SB*, vol. X. No. 2, 1960. p. 53.

caste endogamy. Several studies[20] made in different parts of urban India reveal that a majority of the older as well as younger generation, though there is a change of outlook in the latter generation, still express their desire to marry within their own subcaste. Substantial portions of urban communities in India favouring inter-subcaste marriage strongly uphold caste endogamy.

Why does a large percentage of urban people still emphasize caste endogamy? Principally it is hazardous to act contrary to the custom. People are aware of the adverse consequences that follow in case they break the custom. The chances for marriage of other family members would be reduced since caste members disapprove of any marital relationship with such a family. The couple who have undergone intercaste marriage will be socially isolated within the caste. Therefore, parents naturally turn down any offer of a bride or groom outside the caste in order to preserve their prestige and the interests of the family and extrafamilial kin group. In addition, there is a greater conviction that easy and normal adjustment in family life is possible even in times of crisis, when the partner is from one's own caste and better still from one's own subcaste.

Currently, subcaste endogamy is giving place to caste endogamy in Indian cities, thereby preparing a proper social milieu for intercaste or even inter-religious marriages in future. It is true that "in cities subcastes are on the way to be united into a wider caste group for a number of activities, such as caste magazine, caste scholarship, caste recreational clubs, caste medical services, etc. With this development the circle of endogamy is bound to be enlarged, particularly when the highly educated girls find it difficult to get a suitable partner in the subcaste. What is, however, interesting is the fact that in spite of such obvious advantages, the subcastes are not prepared to lose their identity. The trend in favour of caste endogamy and even intercaste marriage is getting momentum of late, yet people appear to cling tenaciously to their subcastes."[21] How far the various factors such as co-educational schools and colleges, mixed social gatherings and clubs, and mixed employment in educational institutions, factories, firms and offices, would accelerate the tempo of intercaste marriages in Indian cities like Dharwar, is yet to be seen.

We have in this and the previous chapter described some of the major relationships of the kinship system of Lingayats and Brahmans, and have demonstrated the important role of extended kin. The next chapter will analyse the institution of social class and its influence on kin relations.

---

20   Refer, Kapadia, 1959, 1962; Shah, B. V. 1962; Cormack, M. C. 1961. p. 87; Kuppu-swamy, *J. Psy.* 1956; Ross, A. D. 1961. pp. 35–66.
21   Kapadia, K. M. *S.B.*, vol. XI, 1962, pp. 85–86.

CHAPTER SIX

Class and Community

THE PURPOSE of this chapter is to delineate the social stratification structure in Kalyan and Gokul and to examine the impact of modernization on kinship relationships. Urbanization, modern economy and education will be used as variables. We shall discuss the channels of social mobility such as occupation, education, and marriage. An attempt will be made to answer questions such as: Is class a barrier in kin contacts? Do migration and social mobility adversely affect kin relations? The pattern of interaction with friends and neighbours and other aspects of the community will be discussed tangentially. The general statements on social class and mobility of the Lingayats and Brahmans are based on the author's observations and on data gathered through interviews.

A universal feature of every known society is its social stratification, that is, the ranking of individuals or groups in a hierarchy according to some valued attribute, or attributes, such as ancestry, wealth, skill, or power. Every human community tends to develop a system of values in terms of which persons judge themselves and one another. Standards of evaluation which determine socio-economic status of persons differ greatly from society to society. Kalyan and Gokul are no exception to this fact. Within each caste, subcastes are hierarchically arranged, but class cuts across the ritual hierarchy of subcastes. Within a subcaste, class to which a person or family belongs is determined mainly by property, occupation and income of the social unit concerned. People are conscious of such class differentiations within the caste and subcaste.

Social classes in modern societies are considered as categories of individuals who, through similiarity of property, education, occupation, income, power and prestige, have come to have a similar mode of life, values, attitudes and forms of behavior and who, on any or all of these grounds, meet one another on equal terms and regard themselves, although with varying degrees of explicitness, as belonging to one group. Among Lingayats and Brahmans the crystallization of social classes manifested in their material possessions—land, gold ornaments, behavior, dress, education, speech, values and attitudes—can be ascertained. Within the same class people meet on terms of equality and tend to feel at ease. When they are in contact with members of a higher class in the social hierarchy, they feel inferior and their behavior implies deference or submission; when they are in contact with those below they feel superior and their behavior implies self-confidence and dominance. The members of the upper class maintain social distance from those of the lower class.

Max Weber's[1] concept of class built upon the possession of economic means, power and prestige would be useful in understanding the class structure in Dharwar. We need not repeat here the enormous literature on "class" in sociology.[2] In the present analysis, however, by taking into account the life-styles of the Lingayats and Brahmans one can discern a social class structure composed of the upper, middle, and lower or working classes. Criteria such as possession of property, income, education, and occupational prestige determine the class position of families in Kalyan and Gokul.

In Kalyan, 60.86% are engaged in agriculture as a means of their liveli-hood. The size of the cultivable land possessed by the family tends to determine socio-economic status. The upper class is composed of families possessing about 50 to 100 or more acres of land and those families following trade and profes-sions. Annual income of these families ranged from rupees 8,000 to 15,000 and over. Adult members were high school and college graduates. Their occupation commanded higher prestige than the middle class occupations. Of the house-holds in Kalyan, 10.43% belong to the upper class. By local standards these families can afford to spend money on comforts and luxuries, to save enough and also to provide higher education to their children. They are relatively more modernized and are held in high social esteem by the people belonging to other social classes in the suburb. The upper class is the most clearly defined in that its membership is acknowledged practically by everyone in Kalyan. Its members tend to associate more among themselves and marry among equals than with people of other classes. Though the upper class is numerically the smallest social category, it wields considerable influence over other classes.

The middle class is composed of owner cultivators with medium size hold-ings of approximately 20–30 acres, tenants, traders and those employed in government or private organizations as clerks, school teachers and the like. The middle class family income ranges from 3,000 to 7,999 rupees. Generally, middle class people have high school and in some cases a few years of college education; and their occupations possess higher prestige than the lower class occupations. In Kalyan 64.35% of the households belong to the middle class.

Although the number of acres of land owned by agricultural middle class families varies, the pattern of their economic and social life is similiar. General-ly, they own two working bullocks, milch cattle and agricultural implements. "Such farmers may in fact be considered to be engaged in farming business of 'economic size' in the sense that even though there is no surplus or margin of profit yielded by the business there is generally no net loss under normal con-ditions."[3] Men, women and children of the family work as a team in the

1   Weber, Max. (Tr. & Eds.) Gerth & Mills C. W., From Max Weber: Essays in Sociology, New York, Oxford University Press, 1946.

2   Refer for example: Bendix, R. & Lipset, S. M., Class, Status and Power, New York, The Free Press, 1966; Lasswell, T. E., Class and Stratum, Boston, Houghton Mifflin, 1965; Heller, C. S. (ed.), Structured Social Inequality, New York, Macmillan, 1969; Eisenstadt, S. N., Social Differentiation & Stratification, Glenview, Scott Foresman, 1971.

3   Gazetteer, 1959, p. 557.

cultivation of their own farms. The middle class families are able to make some savings partly in cash, partly in the form of ornaments or in other kinds of investments. When faced by some unforeseen contingencies they depend upon previous savings or borrowing.

Members of the middle class have greater social interaction amongst themselves than with the upper or lower class people. They consider it a privilege to associate themselves with the upper class but look down upon the lower class. While there is a general agreement that the differentiation between the classes is based mostly on occupational and economic factors, the line of demarcation between the classes is sometimes blurred at the peripheries.

The lower or working class is at the bottom of the social scale. In Kalyan 25.22% of the households belong to this class. Members of the lower class earn less than 3,000 rupees per annum and have primary education or no formal education. Their occupational prestige is low in the community. They are mostly landless manual labourers earning daily wages either on one farm or in the city offices, factories and other establishments. The women and even children have to work and earn wages to supplement the family income.

There exists a considerable social distance between the middle class and the lower class. The upper and middle class people think that the lower class members are dirty, live from hand to mouth, and have mean habits. The people in the lower class are usually conscious of their own socio-economic status and what other people think of them. They accept their lot, show indifference or criticize the other classes for their attitudes. They, however, are economically dependent on the middle and upper class. This interdependence among classes reduces to a certain extent the class conflicts that may otherwise arise or become serious.

Although each class has a social reality of its own, it has position only in relation to other classes and the features of any one class have practically no significance when isolated from the social system as a whole. It can be observed that the pattern of intimate social relationships such as close friendships, mutual aid and advice, choice of guests at meals, marriage alliances, etc., are all influenced by the class system in Kalyan. Although there are "social climbers", the opportunities for them are limited.

The local economy and occupational structure present significant features of kinship solidarity and mobility patterns. The members of the family and kin group work as a team. Here kin group and work group tend to overlap. In fact their common agricultural activities reinforce their kinship and make the father-son tie preeminent. Likewise, married daughters do the same work as their mothers—cooking, upbringing of children, house-keeping and working on the farms. In the case of women, the family life and work life are not separate. In Kalyan where the peasant economy is predominent there are no organizations exclusively charged with tasks of production. More often than not, the bonds of kinship which structure families, lineages, and kingroups are those which organize economic activities also. Moreover, territorial groupings of kin create and reinforce local producing organizations. This kind of dependence of economic units on pre-existing kinship relations has a characteristic series of consequences. Productive units tend to become multipurpose units and their economic activities are only one aspect of the many things they normally do.

Among the peasant families of Kalyan almost "everybody is related to everybody else". In fact the structure of farm families and their kin groups is closely related to occupation and use of land. Here it is the farm family, the household, which is the basic unit of economic production. Agricultural operations require the cooperative enterprise of many people. Significantly kin groups constitute such cooperative economic units. Nearly 80% of the male labour on farms is provided by farmers, their sons and grandsons and other relatives, and approximately 90% of the female labour is provided by their wives and their sons' wives, daughters and grand-daughters and other female relatives.

The ideal farm family is one that can be run without the help of hired labour. This requires in most cases that every member of the family play his or her part in agricultural activities. The absence of hired labour or minimum employment of labour on most farms implies that every member of the family works very hard. Even school-going children are expected to do work on several occasions. School teachers in this suburb reported that children remain absent for a considerable period of the year and it is difficult to enforce compulsory attendance rules. Because of poverty children are an economic asset and parents need them in herding cattle, protecting crops or for assisting in manuring, sowing or harvesting, etc. There has been, in recent years, an acute shortage of seasonal hired labour. Farmers find it extremely difficult to employ men because of high wages. They find it easier to employ their own children for reasons of economy, honesty and sincerity in their work which non-kin labour lacks.

Cooperation in Farming

Often farm families call upon their relatives to help in their economic activities. In this respect mutual aid among kin is quite common. "At times work may be held up even for want of a needle. Reciprocal help among kin, thus, becomes inevitable," said one of the respondents. Practically, the effective kin group functions as one unit especially on those occassions when the agricultural work demands relatively large numbers of men working together, such as sowing, transplanting, harvesting and threshing. Relatives help one another not only in activities such as those of ploughing and harrowing, but also in transportation of manure, grains and fodder. Farmers frequently borrow and lend bullocks, implements, seeds and the like. In times of drought, poor harvests or other economic stress, farmers can always rely upon their relatives for help and sympathy. Financial aid among kin is meagre but whenever they lend money to their relatives, they do not charge interest.

Mutual aid on farms was greatest among brothers. In order of importance, reciprocity exists between father and sons followed by the help that Ego (male) receives from kin on the side of his wife and married sisters and to a very lesser extent from his relatives on the mother's side and married daughter's side. The widows also reported that their relatives helped them in the cultivation and/or management of their lands. It is in the peasant economy that one finds the paternal authority well developed. The father is the head of the family in many respects. Naturally, his children are economically and psychologically dependent on him. One can observe here the functional interdependence of economy and society. Since the same persons are actors in the economic, the kinship and the religious spheres, the role of the farmer, the father and the worshipper of gods and goddesses practically coincide. This kind of reciprocity, interdependence and unity in their economy and religion reinforces their kinship solidarity.

From the foregoing discussion it is evident that similarity of occupations brings members of the family and kin group together. To what extent do the sons follow the same occupation as their fathers? It would be interesting to examine the extent of occupational mobility through generations and among members of the same generation.

Occupational Mobility

An analysis of occupations followed by adult male members of 115 households in Kalyan revealed significant patterns of stability and mobility. In the case of 61 (53.05%) households, when the eldest members in the household pursued agriculture his younger brothers, sons and grandsons also took up farming. In 20 (17.37%) households the non-agricultural occupation of the eldest person is followed by his younger brothers, sons and grandsons. But in 15 (13.04%) households when eldest male followed agriculture his brothers and/or sons and grandsons have taken to non-agricultural occupations characteristic of modern urban life. In the latter case, there is a complete departure from the traditional to the non-traditional occupations. However, in 19 (16.52%) households interestingly enough, when eldest person is a farmer, only one or two younger brothers or sons followed the same occupation whereas other brothers and sons have jobs in the city. This change of occupations by some members of a single household illustrates the impact of urbanization.

We find that 70.44% of the households' working members, both old and young, have not changed their occupations—agricultural or non-agricultural. So the major portion of the present occupational structure of Kalyan remains deeply rooted in the traditional pattern. The process of mobility in the occupational structure is manifested in the case of 29.56% households. The urban-industrial occupations pursued by them range from their employment as peons, clerks, typists, police-constables, truck drivers, electricians, and compositors to the employment in factories and mills, colleges, hospitals, government offices, banks, railways, posts and telegraphs and radio broadcasting station. This occupational diversification tends to lead people from the intimate kin orientated personal environment to that of an impersonal world of work where kin seldom have the opportunity to help and cooperate.

Education

Other things being equal, the educational achievements of family members raise the prestige of individuals and families. In the past, Kalyan parents trained their children in the traditional occupations, and for generations transmitted requisite knowledge and skills for earning a livelihood. Now the modern society demands various specialized skills which cannot be imparted by the family. So the formal systems of education have developed to cater to the needs of urban and industrial communities in training the young to handle complex and varied tasks.

As the majority of people of Kalyan are occupied in agriculture, formal schooling is of little use. In this suburb there are 121 illiterates. Such illiterates are mostly in Ego's father's generation and relatively few in Ego's own generaration, where Ego is a middle-aged person. There are 333 persons who have received primary education, 33 secondary education, 30 matriculates, 8 undergraduates and seven graduates in all. A large percentage of illiteracy and the major percentage of people with primary education are indicative of the fact that need of and motivation for formal education are not quite sufficient. "If we know the three R's—reading, writing and a bit of arithmetic, that is enough. After all we don't go in for skilled jobs," told most of the farmers. Most of them cannot afford the luxury of modern education. "Why should we waste so much money on education of children? Look, my son is a matriculate, can work as a typist—still he is unemployed. What is then the good of education?" asked another. In their value structure, education of girls does not claim much importance as they after all are to be good housewives engaged in cooking and caring for children and other members of the family.

A three-generation study of Kalyan community reveals a changing pattern of literacy and education. Barring a few exceptions, people are illiterate in Ego's parental generation, and those of Ego's own generation have been receiving secondary and even college education. Though the need and urge to have higher education is relatively less among people of Kalyan the spread of modern education in recent years is significant. Not only will it bring about a change in their traditional ways of living but may also help to introduce new values and aspirations.

Modern education is a principal means of acquiring higher social status. In fact ten families have attained a higher social status because of the higher educational achievements of one of the family members. These families have been exposed to new contacts and ideas. Fifteen college educated young men have changed their values and behavior from traditional to modern with regard to subcaste endogamy, commensal taboos, selection of mates and age of marriage, friendship, dress, speech and habits. The deviation from traditional norms on the part of young educated men sometimes tends to create frictions and tensions between the older and younger generations. By and large the educated young men try to adjust their behavior in order to avoid overt conflicts with parents. There is a social gulf between the educated few and the majority of their illiterate kin; and there is a tendency on the part of the educated young social climbers to look down upon their relatives who have no formal schooling. On the other hand, the uneducated elderly kin label the educated young as "ultra-modern", "high-brow", "devaints" and the like. However, the older generation fails to recognize the high status of educated young people.

Certainly, educational achievements and other factors do influence the nature of occupation and income. The differential valuation of occupations in this community can be gathered from the saying, "Best is agriculture, trade is middling, while service is the lowest" of occupations. Inadequate income from agriculture and the relative security, power and privileges of urban jobs, have made them realize the importance of urban occupations. However, despite the uncertainties of agriculture and the attraction of the city jobs, agriculture remains the basic and predominant occupation.

Marital Bonds

Besides education, occupation, wealth and income, marriage is a channel through which "social climbing" or "social sinking" in the social status scale is possible. The desire to change one's class through marriage operates and affects significantly a caste structured society. As a result, the inter-class marriages, along with the inter-subcaste ones, become a matter of social ostracism. Class endogamy is as important a social phenomenon as caste endogamy. The general rule is that one must marry within one's own class. A girl who belongs to the middle class should marry a person of her own class or that of the upper class but she must not marry a man belonging to the lower class. If she does marry a lower class man, not only she but also her parental family sink in the social scale and a social stigma is attached to such an alliance.

In Kalyan, marriage is a channel for social mobility. Marriages in which the wife came from the class immediately below that of the husband constituted 10% of those under study. In such cases social ascent was possible for the woman and her parental family. But it is a widespread custom that a person is expected to seek his mate in his own class. In 80% of the marriages, husband and wife belonged to the same social class, and in only 5% of the marriages the wife was from a class higher than that of her husband. Hence, there is a good deal of non-mobility through marriage. However, in recent years there has been a gradual increase in social mobility through marriage.

Is Class a Barrier in Kin Contacts?

Usually class is no barrier to kin contacts. Of those studied 35% reported that their wive's relatives who were richer than them did help in times of need. Blood bond is stronger than class differences. Not only in agriculture but also in trade, purchase of land, litigation, education of children and the like, the rich help their "poor" kin. "It is," as they say, "kin who mingle together in times of crisis and not others."

This, however, reveals only one side of the picture. There is also the other side: the kinship system is subject to the influence of class structure. We find that 45.22% of the respondents indicated that class acts as barrier in kin contacts, whereas 54.78% said that it does not. Wealth and poverty create differential nature of kin contacts. In 3% of the families when Ego had a sudden loss in trade and property, his relatives who used to visit his household frequently minimized their relationships. In one instance the informant reported: "Class acts as barrier in mutual relationships among kin. Some of our relatives who are economically better placed maintain a high social prestige and look down upon their poor kin. If we are rich all come to us, if we are poor all kin desert and avoid shouldering the miseries and economic burden of the not so well-to-do."

Some respondents expressed similiar experiences and feelings of class rupture among kin:

"Money is everything and it is respected like father's elder brother." "Ants cluster where there is sugar." "Everyone is kin to the rich man including his enemy. But for the poor man even his relatives become his enemy." Although there is some exaggeration in these folk-sayings there is a grain of truth. The attitudes of the rich towards their poor relatives is one of:

> "You are my kin all-right,
> I love you so well,
> But touch not my purse."

People experience a significant change in kin relationships when a member of a kin group rises to a class above that of most group members or when another sinks to a lower class due to economic loss or otherwise. In such cases loyalty to one's kin, which is a *sine qua non* of the kinship system, is strained and to a certain extent there emerge different segments of the same wider kin group based on class differentiations. However, it should be made clear that such subtle polarization and repulsion among kin do not always arise on account of economic forces alone. The degree of kinship relations, the extent of intimacy, and personality factors cross-hatch the economic ones.

In one extreme case a respondent said, "We are poor; we have no relatives. Rich relatives for us are dead." In the case of twenty-four households social tensions, frictions and overt conflicts were reported among male siblings especially after their marriage. These were mostly due to cantankerous nature of women, jealousy and hatred arising out of partition of the joint-family property, socio-economic and other differences.

However, despite the tensions and conflicts arising from class differences, kinship solidarity has largely remained intact. It manifests itself not only in matters of economic activities but also in favouring the relatives in matters of employment. Of them 9.3% were helped by their kin in securing jobs. Since a majority of the respondents were peasants they were not in a position to help their kin in securing jobs in the city. But even the limited extent of nepotism is sufficient to indicate family and kinship loyalty. In normal and in difficult times people forget class differences among kin and help one another.

Geographical Mobility

Spatial non-mobility is one of the characteristic features of the Kalyan community. Barring the emigration and immigration of women on their marriage, the rate of migration of men folk from Kalyan to other places is insignificant. Approximately 80% of the families have been residing in this suburb for the last four or five generations. Nearly 17% of them have migrated to or from villages within a radius of five to ten miles. Here the unit of migration is either an unmarried adult individual, or a married couple with or without children and/or sometimes with other dependent relatives. The data on migration suggests that the direction of migration of individuals of Kalyan is mostly determined by kinship. A tendency reflected in the genealogical material shows that a man tends to migrate to a place to which his elder brothers, own or classificatory, or other relatives have already migrated. This kind of kinship-oriented migration is quite pronounced.

Only 25% of the people, mostly the younger generation, have migrated to other places within the same district or adjacent districts on account of job requirements. There is only a handful of persons who have migrated to another province. This remarkable lack of mobility is mirrored in their responses. Only 6.96% are willing to take jobs outside Dharwar. The rest 93.04% are unwilling to work outside the city.

Of all the pull factors that operate in the process of immigration and attract the immigrants to a particular city, the presence of relatives, who encourage and support job-hunting and help in settlement, constitute the most powerful consideration. This trend was observed among the immigrant families in the adjoining city of Hubli.[4] A few individuals and families who have migrated to and from Kalyan have maintained close links with their native place. Most of them visit their kin more than once a year. The frequency of visits and the degree of attachment to their kin and place of origin are largely determined by the presence of kin, existence of property at the native place and the spatial distance.

Kin first and Friends next

Besides social contacts with relatives, people of Kalyan have active relationships with neighbours and friends. For every family the contiguous houses to the right, and left and opposite, and unrelated persons living in the same street, constitute "the neighbours". The importance of physical proximity as a basic factor in the social structure cannot be underestimated. Although to a

---

4   *VIDE*, Dhekney, B. R. 1959, p. 61.

certain extent the attachment to relatives tends to be at the expense of attachment to neighbours and friends, the family and kinship ties do help in promoting contacts with non-kin. In fact each relative functions as a bridge—a liaison officer—between the individual and the community.

Good neighbourliness prevails. This is manifested in the lending and borrowing among neighbours. The lending or borrowing between women range from salt or sugar, red chillies or a kilogram of wheat to clothes, ornaments and money. Men, on the other hand, maintain reciprocal relationships in the lending and borrowing of bullocks, bullock-cart, agricultural implements and personal services. The farmer's concept of a neighbour extends beyond that of people residing in the vicinity of his house. On his farm he counts the adjacent cultivators as his neighbours. A farmer is never too well supplied with farm implements or labour. He does need his neighbours, help sometime. "A stone, however big, does need the support of even a small stone" said an informant summing up the underlying philosophy and sociology of the people.

The intimacy among neighbours can be best observed when they frequently visit one another's houses without prior notice or engagement. Neighbours are so familiar with one another that a casual observer may find it difficult to ascertain the real composition of a family. Often, during the day time, children of neighbours freely wander in and out of one another's houses, sometimes joining the neighbouring families at breakfast or lunch. Cooperation among neighbours is constantly established and strengthened from one generation to another. Frequent personal contacts among neighbours, typical of this suburb, help to strenghten the bonds of neighbourliness. The high degree of physical proximity in Kalyan usually makes the neighbour relationship strong and intense. But where neighbourlines develops to an optimum point and when frequency of contacts and intimacy increases, even the little things that happen in one house rarely escape the knowledge of people in neighbouring houses.

People in the neighbourhood are familiar with one another and form an informal group which controls individual behaviour through social ridicule, ostracism, gossips, and other negative sanctions. To a certain extent neighbour groups in this suburb resemble kin groups in that they function as a control over behaviour of the individual in the community. However, the neighbour group is much less structured, and the psychological bonds which unite it are weaker than those of the kin group, and the intensity of the interaction is correspondingly less. The neighbour group is not capable of collective action whereas the kin group is.

All neighbours are not friends and all friends are not neighbours. Kinsmen and neighbours exist whether one likes them or not. One has to tolerate them in as much as one does not have freedom to choose. But in the case of friends the individual has freedom to pick and choose. The polarization of individuals who have no kinship relations indicates the extent of their desire to maintain social relations outside the orbit of kinship.

Friendship ties in Kalyan are based on similarity of caste, and subcaste, class, age, common interests and the degree of mutual aid. While the majority of people are aware of the distinction that prevails among kin, neighbours, friends and others, a few informants did seem to confuse kinship with friendship. Friends are unrelated individuals with mutual attachment, intimacy and disposition to promote one another's good, residing in the same neighbourhood or different neighbourhoods. Friendships are not confined to the neighbourhood or the suburban community alone but extend to other parts of the city or beyond.

Loyalty to one's friends is expressed during normal and crisis situations at home and on farms. While purchasing land or bullocks, or building a house, monetary aid is extended more often by friends than by kin. Relationships among friends are of the fraternal kind. Most informants said, "If our relatives do not give us help in times of need even when expressly demanded, it disturbs our minds and leads to strained relationships. In the case of friends, normally, there is reciprocity. Even if a friend does not help for some reasons or the other we do not take it to heart. Generally, there is mutual give and take among our friends". Several instances were given of how friends helped in cash and kind, in matters of agriculture, business, matrimony, securing jobs and so on. They went together to fairs and festivals, marriages, movies and dramas. Practically everyone recieved some kind of help from his friends. In Kalyan, 35.65% of the respondents had friends belonging to their own caste, while the majority (64.35%) had friends of other castes. Thus, friendships cut across caste barriers. However, several people expressed, in confidence, that, barring a few exceptions, a caste friend was generally more intimate and reliable than any other.

Traditionally, women confined friendships to their neighbourhood group. Women of Kalyan come in contact with women other than their kin on farms and in the city. The modern urban way of life has its influence on female members of the family, who are beginning to extend their ties of friendship.

While tributes were paid to neighbours and friends for their timely help on several occasions, 82% of the people of Kalyan stressed the importance of kin over non-kin, neighbours or friends. "Friends are there only for drinks and dinners and not for help when there is a need", remarked a middle-aged man. "Friends are rich in giving lip sympathy and nothing more", told a housewife. "In times of crisis, it is mainly our kin who come to our rescue and not so much our neighbours or friends", an old widow remarked. Such statements make clear the pivotal role of kin in mutual help and cooperation throughout one's life in contrast with that of non-kin.

Social contacts in Kalyan also include the services and guidance of the key personalities such as the carpenter, blacksmith, the priest-astrologer, the school-master, and the barber. Inter-caste and intracaste relationships are friendly and harmonious. People have courtesy (ritual) kin, and appropriate kinship terms of address are made use of in social intercourse, not only within the caste but across caste lines. Sometimes, a casual observer is likely to confuse the fictitious kin with real kin. Unlike those of real kinship ties, these fictitious kinship relationships involve little or no obligations.

The foregoing analysis reveals the influence of class on kinship. It also demonstrates that, although the people of Kalyan live in a strongly kin-oriented environment, neighbours, friends and other members of the community complement rather than compete with kin.

Gokul

In Gokul, occupational categories provide the initial frame of reference for the class structure. Of the families studied, 8% depend mainly on the rent received from land. Those persons whose income is mostly or solely derived from the land, style themselves as "Land-Lords". Today, sons of these "Land-Lords" are being educated and are entering modern professions and services. There are physicians, engineers, lawyers, professors, businessmen and a few high salaried government officers who form the "modern elite", upper class, because of their wealth, education, occupation, income, power and prestige. In Gokul, 20.00% of the households belong to the upper class. The upper class families have an annual income ranging from rupees 8,000 to 15,000 and over.

The members of the upper class, with their distinct values, material possessions and behaviour patterns, enjoy higher social status. In Gokul they are more influenced by the process of modernization in their tastes and interests, way of life and aspirations than that of the upper class of Kalyan. The rich are able to save enough for the exigencies of life and they can be easily distinguished by the type of houses they live in. Generally, they spend more on education, clothes, jewellry, entertainment and other items which have considerable ostentation value. Their speech and manners reflect the upper class consciousness in the suburb. Effective and close social contacts are mainly confined to members of the same class. They marry in their own class rather than others of their community.

One finds that 62.61% of the households belong to the middle class, which is comprised of clerks, school teachers, middle strata of salaried persons in government or private offices, and a few medium-scale traders and those in professions with an annual income ranging from 3,000 to 7,999 rupees. "The size of the family is generally larger for this class than for the others. Cases of joint families occur not infrequently".[5] Since the middle class Brahmans are mostly dependent on urban employment for their livelihood, it is essential that they equip themselves with modern education. Parents have responsibility and great concern for their children's education. Educational and economic opportunities, which are on the increase in urban areas, have been giving rise to new ambitions and aspirations among the middle class.

Though middle class persons interact amongst themselves, motivations for upward social mobility are present. Though they do not have a feeling of inferiority in relation to the upper class, they seem to have developed a feeling of superiority to those below them in the class hierarchy. Class differentiations, nevertheless, do not exclude the social fact of their interdependence.

---

5 Gazetteer, 1959, p. 568.

It is difficult to characterize the lower or the working class with any degree of accuracy since many of the studies of the working class include a wide social spectrum ranging from skilled workers to the unemployed and the social misfits. Furthermore, these difficulties are compounded by the Brahman's higher ritual status in the caste structure. Under these conditions, absolute precision of exposition is not possible. However, 17.39% of the households in Gokul constitute the working class. This class is composed of factory workers, artisans, priests, astrologers and cooks, with less than 3,000 rupees annual income. These people are hardpressed due to the rising cost of living in the city, and they struggle hard to make ends meet. In fact, these people may be said to belong to the upper-lower class which is made up of "poor but honest workers" in terms of Warner's class structure as documented in "Yankee City".[6]

The upper and middle classes maintain considerable social distance from the lower class. However, on various religious and social occasions the services of priests, astrologers and cooks are demanded. In fact, such men, though they belong to the lower class, enjoy higher ritual status. In this context, ritual and secular statuses do differ and exert influence in their sacred and secular spheres of life.

The network of close social relationships and marital ties shows the impact of the class system in Gokul. The Brahmans make use of modern urban opportunities for vertical social mobility. The members of all classes have before them higher goals to achieve. There are controlling mechanisms which tend to enforce conformity to a set of norms and behaviour patterns along class lines. Different social classes have different reference groups. Social ascent is normally directed towards the kind of groups whose standards of life one aspires to have. Within the wider kin group, class determines which members of the kinship group are more in contact and talked about, who associates with whom, and the sociometric cliques and cleavages. The class also influences the members in their beliefs and attitudes, decisions and social actions.

Occupational Roles

As already noted, Kalyan kinship roles have strong associations with occupational roles, and some kind of economic cooperation with kin is a dominant feature. In Gokul, owing to heterogeniety of the occupational structure and the existence of several complex organizations, occupational roles very often differ from kinship roles. Only in six households, Ego, his sons and/or his brothers were engaged in the same economic activity, that is, they worked together in the same business or profession. In 58 households the occupation of the head of the household differed from that of his children and/or brothers. In another ten households, the head, his children and/or brothers followed more or less similar occupations but they worked at different places. Hence, father and son or brothers, or members of the extended family and kin group, could

---

6　Warner & Lunt, 1941.

seldom meet outside the home in their everyday occupations. Evidently this deprives kinship relations of an important element of kinship cohesion.

The modern type of occupational organization demands persons with special educational qualifications and skills to fit the specialized jobs. Thus, the traditional connection between family and social status is weakened. In the contemporary urban Indian society, the assignment of occupational roles and thereby of social status depend mostly upon an individual's performance in the non-kin-oriented and impersonal educational and occupational organizations, which have the responsibility of training and selecting persons mainly on merit. However, this does not mean that the family has no part to play in allocating social status to the individual. As long as the family continues to rear and train children, families with higher socio-economic status will be in a position to provide, initially at least, differential opportunities and advantages to their children. In Gokul, however, factors such as heterogeniety, anonymity and impersonal urban life considerably limit the family's scope for exercising influence in determining social status of its members.

Urban Life and Occupational Mobility

The complex occupational diversity, so prominent in modern urban life, leads to a situation where economic cooperation with kin is hardly possible. The life of an adult is now geared more to an impersonal place of work where one will not get the assistance from relatives which one formerly experienced. The modern occupational system plays a decisive role in the system of social stratification, and coexists in Gokul with a good deal of institutional emphasis on kinship ties. It seems as though the kinship structure is developing in such a way as to give enough scope for occupational mobility, while at the same time maintaining kinship solidarity.

Unlike the relative lack of mobility in the traditional occupational system of Kalyan, there is greater mobility in the modern occupational system of Gokul. Since the Brahmans have been traditionally a class of priests, teachers and non-cultivating owners of land, the recent abolition of absentee land-lordism through legislation and other social, economic and political changes has further forced them to seek new jobs. Urbanization and new values of life have been influencing their occupational patterns and various other dimensions of the social system. As the occupational system and the family are closely inter-related and influence each other, analysis of inter-generational and intra-generational occupational mobility in Gokul is of great significance in understanding the Brahman kinship values and behaviour.

Only in 5% of the households was there occupational stability. That is to say, the eldest male member and his sons were in pursuit of the same occupation. In 90% of the households, the occupations followed by the eldest male, his brothers and sons were all different. It was not unusual to find, for instance, that, in a family where the Ego was a teacher, one of his younger brothers was a clerk, another a salesman, the third an engineer and the fourth a lawyer. This kind of occupational diversity among siblings is more common in Ego's children's generation than in Ego's own. When the father is a landlord one can observe his son being a physician, professor, or an army officer. There were instances of the father being a watch-repairman and his son a telephone-operator; the father being a physician and his sons being a college professor, a chartered accountant and a sales manager. There was a father, a compositor in a printing press, whose son was a chemical analyst in the chemical laboratory; another was a clerk whose son was a stenotypist; a third was a schoolteacher whose son was a professional photographer. There was a father, a railway station master, whose three sons were civil, mechanical and radio engineers. Such instances of inter-generational and intra-generational occupational mobility can be multiplied. This suggests that usually father-son solidarity through common economic activity is no longer possible.

Furthermore, this occupational mobility has not caused any substantial change in their social status. Out of the fifty households, twenty-six experienced change in occupations between two generations, with more or less the same status retained, leading only to horizontal social mobility. In eighteen households, however, vertical social mobility was experienced. There is upward social mobility in ten households and downward social mobility in eight households, although 21% of the Brahmans follow the traditional callings. Secular urban-occupational patterns, characteristic of the Brahmans, are different from occupational patterns of the Lingayats; and among the Brahmans the lack of joint economic enterprise among kin seems to be an important factor in the transformation of kinship values and behaviour.

Vertical social mobility, though confined to a relatively small percentage of households, has occurred with greater frequency between the middle and upper strata than the lower class. Several individuals, through hard work, education, job, higher income, power and prestige, personal efforts in professions and business, and marital ties have been able to move from the middle to the upper class. Of course, not all individuals have been able to move up. The social gulf created between relatives as a result of social mobility sometimes lessens the frequency of contacts and cooperation. The rich look down upon their relatives who are economically worse off. Higher socio-economic status coupled with pride and snobbery sometimes creates socially isolated configurations of kin. Misunderstandings and tensions between relatives emerge because of class differences. But in general, class barriers do not operate so as to disrupt kinship relationships.

Education

Educational achievement constitutes the major source of livelihood among men of Gokul. Being educated is not merely a matter of prestige. It is the parents, responsibility to educate the children. It was not uncommon to observe Ego having his siblings' children also in his home for purpose of their education. Sometimes wife's siblings or wife's siblings' children are also provided with free board and lodge while they attend school or college. This kind of educational aid by the intimate kin group is more pronounced in Gokul than in Kalyan.

Children of all classes in Gokul are encouraged to achieve formal education. It serves as the main channel through which "social climbing" becomes possible. In this struggle to attain the goals, the individual is helped by his family and intimate kin group. When the individual is wellplaced in society he is expected to help in return his parents, younger brothers and sisters and other relatives. The ambitious youth, however, may feel pushed and pulled by the forces of ever-increasing desires and needs and a high cost of living in the urban milieu, on the one hand, and kinship ties and obligations on the other.

Since almost all the Brahmans of Gokul depend upon urban occupations for their living, the achievement of requisite formal education is of great importance. There are 42 illiterate people, mostly women above fifty years of age. There are 166 who have received primary education, 138 who have attended secondary schools, and 164 who have passed secondary school certificate examination. Sixty-two persons have attended college for a few years, a dozen of them with diplomas in science and technology. There are 64 graduates in arts, science, education, law, medicine, engineering, etc. The high percentage of literacy and the presence of a great majority of people with primary, secondary and even college education indicates that the Brahmans have continued to be the "literati" of contemporary society as they were in the traditional Hindu social system.

Education in modern India is generally geared to the task of preparing individuals for entry into the urban occupational structure. The urban Brahmans constitute, in the main, the modern intelligentsia for whom the urban community offers job opportunities. The occupational and social mobility patterns appear to be determined by the traditional social structure. The Brahmans, by virtue of their traditional stress on learning, education, work, professions and the like, and also because of higher educational attainments, have a wider choice of modern occupations.

Education of Brahman girls has become necessary not only for enabling them to get suitable bridegrooms and to be intellectual companions to husbands but also to minimize the amount of dowry to be paid to the groom's party. A minimum of secondary school education or even college education for girls is preferred by Brahman young men so that they can be "good" partners in marital life. Parents educate their daughters to qualify themselves for marriage and also to enable them to earn and supplement family income if need arises.

Besides women with primary and secondary education, especially women below thirty-five, there are fifty having secondary school certificates, eleven undergraduates and nine graduates. Although traditionally the Brahman women are not allowed to work outside their homes, during the last few years educated young women are beginning to take up urban occupations. In Gokul, six women (five of them unmarried) are employed as teachers, clerks, and telephone operators. Several other young girls, who have been receiving high school and college education are also becoming career-conscious. A generation ago, among the Brahmans, employment of women in any kind of occupation, outside their own homes was prevented by forces of religious taboos and social practices. A woman working outside her home was looked upon with great disfavour. The traditional idea of marriage and home being the main career for a girl still has a strong hold in the Brahman community. This idea, together with the social restrictions on employment of women, is undergoing change.

With increasing urbanization, spread of modern technology, growing employment opportunities and better conditions of work for women, the general attitude of the Brahmans towards woman's employment is becoming favourable. In contrast to the Lingayats of Kalyan, the Brahmans of Gokul allow and even encourage their daughters and sisters to receive education. But employment of a few women of Gokul appears to be an activity during the waiting period and it continues only until they get a life partner. This suggests that the employment of women in services and professions has not yet become so much a part of normal life.

Generation after generation, the Brahmans have been receiving more and more advanced and specialized education in order to qualify themselves for more skilled and better paid jobs. As a rule, Ego's children are better educated and employed in those jobs that would bring more income and prestige than Ego's job did. Such an educational advancement of the community decade after decade has tremendous repercussions. As observed by Talcott Parsons, "the primary meaning of education", in Gokul also, "seems to be that it serves as a path to future occupational (and partly marital) status".[7]

The Brahmans, being highly educated, they prefer to be in the white-collar jobs and normally shun manual work because of their traditional background of hereditary callings—priestly, teaching and ministerial. Unlike the people of Kalyan who extol agriculture and demean service as the lowest of occupations, the people of Gokul seem to appreciate service as the most suitable, if not the best, of all occupations.

The acquisition of formal education by the younger generation is still largely influenced by social class factors. Despite the fact that the Indian government's egalitarian ideology and social welfare policy try to minimize class differences by providing free primary and secondary education and the extensive programmes of financial aid, such as scholarships, fellowships, and loans in the colleges and universities, many young men and women with necessary talents and aptitudes are denied educational opportunities because of their class position. The increasing social mobility facilitated by the modern educational system tends to bring conflicts of values and behaviour patterns between generations thereby bringing to the surface the problems of youth and old age in contemporary Indian society. The democratic values imparted by the modern school to the growing child are not always easy to accept. They have to compete and sometimes come in conflict with traditional values imposed by the family, caste, and neighbourhood. Formal education,

---

7   Parsons, T. 1958, p. 428.

which is increasingly becoming a principal means of social control in India, thus has to face competition and conflict at times with other means of social control. In spite of such limitations, one cannot underestimate the paramount role of modern education in bringing about far reaching changes with regard to the values, aspirations, behaviour and outlook of the Brahmans.

In Gokul, formal education is an important channel of social mobility. Obliged to meet the requirements of modern age, parents incur the financial burden of educating their children. People sacrifice a good deal of their own comforts in order to educate children of their own, and their siblings' children and sometimes children of their spouse's siblings, as well. The sufferings and sacrifices of parents and intimate kin in this respect are gratefully remembered by the children, and through their feelings of loyalty and obligations to their parents and intimate kin, the kinship solidarity is further reinforced The greater and varied opportunities of education and jobs elsewhere have caused children to move away from the city and reside in an environment relatively free from the direct control and influence of family and intimate kin group. In most cases, this process whether one likes it or not continues because of educational and economic exigencies. But the staying away from the family and intimate kin group has not made for any significant weakening of the kinship ties. The possible adverse consequences of geographical and social mobility are being offset by frequent visits, mutual aid, exchange of gifts, counseling, and correspondence among kin.

Marriage and Mobility

Marriage also acts as a channel in the process of social mobility. By and large, the dictum "Equals should marry" holds good. While selecting mates for their children, parents choose brides or grooms from families with similar socio-economic and cultural background. Significantly enough, nearly 70% of the marriages in Gokul are confined to persons from the same social class, thereby confirming the existing system of social stratification.

In 17% of the marriages, men have married into a higher social class, that is, parents of wives belong to a higher class than husbands. The father who finds it difficult to get a suitable bridegroom for his daughter, for reasons of dowry, is at times forced to give her to a man of moderate means belonging to a lower class. In 13% of the marriages, however, the wife came from a lower class than her husband's.

Though some individuals have married across class lines and there has been some social mobility, it does not mean that men and women of an upper class readily marry into a lower class. Social class differences to a little extent is tolerated, but if there is a wide social distance between the classes it is indeed a significant barrier for marriage. Therefore, in reality, individuals normally tend to marry persons belonging to the same class.

As a rule, class differences do not come in the way of kinship relationships. Relatives normally forget their class differences and help one another in normal and in difficult times. At various ceremonies a constellation of kin is formed and it knows no class boundaries. The predominance of kinship bonds over class in Gokul is largely felt by the majority of people and 72.1% of the respondents said that class is no barrier in kin contacts.

But the class structure does influence the attitude and interpersonal behaviour among kin in a very subtle way. In a way "it determines what members of the kinship group are remembered and talked about, it enters into judgments of people, behaviour and institutions".[8] The disparities in the economic conditions of different families of the same wider kin group have repercussions on social interactions. Misunderstandings and tensions arise due to financial matters and marital affairs. Some relatives expect more help which cannot be given for a variety of reasons such as the rising cost of living. Similarly, the poor economic conditions of Ego keep him aloof from rich and snobbish kin.

Responses similar to those already recorded in Kalyan were reproduced almost verbatim, though less frequently and with less intensity by the people of Gokul. "Money is all important like father's elder brother" and "If one is rich there is world of strength". In six cases respondents stated that the rich have looked down upon their kin who were poor. Anyway, the general attitude of the Brahmans is one of avoidance of areas of social friction among kin. They feel ashamed of asking for financial help especially from in-laws as it is a matter of maintaining prestige with equals. Nevertheless, non-monetary mutual aid continues to be a strong characteristic of the Brahman kinship system. The increased social mobility, the growing influence of egalitarian ideas and other modern values of life have kept class tensions among kin at a minimum. Only 27.83% of the Brahmans, as against 56.78% of the Lingayats, say that class influences kinship relationships adversely. The researcher seldom heard reports of tensions or overt conflicts among male siblings and other kin in Gokul.

As the Brahmans are increasingly dependent on modern urban occupations, nepotism—a function of family loyalty and kinship solidarity—is more evident in Gokul than in Kalyan. In Gokul, 26.96% of the men in employment secured appointments through the favours and good offices of their relatives. This demonstrates that in urban India, kinship functions as a "Bureau of Employment" and influences the social, economic and political life of the country. To what extent such nepotism, that is, the employment or the award of special favours on the basis of family instead of merit, leads to inefficiency, corruption and adverse effects on the morale of nonfamily workers is difficult to assess.

Nepotism as manifested in Gokul seems to be widespread throughout the country. It has attracted the attention of political leaders as an element seriously hindering the social and economic progress and the national unity of India. Public and private agencies are making efforts to fight the harmful effects of nepotism. Despite the fact that public opinion condemns the practice of nepotism, family and kinship loyalties influence the behaviour of people

---

8   Mogey, 1956, p. 142.

considerably in bestowing undue favours on their kin in public life. In the kinship oriented society of Dharwar, failure to give letters of introduction or refusal to use one's power and prestige in order to get jobs and other favours and privileges for their relatives is still considered a serious ommission in the fulfillment of kinship obligations. Such nepotism helps Brahmans in their upward social mobility.

Migration and Social Mobility

Social mobility is closely linked with geographical mobility. Job requirements have necessitated migration of Brahmans to major cities such as Bombay, Bangalore and Poona. In Gokul, 19% have migrated outside Mysore State to different parts of the country. However, among the migrants 15% have gone to the neighbouring Maharashtra State. The unit of migration is often the unmarried individual or the married couple with or without children. In addition to education and employment, marriage is also a factor accounting for migration.

Social mobility often requires geographical mobility. The upward mobility goals held by the lower and middle class youngsters are reinforced and encouraged by the family, the school, peer group, state activities, and mass communications. These provide informal training in the various motives and attitudes, and also social skills necessary for mobility. Social class values such as need for achievement, wealth, power and status, not only instill motivation and provide the initial leverage to propel the lower and middle class youth for upward mobility strivings but also tend to sustain such mobility patterns.

The individual is exposed to an environment wherein the norms and behavioural traits of others influence in accelerating social mobility. The increasing reliance of individuals for guidance and role models on extrafamilial reference groups such as the peer group, work group and the media of mass communication implies a gradual decreasing dependence upon the family and kin group. In this regard, Merton's[9] hypothesis of the "disassociative" consequences of social mobility needs to be considered. He points out that "membership in a group which has involved deep-seated attachments and sentiments cannot be easily abondoned without psychological residue". The probable consequence is one of ambivalence toward parents and other elders, the youngsters in such situations experiencing some difficulties. Although it is expected that social mobility brings with it initial stresses and strains, social isolation and nervousness, role strains and conflicts, the present data do not suggest social or psychological disintegration in any significant way.

Social frictions, conflicts, disintegration and dissociative consequences have not been manifested probably because of relatively lower rate of social mobility and social change on the one hand and the insulating mechanisms of traditional sociocultural constraints on the other.

9   Merton, R. K. 1962, pp. 269–275, 293–294, 302–304, 329–330.

Contrary to common assumptions, the foregoing analysis suggests that social stratification in modern urban India, though based on caste, is not closed, rigid and immobile but is open, flexible and mobile. It is not only adapting itself to the modern environment but the class structure within the caste system provides opportunities and motivations for social mobility. And in this process of social mobility, the individual is aided by his family and intimate kin.

The Five Year Plans of the Republic of India, which have been in force since 1950, have been responsible for accelerating the rate of industrialization and urbanization and along with it the rate of social mobility is most likely to increase in the future. The Constitution of India guarantees fundamental rights to all citizens, irrespective of differences in their caste, creed, religion or race, etc. All Indians are equal before the law. Moreover, the value premises of modern Indian society are formulated in the Directive Principles of State Policy enshrined in the Constitution of India. Among others, these directive principles are aimed at a casteless and classless society.

Especially during the last two or three decades, there have been significant social changes in urban India.[10] Traditional caste hierarchy and the privileges and/or disabilities associated with a caste have lost their former significance in the secular life of urbanities. Rigid rules of caste are not being observed. Taboos regarding commensalism have disappeared. When compared to the previous generation rules pertaining to connubial relations are not rigidly adhered to. People change their occupations from the traditional to the non-traditional without caste restrictions. Occupational mobility is now greater than ever before. Status by achievement rather than status by ascription assumes greater importance.

Social class seems to operate within a caste framework and across castes. Though both caste and class appear to co-exist and crosshatch, people are becoming more and more conscious of their class position in secular life. Modern education, increasing secularization of the life of urbanites and egalitarian "ethos" have a tremendous impact especially on the younger generation. Industrialization and urbanization have tended to reduce social distance among different castes. All these forces seem to increase social mobility in urban India.

Higher incidence of geographical mobility through generations and even within the same generation is manifest. The Brahmans with their educational attainments and specialized skills are pushed and pulled to the towns and cities. Wider geographical distribution of kin is also made possible through marriage, partly because of their rigid rules of clan exogamy and lesser frequency of inter-kin marriages. We find that 50% of the migration is confined to the district itself, 30% takes place within the state and as many as 19% of the people go out of Mysore State to different cities and towns for purposes of education, employ-

---

10   Refer Kuppuswamy, B. 1972; Singer, M., 1972; Srinivas, M. N. 1966; Turner, R. 1962; Issacs, H. 1964; Unesco, 1956.

ment and marriage. A little less than one per cent have also migrated to countries like East Africa, the United Kingdom and the United States.

With the increase in geographical distance, the frequency of kin contacts, personal or otherwise, decreases unless close kinship relations prevail. One informant told that he could not visit frequently his married daughter in Bombay because of distance. Another reported that instead of attending the wedding ceremony of his FaBrDaDa and spending money on a long journey he sent a wedding gift. Mutual visits and attendance at important family ceremonies, help and cooperation, correspondence and exchange of presents, though on a lesser scale, mark the relationships with relatives who have migrated to many distant places. Although a few informants remembered names of their kin who migrated two decades back to Calcutta and Delhi, and in one instance to East Africa, they do not know the names of children of these migrants. But it is significant that they are at least aware of the fact that a particular branch of their lineage or kin group is in a particular place.

The pattern of migration within the district and within the province reflects a tendency of individuals of going to places where their relatives have already gone and settled. Various types of help such as food and shelter, education and acquaintance with urban ways of life and provision of job to the new migrants are provided through relatives and their friends. Such kin-oriented migration within the province is not always possible outside the province. Nevertheless relatives still continue to be an important source of social, economic and emotional support. UNESCO studies[11] of the social implication of industrialization and urbanization in South Asian cities like Bombay, Dacca, Bangkok, etc., also reveal the importance of help extended to the newcomers by their relatives residing in the cities.

Despite the fact that many members of the kin group are relatively remote from one another—at Bombay, Bangalore and Poona—both geographically and genealogically, much importance is attached to such kin and some kind of relationship is always maintained with them. In addition to kin contacts, 30% of the people of Gokul are ready to go out of Dharwar for jobs compared to 6.96% from Kalyan. This willingness for geographical mobility among the Brahmans is a value-orientation different from that of the Lingayats of Kalyan. Since economic and kinship relationships often tend to be different in Gokul, wider geographical dispersion of kin is on the increase. But it seems that the disruptive influence of migration is overcome by frequent contacts and exchange of help and gifts on various occasions which tend to revitalize the bonds of kinship.

Friendship

Friends and peers play an important role in the life of the Brahmans. The friendship circle of the Brahman is wider than that of the Lingayat because

---

11   Unesco, 1956.

of the greater social and geographical mobility of the former. Childhood companions, class-mates in school and college, work-mates and those sharing common interests reinforced by mutual goodwill and help are considered friends. Friendship develops mostly along caste lines. In Gokul 46.09% of the people have friends of their own caste. The friendship ties of the rest, however, cut across their caste limits. More often than not, the Brahman comes in contact with members of various other castes in educational institutions, at places of work and in the community at large.

The influence of secular and democratic ideals, and the necessity of coordination and teamwork in various spheres facilitate friendship beyond one's own caste. Yet, barring a few exceptions, it seems friends of the same caste are more intimate, helpful and reliable than those of other castes. Friends give advice on various problems and extend their sympathy and emotional support in times of distress. At the wedding and initiation (*Upanayana* or *Munjive*) ceremonies, during illness and at funerals, friends along with kin play a significant role. In times of financial crises, usually friends come to the rescue. The importance of mutual cooperation of friends in matters of school studies, securing job and in work life, cannot be underestimated.

The respondents remember with pride and pleasure the exchange of ideas and the cooperation of friends with regard to religious, social, literary, academic, political and other activities. People in Gokul carry pleasant memories of their association with friends whether they be of the same or different caste. Greater social interaction, and mutual aid and intimacy which characterize friendship make the Brahmans believe that a "friend in need is a kin indeed", especially when relatives are scattered and contacts are correspondingly less.

People spend their leisure time over evening walks, picnics, indoor games, visits to restaurants, theatres, clubs and other centres of recreation and entertainment besides informal chats and discussions. Friendship ties among middle-aged women, much influenced by the Brahmanic traditions, are mostly confined to the neighbourhood. Young housewives and girls attending schools and colleges have many friends from different castes who help one another in shopping, child care, school studies and the like. Teenage girls learn from one another the arts of knitting, embroidery, tailoring, music, etc. Friendship relationships among the Brahman women are not strong or continuous, and seem to be ephemeral unless after marriage they continue to live together in the same suburb or city. Educated young girls, however, confide more in their friends than the kin. Heterosexual friendship is being looked askance, though a few college boys and girls venture to develop it.

In times of difficulty men approach their intimate friends for help. The preference for friends is greater if they have to approach the affinals. Help and sacrifice among friends are reciprocal. The rule seems to be that friends supplement kin rather than substitute them. Generally an increasing number of friends means increasing influence on one's attitudes and behaviour. New values and interests activate young men as a result of inter-caste and inter-regional friendship. Rigid caste taboos as regards food and drink, ceremonial purity and the like have weakened. Moreover, the increasing time spent among friends at educational institutions, place of work and leisure, and the greater dependence on friends to acquire modern skills and the satisfaction of certain interests in their company, have led to a gradual trend away from the company of relatives. Kinship obligations are being shouldered, at least partly, by some intimate friends.

People without kin tend to develop greater attachment to neighbours and friends. The substitute relationships provide, to a certain extent, companionship and help even though friends cannot wholly replace kin. Relatives, far from being a barrier in establishing contacts with the unrelated individuals in the community, function as an influential channel to link people effectively with the wider society.

Neighbourhood

The greater social and geographical mobility in Gokul not only keeps the people away from their kin but also makes them rely more on their neighbours for their immediate needs, help and guidance. The everyday lending and borrowing is primarily confined to neighbours. Women in the same neighbourhood, though not relatives, meet often, attend family rituals and ceremonies, exchange news and views, and indulge in gossip on local and national affairs. Good neighbourliness is a thing desired by almost all. One housewife said, "Ever since my marriage I am away from my former neighbours and friends. Most of my kith and kin including my sisters and daughters are living in different places. So I cannot expect help at every moment from our relatives. But our neighbours are always a great help in times of need." It is the close physical proximity that brings them together to share the common joys and sorrows of life.

The service rendered by neighbours may not be of the same kind and degree as that by one's kin, but what is appreciated most is their help at the very moment of the crisis. Unlike the neighbours of Greenleigh in London,[12] the neighbours of Gokul in Dharwar are not "unfriendly" or "do not keep themselves to themselves". The Brahman adult male not only spends his time with his most intimate kin but also keeps contact with his neighbours, at least on Sundays and holidays.

Social relationships among neighbours are reflected not merely in the exchange of greetings in the street. They are also expressed in mutual visits and help. As contrasted with neighbourhood relations in Kalyan, frequency of social interaction among neighbours in Gokul is less and relationships seem to be relatively formal. Women often seek the company of neighbours and have more contacts with them than men. People having fewer relatives or no relatives in the suburb or in other suburbs of the city maintain correspondingly more intimate relationships with their neighbours and rely more on them for help

---

12   Young and Willmott, 1957, 147 ff.

than those who had relatives in Gokul and in other suburbs of Dharwar. Intra-caste neighbourly relations seem to be effective.

Although the Brahmans had less intimate relationships with neighbours, each household maintained close contacts with at least one neighbouring family. Despite the relative lack of intimate relationships amongst all neighbours, Gokul residents are conscious of neighbourhood unity. Sociologically, neighbourhood has its social significance in Dharwar in the sense that the mere fact of close physical proximity and long residence draws people together spontaneously to tackle some common problem or for some local organization where concerted action is believed more likely to be effective than individual action, or simply from the human need of gregariousness. Neighbourhood solidarity is further reinforced by the strong bonds of caste.

In Gokul community, the persons who wield influence not only in sub-urban but also in city life, include the teacher, lawyer, doctor, merchant and publisher. Some of the civic activities revolve around these functional leaders. Caste consciousness is strong and the Brahmans make efforts to protect the interests of their own caste members in educational institutions, government, and other organizations.

Although kinship is not a territorial group in Gokul, the very fact that people occupy a common territory for a considerable period of time has developed a feeling of attachment to the physical and social environment. The solidarity of the Brahman community is exhibited in their religious, social, political and cultural activities. But the relatively formal and impersonal relationships characteristic of the city life have not encouraged ritual or courtesy kinship ties.

In Kalyan the influences of agriculture, illiteracy and conservatism restrict geographical and social mobility. Correspondingly its impact on kinship values and behaviour is less. But in Gokul, people are more educated and earn their living mainly or wholly by modern urban occupations. The foregoing evidence suggests that the greater degree of assimilation of modern values, and greater social mobility and migration have to a certain extent influenced the Brahman kinship values and patterns of behaviour more than the Lingayat kinship.

Urbanization, education, and intergenerational occupational mobility appear to be important in precipitating changes in kinship values and behaviour. However, a high frequency of mutual aid tends to reinforce bonds of kinship. With very few exceptions, class is no barrier to kin contacts. The possible adverse effects of migration are offset by frequent visits, exchange of gifts, family get-togethers, counseling, and help in crisis of life. What is more significant is the fact that in the process of social mobility the individual is aided by his family and intimate kin.

After this analysis of the interaction of the kinship and social stratification in this chapter, it only remains now to consider the modernization of law and its influence on family and kinship.

CHAPTER SEVEN

Legislation and Welfare

THIS CHAPTER seeks to examine the modernization of law and its impact on family and kinship in Kalyan and Gokul. Of the various activities of national reconstruction, such as social and economic planning, legislation and welfare activities of the Indian government since independence (1947) have assumed new significance in influencing the values, public opinion and behaviour of the people. We shall attempt to examine the role of social legislation and welfare services, and their repercussions on the kinship system of Lingayats and Brahmans.

Social Legislation and Social Welfare

Social legislation generally refers to "laws designed to improve and protect the economic and social position of those groups in society which because of age, sex, race, physical or mental defect or lack of economic power cannot achieve healthful and decent living standards for themselves".[1] It also implies that legislation which serves present social and economic objectives of the nation deals adequately with current social problems. To achieve social justice, social legislation aims at the protection of social and economic interests of the people who suffer from certain social and economic disabilities. In this sense most of the laws of the State may be termed as social legislation. Social legislation differs in space and time. During the nineteenth century, social legislation in India dealt with the social evils such as *Sati*, female infanticide, infant marriage, social ban on widow remarriage and the like. Today it is concerned with the elimination of the rigidities of caste, recognition of equal rights for women in social, economic and political life, child and labour welfare, land reforms, rehabilitation and care of the socially, mentally and physically handicapped individuals, public health, housing and education, etc. Such a comprehensive concept of social legislation forms a part of the concept of the modern welfare state.

For the present study social legislation is mainly confined to laws pertaining to marriage, family, maintainance, rights of inheritance of property and other related legislation applicable to Hindus in particular. The Government of India since independence has been making attempts to codify the Hindu law which until recently was a complicated structure made up of different schools and a maze of customs prevailing in different parts of the country. Among the

---

1 Fairchild (ed.), 1961, p. 285.

laws formulated by the Parliament, mention may be made of the Hindu Marriage Act of 1955, the Hindu Succession Act of 1956, and the Dowry Prohibition Act of 1961, which have initiated significant changes in the traditional life of the people.

Kinship and Legislation

To what extent has State legislation recognized the rights and obligations of kinship? What are the expectations and aspirations of people? How far does the present legislation correspond to social reality? Is it lagging behind the prevailing customs, mores and public opinion or is it ahead of them? What are the repercussions of the new social ideals set by recent legislation? To what extent are they effective? To what extent can social legislation be used to prevent kinship break up? Do they need modifications? What is the desirable social policy to be pursued by the State in the interest of kinship cohesion? These are searching questions that necessitate factual investigation with particular reference to the Lingayat and Brahman communities. The present analysis, however, does not take note of the problem, though fundamental, of whether or not the kinship break up is "good".

The people of Kalyan are "bilegal" and make use of the traditional customary law and also the statutory law in the administration of justice. In the realm of personal laws of Lingayats pertaining to family and property, customary law is more influential and effective than the State law. With regard to marriage, Lingayats of Kalyan, as noted already, follow the rules of sub-caste endogamy, prefer inter-kin marriages, celebrate pre-puberty marriage, allow polygyny, permit divorce, and allow remarriage of divorcees and widows. Such a pattern of marriage is in keeping with the traditions and customs of the people and hence it is approved and practised by them.

The Law of Marriage and Divorce

The Hindu Marriage Act of 1955, while reinforcing some of the marriage practices of the Lingayats, intends to initiate changes in some of their social norms and customary behaviour. According to the Act, the necessary conditions for the solemnization of a marriage between any two Hindus are that neither party has a spouse living and that neither is an idiot or a lunatic at the time of the marriage. The bridegroom must be 18 years of age and the bride, 15 years, at the time of the marriage. The parties must not be within the degrees of prohibited relationship or must not be *Sapindas*,[2] unless the custom or usage

---

2   "Sapinda" refers to agnate or cognate who shares in "Pinda", that is, rice-ball offering made to the ancestors. The degrees of Sapindaship are three degrees counting through the mother of either party and five degrees counting through the father. The party himself is counted as a degree in the traditional Hindu method of counting. If, counting in this manner, one reaches a common ancestor or ancestress, the marriage would be void because the parties would be sapindas.

governing each of them permits marriage between the two. Where the bride has not completed the age of 18 years, the consent of her guardian, if any, must be obtained for the marriage.

This law established monogamy and abolishes polygyny, which has been in practice though rarely among Lingayats. It does not recognize caste differences, and allows inter-caste marriages. To this extent, law sets up new social ideals which are ahead of the prevailing norms and practices of Lingayats. Lingayats have been tenaciously sticking to the rules of subcaste endogamy, which has been seldom violated in recent years. Therefore, people resent and disapprove of such provisions of the law allowing and recognizing inter-caste marriages. Because of the traditional and conservative outlook at present, they cannot even think of inter-caste marriages. Despite initial ineffectiveness of the new law and resistance to it in course of time, the spread of education, changes in occupation from the traditional to the modern, and internalization of modern urban values by people may lead to changes in their attitudes and behaviour patterns with regard to the law. In this context, law as a means of social change can become strong and effective through persuasion and education. In the long run it can help to bring about the amalgamation of different castes and subcastes among the Hindus, thereby breaking the caste patriotism and reducing rivalry and conflicts among various castes which corrode national life today.

The minimum age at marriage for girls (i.e. 14 years) as laid down by the Child Marriage Restraint Act, 1929, was practically ineffective. The Census of 1951 states that among the girls belonging to the age group 5–14, there were 6,188,000 married and 134,000 widowed or divorced. Among the Lingayats of Kalyan, 80.53% of the females married when they were below 15 years of age, and the average age at marriage of females is 12 years for all age groups. Such a large number of prepuberty marriages occur in Kalyan because of prevailing social norms, preference for inter-kin marriage, and the relatively poor economic conditions. However, the average ideal age for females according to the verbal responses of the older generation (i.e. 35 and above) and younger generation (i.e. below 35) should be 14 and 15 years, respectively, despite the fact that in reality, marriages of girls take place much earlier than 15 years. The data abundantly make it clear that people of Kalyan have been violating the Hindu Marriage Act, 1955, with respect to minimum age of marriage of females.

The punishment for contravention of this clause is that every person who procures a marriage of himself shall be punishable with simple imprisonment which may extend to 15 days or with fine which may extend to one thousand rupees, or both. So it is the parties to the marriage alone who can be punished under the Hindu Marriage Act, 1935. The parents, guardians, or other relatives who are mainly responsible for arranging such early marriages cannot be punished under section 18 of the Act. But in punishing the parties to the marriage, instead of the parents who actually arrange the marriage, the law punishes the wrong parties.

Paper Law and Law of Action

The very fact that of the many violators of law in this regard very few are punished indicates that the law exists on statute books only and not in actual practice. To what extent is law ineffective due to the indifference and inefficiency of the machinery of execution? If the objectives of law are to be realised, the "paper law" needs to be translated into action. Moreover, the implementation of law pertaining to the minimum age of marriage is due to a rather basic handicap. Since there is no legal compulsion for the registration of births, it is difficult to prove the age at marriage of parties. In order to prove the age of the girl legally, the law must provide for compulsory registration of all births, thereby facilitating the punishment of deviants and abettors.[3]

The average age at marriage of women (12 years) in Kalyan and the fact that almost all girls between the ages of 15–20, said to be the most fertile period, are married, have made for a high rate of reproduction. In view of the alarming growth of population in India, inadequate exploitation of resources, and in the interests of desirable living standards, some scholars argue that it is imperative to postpone the age of marriage.

In accordance with the directive principles of state policy as laid down in the Constitution of India, the Hindu Marriage Act, 1955, in providing a uniform code for all Hindus, sets new ideals, allows intercaste marriage, and paves the way for the emergence of a casteless society. Law as the initiator of social change may be met with resistance, as in Kalyan, when it requires the customs to adapt to the new legal ideals. To that extent law as social control may be ineffective, initially at least. Law, if it is to exert its influence on human behaviour, should provide an environment which will enable the legally deviant persons to internalize the values embodied in it.

Despite the fact that the Lingayats of Kalyan are placed in the urban milieu, the degree of internalization of modern values is limited due to the peculiarities of caste, occupation, lack of education and various other socio-economic conditions of the people.

If some provisions of the Act—minimum age of marriage of females, inter-caste marriage, and monogamy—are ahead of the prevailing values and social customs there are others which reinforce certain existing values and customs of the Lingayats in this suburb. Although uncle-niece and cross-cousin marriages fall within the category of legally prohibited degrees of relationship, the law allows such marriages and considers them valid because the customs or usage governing each of the parties permits this type of marriage.

Besides provisions for the restitution of conjugal rights and judicial separations, section 13 of the Act refers to the right of divorce. One of the distinguishing features of the sacred Hindu law has been the indissolubility of the marriage tie. The Brahmans and other "upper castes" followed this norm. To

---

3   A Bill was introduced in the Parliament for compulsory Registration of Births and Deaths on 2, Oct. 1964, and was passed subsequently.

them, the present Act which expressly confers the right of divorce, aims at effecting a revolutionary change in the fundamentals of Hindu law of marriage. However, there have been certain cases within the broader Hindu social system wherein divorce and remarriage have been permitted by custom. Lingayats belong to one such category.

Almost all the Lingayat subcastes (except the Jangam and Banajiga) who seem to be under the lingering influence of the 12th century reformation, allow divorce under certain circumstances and permit the remarriage of widows and divorcees. Since the Lingayats of Kalyan customarily allow divorce and remarriage under certain conditions, to them the Hindu Marriage Act, 1955 does not come as a radical and revolutionary piece of legislation. On the contrary, it reinforces their existing practices. Although divorce and remarriage of divorcees and widows are allowed under exceptional circumstances, it is not socially approved or encouraged, and the parties involved do not enjoy the same social status as that of others (normally married).

In Kalyan, divorce is customarily allowed on grounds of severe cruelty, adultery, serious disease, forced marriage or child marriage, impotency, and other kinds of incompatibility between spouses. Section 13 of the Hindu Marriage Act, 1955 provides some grounds for divorce.[4] It should be noted that the court is allowed to entertain any petition for dissolution of a marriage by a decree of divorce three years after the date of marriage, and before this 3 year period only in case of exceptional hardship to the petitioner. It is obvious that to obtain a decree of divorce from the court of law is a waste of considerable money and time. Hence the people of Kalyan prefer to settle their matrimonial disputes through the traditional caste *panchayat* (Council of Five). The members of the caste *panchayat* are generally familiar with the facts of the case and can decide it expeditiously, with little or no cost.

As yet dowry has not become a social problem among the Lingayats of Kalyan. The Dowry Prohibition Act of 1961, defines "dowry" as any property or valuable security given or agreed to be given either directly or indirectly by one party to a marriage, or by the parents of either party to a marriage or by any other person, to consideration for the marriage of the said parties. In this sense, dowry, by and large, does not enter into the marriage proposals and

---

4 Any marriage soleminized, whether before or after the commencement of this Act, may, on a petition presented by either the husband or wife be dissolved by a decree of divorce on the ground that the other party is living in adultery; or has ceased to be a Hindu by conversion to another religion; or has been incurably of unsound mind; or has been suffering from a virulent and incurable form of leprosy or from venereal disease in a communicable form for not less than 3 years; or has renounced the world by entering any religious order; or has not been heard of as being alive for a period of 7 years or more; or has not resumed cohabitation for a space of 2 years or upwards after the passing of a decree for judicial seperation against that party; or has failed to comply with a decree for restitution of conjugal rights for a period of 2 years or upwards after the passing of the decree. A wife may also present a petition for the dissolution of her marriage by a decree of divorce on the grounds of second marriage of the husband, or that the husband has been guilty of rape, sodomy, or bestiality.

agreements in Kalyan and is not decisive enough, by itself, to prevent marriage. In the majority of marriages, presents are traditionally given to either party to the marriage in the form of small cash, ornaments, clothes, or other articles. There is a voluntary payment and exchange of gifts. According to the Act, such presents shall not be deemed to be dowry unless they are made as consideration for the marriage of the concerned parties.

Law of Succession and Kinship Solidarity

The Hindus of this region were governed by the Mitakshara school of Hindu law for purposes of inheritance and succession of property. The mode of devolution of property was by survivorship and not by succession. The conception of a coparcenary was that of a common male ancestor with his lineal descendants in the male line. No coparcenary can begin without a common male ancestor, although after his death, it may consist of collaterals such as brothers, uncles, and nephews. The members held the property in undefined shares which were fluctuating according to births and deaths in the family. Females could not be coparceners though they were members of the Hindu joint-family. The right of property of a female Hindu was a limited one.[5]

In Kalyan on the death of the male head of a family, the sons of the deceased male will have equal share in the movable and immovable property. Traditionally, daughters have no right to claim their share in the parental property. They are entitled to have maintenance until the time of their marriage. The expenses of the daughter's wedding—including ornaments, clothes and other presents made at that time—will be met through her parental property. Even after marriage she visits her parental home occasionally, and may receive, from her parents or brothers, presents in the form of clothes and ornaments, but she hardly thinks to claim her share in the parental property as of right. The cultural milieu in which she has been brought up does not foster such a desire.

The Hindu Succession Act, 1956 brings about a radical change in this respect.[6] According to the Act, in the first instance the basis of the right to

---

5   See, Mulla, D. F. 1960.

6   According to section 8 of the Act, the property of male Hindu dying intestate shall devolve firstly, upon the heirs, being the relatives specified in class I of the schedule, secondly, if there is no heir of class I, then upon the heirs, being the relatives in class II of the schedule, thirdly, if there is no heir of any of two classes, then upon the agnates of the deceased, and lastly, if there is no agnate, then upon the congnates of the deceased. The heirs in class I of the schedule include: son, daughter, widow, mother, children of a pre-deceased son, children of a pre-deceased daughter, widow of a pre-deceased son, children of a pre deceased son of a pre-deceased son, widow of a pre-deceased son, children of a pre-deceased son of a pre-deceased son, widow of a pre-deceased son of a pre-deceased son. The heirs in class II of the schedule include: (a) Fa; (b) SoDaSo, SoDaDa, Br, Si; (c) DaSoSo, DaSoDa, DaDaSo, DaDaDa, DaDaDa; (d) BrSo, SiSo, BrDa, SiDa; (e) FaFa, FaMo; (f) father's widow, brother's widow; (g) FaBr, FaSi; (h) MoFa, MoMo; (i) MoBr, MoSi. As regards the distribution of property among the heirs in class I, the widow of the

succeed to the property of a deceased person lies in kinship with him. Under the Act the term "heir" means any person, male or *female*, who is entitled to succeed to the property of an intestate. For the purpose of the Act, an heir, so far as a male heir is concerned, will mean both the natural and the adopted son of his father. It is relevant to note that the term "*related*" in the act means related by legitimate kinship. But the illegitimate children shall be deemed to be related to their mother and to one another, and their legitimate descendants shall be deemed to be related to them and to one another. Illegitimate children are not deemed to be related to their putative father and shall not be entitled to succeed to his property, whereas they shall be entitled to succeed to the property of the mother.

Attitudes

The present Act introduces revolutionary changes in the patrilineal matrix safeguarded for centuries, by bestowing on the female the rights of succession of property and possession of it as absolute owner. In Kalyan a majority of the people own meagre property. The responses and reactions of them to the new law of succession indicate their dissatisfaction. "If the daughter claims a share, whatever little property we possess will be shattered to pieces. Tensions and conflicts increase between consanguines and affines. It will affect kinship solidarity adversely", said most of the men. "It is unreasonable to claim a share

intestate, or if there are more widows than one, all the widows together shall take one share. The surviving sons and daughters and the mother of the intestate shall each take one share. The heirs in the branch of each pre-deceased son or each pre-deceased daughter of the intestate shall take between one share. Section 14 of the act provides that any property possessed by a female Hindu, whether acquired before or after the commencement of the Act, shall be held by her as full owner thereof and not as a limited owner. According to section 15 of the Act, the property of a female Hindu dying intestate shall devolve, firstly, upon the sons and daughters (including the children of any pre-deceased son or daughter) and husband; secondly, upon the heirs of the husband; thirdly, upon the mother and father; fourthly, heirs of the father and fifthly, upon the heirs of the mother. Quite reasonably it is provided that any property inherited by a female Hindu from her parents shall devolve, in the absence of any son or daughter of the deceased (including the children of any pre-deceased son or daughter) not upon the other heirs mentioned above but upon the heirs of the father. Likewise, any property inherited by a female Hindu from her husband or from her father-in-law shall devolve, in the absence of any son or daughter of the deceased (including the children of any pre-deceased son or daughter) not upon the other heirs referred to above, but upon the heirs of the husband.
Section 30 which is concerned with testamentary succession states that any Hindu may dispose of by will or other testamentary disposition any property which is capable of so disposed of by him, in accordance with the provision of the Indian Succession Act 1925, or any other law for the time being in force and applicable to Hindus. However, this shall not affect the right to maintainance of any heir specified in the schedule by reason only of the fact that under a will or other testamentary disposition made by the deceased, the heir has been deprived of a share in the property to which he or she is otherwise entitled under the Act, if the deceased has died intestate. The foregoing main provisions of the Hindu Succession Act 1956 are pregnant with great potentialities to affect the existing family and kinship system.

in the parental property. We are not entitled to it. Let them (parents and brothers) give the traditional presents such as *sarees* and blouses, ornaments, a cow, maternity benefits, and only in times of need, grain and money. Even otherwise, we are pleased with only the sweet bread of our natal home", expressed a majority of the housewives, young and old.

The women of Kalyan said that they cannot be equal to their brothers in point of industriousness and accumulation of property, and hence they cannot be equal sharers. In any event, a woman on marriage will possess her husband's property. Where then is the need to claim a share in the parental property? The new law, by creating new aspirations, is likely to create jealousies and hatred between brothers and sisters, consanguines and affines.

Until recently, the relationships of consanguines and affines were normally characterized by affection, friendliness, mutual advice and help or they were occasionally marked by tensions and conflicts for predominantly social reasons. The Hindu Succession Act of 1956, by establishing jural relationships between consanguines and affines makes for new stresses and strains, litigation, and disruption of the otherwise integrated kinship system. That is why 40% of the respondents are not in favour of giving a share to the female. There are 52.17% of them in favour of giving some share to the female, but they would like to give a share of the movable property—in the form of traditional gifts and money or food grains—only when she becomes a widow or if the husband's family is unable to maintain her. A minority of 7.83% wishes to give some share in the immovable property to her, provided she has no brothers or in case her husband is poor. Even then the land given to her must be cultivated by her brothers and the income should be given to her.

It is evident then that the majority of men and women do not like the rights of succession and possession of property conferred on the female. Those respondents who favoured such shares for women do so not as a right but as a concession to her when she is economically helpless. They maintain, however, that the payment made to the daughter traditionally is also a considerable part of the property. A share in the family land for women creates subdivision and fragmentation of land, since patrilocal residence compels her and her husband to sell it, possibly to a stranger. So this law is inconsistent with the law of consolidation of cultivable lands. Being contrary to the traditional norms and values cherished by Lingayats, this Act seems to disrupt the age-old relationship within the kin group, thereby leading to kinship fission. In order to avoid the possible serious repercussions of the Act on kinship and community, it appears reasonable to provide, to begin with, only the rights of usufruct of immovable property for women.

Adoption

In the absence of a male child, the married couple, widow or widower feels the necessity of adopting a close relative. The need for maintenance and care in old age, and the desire for perpetuating the family name and settling succession to property in accordance with one's own wishes—being rather strong and further reinforced by religion—have led to the artificial creation of kinship through the custom of adoption. The old Hindu Law allowed adoption of a son, not a daughter, in accordance with the traditional customs. But the Hindu Adoptions and Maintenance Act, 1956 goes a step farther and provides, on satisfying the prescribed conditions, for the adoption of not only a son but also a daughter. Now the female both as adopter and adoptee enjoys equal rights and privileges.

By the establishment of such new kinship relationship through adoption, a person ceases to be the child of his or her natural parents and becomes the son or daughter of his or her adoptive parents, provided the legal requirements and formalities are fulfilled. Moreover, a valid adoption cannot be revoked or renounced by any of the parties thereto. The bonds of kinship created thereby are regarded as good and lasting as those acquired by birth, but with the difference that an adoptee cannot marry any one within the prohibited degrees of relationships, not only in his adoptive family but also in the family of his birth.

In Kalyan, people shun the idea of adopting a daughter because it does not satisfy any of their motives for adoption. The traditional Lingayat cultural complex does not encourage adoption of a daughter, since it is opposed to the patrilineal norms of society. Even if a man has only one daughter and no male issue, he invites his daughter's husband to stay with him and inherit his property. There are some such instances in Kalyan, whereas there is not a single case of adoption of a daughter. Of the 13 cases of adoption of a son, in the 6 cases when the adopter is a widow she usually adopts her younger brother, BrSo, or DaSo. In seven other cases when the adopter is male, the adoptee is either his BrSo, FaSiSo, FaBrSoSo or his DaSo, SiSo, WiBrSo. Hence the adopters prefer both agnates and cognates as adoptees, and in any case it is always preferable for them to keep property within the intimate kin group.

On adoption, the adoptee takes the family name of his adopter and possesses all the rights of a real son in the adopted family. From the date of adoption for all purposes, even though the adoptee's ties with his family of birth shall be deemed to be cut off and replaced by those in the adoptive family—legal severance apart, the adoptee nevertheless maintains social relationships with the members of the family into which he was born. Though the adoptee's kinship status and role change legally, in reality he continues more or less with the same old patterns of relationships that existed prior to adoption; this is indicated by the use of same kinship terms of address. The adoptee is more affectionate and inclined towards helping his natural parents and siblings rather than the adoptive kin.

The Law of Maintenance

It is a kinship obligation of paramount importance to look after, support, and maintain those members of the family and intimate kin group who are unable to stand on their own because of certain physical, social, economic, or other disabilities. To what extent have the rights and obligations of main-tenance been recognized by law? Under the old Hindu law it was the rule that every member of the joint family who was entitled to reside in it was to be maintained out of the joint family funds. On partition of the joint family, members not entitled to a share in the joint family property were entitled to a provision for their maintenance. The head of the joint family was bound to maintain its members, their wives, and children; and to pay the expenses of their marriage and other *rites de passage* and meet other expenses for their physical support and spiritual well-being. Maintenance as defined by the Hindu Adoptions and Maintenance Act, 1956, however, includes, in all cases, provision for food, clothing, residence, education, and medical care. In the case of an unmarried daughter, maintenance also includes the reasonable expenses of and incidental to her marriage.

The persons entitled to maintenance are one's wife and children, aged parents, daughter-in-law, and some specified dependants. From the date of marriage, the husband is under a personal obligation to maintain his wife. As long as she resides with him, the dispute as to her maintenance does not arise. The wife's right to separate residence under certain circumstances is almost interlinked with her right to maintenance. According to the Hindu Marriage Act of 1955, the causes of disputes between married couples that call for judicial interference have been the restitution of conjugal rights, judicial separation, annulment of marriage by a decree of nullity, and dissolution of marriage by a decree of divorce. It is significant that under the Hindu Marriage Act, 1955, a petition for any of the reliefs can be presented not only by the wife but also by an indigent husband to claim maintenance even during the pendency of matrimonial proceedings and for the grant of necessary expenses to prosecute or defend the same.

A wife forfeits her right to maintenance by her husband if she is unchaste or ceases to be a Hindu by conversion to another religion. After the death of her husband, she is entitled to be maintained by her father-in-law to the extent she is unable to maintain herself out of her own property or earnings or from the property of her husband, parents, or children or their estate. But the obligation of the father-in-law will not be enforceable if he has not the means to meet his obligations from any coparcenary property in his possession out of which the daughter-in-law has not obtained any share. Of course, such obligation shall cease on the remarriage of the widowed daughter-in-law.

Prior to the Hindu Adoptions and Maintenance Act, 1956, the Hindu law provided that a father was personally bound to maintain his son until he attained legal age, a daughter until her marriage, and his parents when they became old and infirm. An illegitimate daughter was not entitled to maintenance. But the Act of 1956 provides for maintenance of children of both sexes, whether legitimate or illegitimate, and of aged parents. "Parents" do not include grandparents and "children" do not include grandchildren. The word "parent" includes a childless step-mother, and a "legitimate child" includes an adopted child. It should be noted that while it is a legal obligation for a Hindu during his or her life-time to maintain children, so long as they are minors, the question of maintaining aged or infirm parents or an unmarried daughter would arise only if any of them is unable to maintain himself or herself from his or her own separate earnings and property.

The law relating to maintenance of the dependents of a person prior to the codification of Hindu law would seem to have included all the (near and distant) members of his family, who were dependent for their support on him. There could be no dependents of females, because they themselves were considered to be dependent on males. But under the Act of 1956, dependents have been defined with reference to women also. As defined by the Act, dependents mean only those relatives of a deceased person who are specified therein, some of them only under specified circumstances. The dependents of a deceased male Hindu are his father, mother, widow, son, etc.[7] The dependents of a deceased female Hindu are her father, mother, son, unmarried daughter, minor illegitimate son, and unmarried illegitimate daughter. So the law of maintenance recognizes the members of the intimate kin group as dependents. In Kalyan, the resentment of the people towards this law is mainly against the maintenance of illegitimate children who are not socially recognized as members of the family in the Lingayat kinship system.

In the absence of parents and their property, the eldest male is under a kinship obligation to look after and maintain his younger brothers and sisters. He has to provide for their food, clothing, education, medical care, and marriage. Such sibling solidarity is often manifested in Kalyan. Even the widowed sister takes refuge under the care of her brother. The law, however, does not recognize such a responsibility of kinship, and no privileges are granted to the brother for performing the function.

Guardianship and Kinship

The law of guardianship is based on the incapacity which law attributes to minors and persons deficient in mental capacity in the matter of looking after themselves, managing their property, or entering into contracts, and the consequent necessity of entrusting the management of their affairs to the care of proper guardians. Under the Hindu Minority and Guardianship Act, 1956, a "minor" means a person who has not reached the age of 18 years. A "guardian" is a person who has the care of a minor's person or property or of both.[8]

---

7 Other dependents of a deceased male Hindu include: son of pre-deceased son, son of pre-deceased son of pre-deceased son, unmarried daughter, widowed daughter, son's widow, minor illegitimate son, unmarried illegitimate daughter.

8 The natural guardians of the person and property of a Hindu legitimate child, in order of preference are—where the minor is a boy or an unmarried girl: (i) the father, provided that the child is below 5 years of age, its custody ordinarily belongs to the mother, (ii) the mother. Where the minor boy or the unmarried girls are illegitimate(i) the mother (ii) the father; where the minor is a married girl her husband; where the minor is an adopted son: (i) the adoptive father, (ii) the adoptive mother. So far as natural guardianship is concerned

The Hindu Marriage Act, 1955, provides a list of guardians in order of priority who are entitled to give consent to the marriage of a minor girl. A guardian, natural or testamentary, is entitled to do all acts which are necessary or reasonable and proper for the benefit of the minor or for the realization, protection, or benefit of the minor's estate. The court in appointing a guardian, takes into consideration among other things his nearness of kinship relationship to the minor. It may be pointed out that the law of guardianship has not given due priority to the mother's brother who plays an important role in looking after the welfare of his sister's children in Kalyan.

The foregoing analysis of legislation pertaining to marriage, family, and kinship, inheritance of property, adoption and maintenance, minority and guardianship reveals the zeal of Indian legislators, after Independence, to give equal rights and privileges to females in different spheres of life. In their enthusiasm to place women on an equal footing with men, the policy-makers have, it appears, lost sight of the possible adverse effects on kinship cohesion and solidarity. The new legislation incorporating modern egalitarian values which are strikingly opposed to the traditional norms and values tends to rupture kinship relationships. In the future, frictions, tensions and conflicts are most likely to increase within the intimate kin group unless the law changes or has some restraining effect.

Since the majority of the inhabitants of Kalyan are farmers, with small land-holdings, the land reforms legislation and the taxation law have not affected the kinship system to any considerable extent. Similarly the social security schemes, such as that of pension, provident fund, insurance, etc., have not made their impact.

Gokul

The cultural milieu of the Brahmans being different from that of the Lingayats one can easily notice the differential effects of the same law on the Brahmans. Brahmans do not follow the rules of sub-caste endogamy as rigidly as Lingayats. Inter-subcaste marriages are quite common in Gokul but inter-caste marriages are still an exception and meet with severe social ostracism. Traditionally, inter-kin marriages are preferred but to a lesser extent when compared to those of Lingayats. Post-puberty marriage is the norm. Marriage of individuals of the same *gotra* is prohibited. Polygamy, which is seldom found, is tolerated. Divorce is not allowed and there is a strict social taboo on the remarriage of widows.

Marriage a Sacrament

Brahmans recognize the Hindu Marriage Act, 1955 as a radical and revolutionary piece of legislation because some of the provisions of the Act are

---

the terms father and mother do not include a step-father and step-mother. Besides natural guardians there are testamentary guardians and guardians appointed by courts and those appointed under enactments relating to courts of wards.

in sharp contrast to the traditional norms still upheld by them. The law dispenses with caste endogamy and exogamy. The legal recognition and approval of inter-caste marriage and *sagotra* marriage is strongly resented. Moreover, this Act does not allow marriage of two Hindus who are within the degrees of prohibited relationship or who are *sapindas* of each other unless the custom or usage governing each of them permits such a marriage. It is stated that the sacred law of the Hindus does not insist so much on *sapinda* exogamy as that on *gotra* exogamy. According to the Act, *sapinda* relationships with reference to any person extends as far as the third generation (inclusive) in the line of ascent through the mother, and the fifth (inclusive) in the line of ascent through the father, the line being traced upwards in each case from the person concerned, who is to be counted as the first generation.

Only the ritual of *Sraddha* recognizes four generations (inclusive). Under the present Act, whenever the consent of a guardian in marriage is necessary for a bride, the persons entitled to give such consent, in order of preference, are: the father, the mother, the paternal grandfather, the paternal grandmother, the brother, the paternal uncle, the maternal grandfather, the maternal grandmother, and the maternal uncle. The persons mentioned who are entitled to give consent for the marriage of a bride are those related to her within three generations. Therefore, it would be reasonable for the law to lay down the observance of *sapinda* exogamy within three generations even where the custom or usage governing each of them does not permit such a marriage. Cross-cousin marriage and uncle-niece marriage, even though they are within three generations, are allowed on grounds of custom or usage. While giving due recognition to the variations in marital customs it is argued that the best thing that can be done is to dispense with *sapinda* exogamy or prohibited degrees as they constitute legal impediments in marriage.

Pre-puberty marriage, common in Kalyan, sharply differs from the post-puberty marriage that is common in Gokul. Only 24.81% of the Brahman females, a majority of them belonging to the older generation, married when they were below 15 years. Therefore, in this case the problem of the violation of the provisions of the law concerning minimum age of marriage for females does not arise. In fact the marriage practices of the Brahmans including those relating to the age of marriage are far in advance of the legal requirements.

The strongest opposition against the Hindu Marriage Act, 1955 relates to that feature which provides for rights of divorce for both husband and wife on certain grounds. For the Brahmans, marriage has always been a sacrament which cannot be dissolved with at the mere will of the parties. The Brahmanic ideals emphasize the irrevocable marital bond between husband and wife until the death of either of them and the wife is believed to be bound to her husband even after his death. Such a concept of marriage demands the adjustment of interests and ideals and, involves sacrifices from spouses, instead of their preparedness to break the marital tie in case of differences. When marriage was considered a social duty toward the family and the community, the individual interests and aspirations had to be subordinated to the good of the family and kinship, caste and community. The ideals of strict fidelity, utmost devotion and service to the husband have influenced the up-bringing of the female Brahman in such a way that instead of striving for her personal happiness she strives for the happiness of her husband. On the other hand, the moral lapses, personal defects or limitations of the husband were not a matter of great concern. These double standards of morality prevailed when inequality of sexes was taken for granted since it was sanctioned by religion.

To what extent does the divorce law ensure that dissolution of marriage does not take place on flimsy grounds and to what degree does it hasten the breakup of marital bond? The Brahmans are opposed to divorce and remarriage of widows under any circumstances. The law which puts certain obstacles in the way of obtaining a decree of divorce may appear to support their practice. In the first instance the court is not competent to entertain any petition for dissolution of a marriage by a decree of divorce, unless at the date of the presentation of the petition 3 years have elapsed since the date of marriage. It is believed that this 3 year period is necessary to provide spouses with an opportunity for compromise and reconciliation for resolving their conflicts of interests and for mutual understanding. Thus the emotional outbursts of the parties and the possible sudden marital break is prevented.

It is only when the case is one of exceptional hardship to the petitioner or of exceptional depravity on the part of the respondent that the court may allow a petition to be presented before 3 years have elapsed since the date of marriage. Even then in disposing of any application for leave to present a petition for divorce before the expiration of 3 years from the date of the marriage, the court shall have regard to the interests of any children of the marriage and to the question of whether there is a probability of reconciliation between the parties before the expiration of the said 3 years.

The right and willingness to obtain a decree of divorce are also restricted by the fact that at the time of passing of any decree or at any time subsequent thereto, on application made to it for the purpose by either the wife, or the husband, any court exercising jurisdiction under the Hindu Marriage Act, 1955 may order that the respondent shall, while the applicant remains unmarried, pay to the applicant for her or his maintenance and support until she or he remains unmarried or, if such party is the wife, till she remains chaste. Or if such party is the husband, and if he has had sexual intercourse with any woman outside wedlock, the court shall rescind the order to pay maintenance and support. Hence under this Act, divorce is made sufficiently costly. One would think twice before obtaining a decree of divorce. The fears and misapprehensions that this law leads to the distintegration of the family do not seem well-founded. It is obvious that the law gives a decree of divorce as a last resort when attempts at compromise and reconciliation of the couples have failed and when the court is sufficiently convinced of the detrimental effects on the spouses and children if they are made to stay together. It may be difficult to prove the fact of living in adultery especially when the offender is a male, whereas it may be easy to prove the same in case of a female offender in order to obtain decree of divorce on that ground.

As observed by Nimkoff "social legislation may also be an important new influence affecting the family because legislation may introduce a new and even radical concept, although if the concept is too radical, it may prove to be dysfunctional and may be successfully resisted by the massess".[9] The dysfunctional nature of radical legislation is best illustrated in case of the Hindu law allowing widows to remarry. After a lapse of more than a century of the Hindu Widow Re-Marriage Act, 1856, in Gokul there has not been a single case of widow remarriage among Brahmans. This fact makes it clear that when the custom is strong the law as an instrument of social change and innovation proves weak. This, however, need not discourage the law-makers since new legislation can bring about the desired social change provided the law is supported by the necessary socio-economic forces. The modern socio-cultural milieu has brought about certain ideational changes among the Brahmans and 22.61% of them, mostly educated young men, are in favour of divorce under certain extreme circumstances, and 33.04% are in favour of the re-marriage of widows under certain conditions. Behavioural changes in this respect are yet to be seen. It needs strength of character and courage to break the custom and to meet the severe social ostracism. The crux of the problem is that divorcees find it extremely difficult to find a new partner and hence people find it difficult to afford the luxury of divorce.

The Dowry Prohibition Act

When the custom of dowry is widespread among the Brahmans, to what extent can the legislation prevent it? The Dowry Prohibition Act, 1961 lays down that if any person, after the commencement of this act, gives or takes or abets the giving or taking of dowry, or if any person demands directly or indirectly, from the parents or guardian of a bride or bridegroom, as the case may be, any dowry, shall be punishable with imprisonment which may extend to 6 months, or with a fine which may extend to Rs. 5,000 or with both. Any agreement for giving or taking of dowry shall be void. Moreover, where any dowry is received by any person other than the woman in connection with whose marriage it is given, that person shall transfer it to the woman.

Although the punishment prescribed for giving, taking or demanding dowry is a deterrent, the explanation of the Act declares that any presents made at the time of a marriage to either party to the marriage in the form of cash, ornaments, clothes or other articles, shall not be deemed to be dowry, unless they are made as consideration for the marriage. Under the guise of wedding gifts, persons can give or receive or demand dowry although in reality it may be consideration for the marriage. Parents who are more anxious to see their daughter married do not wish the other party to be punished on account of

---

9 Nimkoff, *S.B.*, Vol. VIII, No. 2, p. 38.

demanding or receiving dowry as consideration for the marriage. If they do so, it will further endanger the prospects of their daughter's marriage. The social situation being what it is, the evil of dowry continues unabated and the offenders go unpunished as before. Laws, no doubt, have different ways of effecting social control—through punishment, therapy, and education. The Dowry Prohibition Act alone, however, will not be effective unless an environment is created which will enable the deviant or potential deviant to internalize the values incorporated in the law.

Hindu Succession and Kinship Cohesion

The patrilineal inheritance and succession of property has been a characteristic feature of Brahmans. Traditionally, only the male descendants inherit the parental property. Females, at best, had a limited right to hold property. However, her maintenance and support till marriage, the payment of marriage expenses, the occasional gifts, maternity benefits and the like, have been the responsibility of the natal family. Beyond this, the Brahmanic cultural pattern did not nourish any female sentiments or interests in the parental property.

With the introduction of the Hindu Succession Act, 1956, there has been a distinct departure from the traditional rules of inheritance and succession. As mentioned already, this Act not only grants rights of succession of property but also confers absolute rights of ownership of proprety on the female. The people of Gokul look upon the new law of succession as fraught with serious dangers and explosive potentialities to the kin group. According to 62% of the respondents, the present Act is likely to shake the very foundations of the existing family and kinship system.

Attitudes Towards Law of Succession

While 17.39% of the respondents are against giving a share of property to the female, 39.13% of them are in favour of giving some kind of movable property—which is presented to her traditionally. On the whole, 56.52% of the respondents are actually opposed to the law which recognizes the right of succession and absolute ownership of property of the female. The reasons given for such opposition are as follows: The male descendants have several kinship obligations such as payment of the debts of the paternal kin, maintenance and support of the aged parents, education and marriage of brothers, sisters and children, payment of the expenses on various rituals and ceremonies, medical care, and so on. The female is not burdened with such responsibilities. Even if she is made to shoulder these kinship responsibilities, or even if she wishes to do so, it becomes difficult for her to discharge the kinship duties remaining as she does most of the time in her conjugal family. Equal share for females and males means the property, especially the immovable property, would be divided into small fragments. As the woman is away from the natal home after marriage, this would lead to the disintegration of the family and kin group. Close and intimate kin relationships between brother and sister would be seriously affected. These rights would create jealousy and rivalry among kin. Tensions, conflicts and litigation among affines and agnates would be on the increase.

"On marriage, we are grafted on to our conjugal family. Why should we demand a share in our parental property, since we have our own (husband's)? It is just like robbing Peter to pay Paul. If we insist on our share, mutual love and affection amongst intimate kin withers away. Misunderstandings and miseries on that account tear out the kinship fabric", said several female respondents. Many reactions which voice the feelings of fear on the implementation of the Hindu Succession Act, 1956 are being recorded not only in Dharwar but also in other parts of India. Mayer reports from central India that "when the daughters inherit land, the agnates fear that this property will leave the descent group and never come to rest in the hands of collaterals, however remote. This is the main reason for strenuous attempts by brothers and other collaterals to retain land and not allow sisters or daughters to inherit. Most land disputes have centred around this, some resulting in court cases and others in appeals to the revenue authorities who maintain the land registers. Government policy is against absentee farming, and the daughter may be torn between farming one or other of the lands available to her".[10] In Gokul, although there are some stresses and strains between kin, disputes regarding female succession to property have not gone to the courts for decision. In some cases which arose after 1956, the elders made therapeutic attempts to repair and restore the fractured kinship relationships.

Mayer's speculation on the results of this new pattern of inheritance and the attitudes of kin towards it can be considered here. As he points out, "The main one is that affinal kin are getting more and more involved in property matters. Before, inheritance was almost entirely a matter for agnates; but now, the daughter (and her husband) claims rights as a person having a very high priority. Since the tenure laws now make it hard for the couple to farm at a distance, they will more and more come to live in the wife's parental village if the property is at all sizable; and this will exacerbate the hostility already aroused by the disposal of the property. It will also tend to change the residence pattern, of course, making the village caste group less of an extended agnatic kin group and resulting in more splits of the extended household as men go to their conjugal villages".[11] Such a change in the residential patterns may take place in Kalyan but not in Gokul since the majority of Brahmans pursue non-agricultural occupations. Father-in-law/son-in-law relationships and brother-sister relationships among Brahmans may function on mutual suspicion and fear. The inter-personal relationships and cooperation among kin may be minimized because of the new jural relationships arising from the property rights of females.

Despite such apprehensions, 43.48% of the respondents in Gokul are in

---

10   Mayer, A. C., 1960, p. 244.
11   *Ibid*, p. 245.

favour, at least verbally, of giving a share of the property, both movable and immovable, to the female. Out of these, nearly half wish to give a share to the female only when her husband is poor or when she is a widow or deserted by her husband. There are others, influenced by the modern egalitarian thinking, who say they would like to give a share of property to the female as a right. Those who are in favour of succession of property by the female do not like to discriminate against her on the basis of sex. If these responses were genuine, there would have been no question of the disturbing affect of the legislation on the Hindu kinship. But as our field observations showed, the responses were more verbal than genuine. This means that adverse effects of the legislation do remain. A way to avoid the imminent kinship fission seems to be a modification of the Act to ensure that the change is brought about gradually.

Role of Adoption

When the married couple or widowed persons do not have a male issue they resort to adoption of a son. For a Brahman without a male child, the motives for adoption of a son are strong and varied. The need for care and maintenance in old age, performance of funeral rites and *Sraddha*, succession of property and the perpetuation of the family name are the underlying forces that lead to the adoption of a son. Even in families with daughters, the absence of a son makes the atmosphere relatively unhappy. A son, whether real or adopted, is necessary because there is a belief that a son, and not a daughter, saves his parents from going to a certain type of hell after death. In Gokul, practically no one showed a tendency to adopt a daughter, which is allowed by the Hindu Adoptions and Maintenance Act, 1956, as it is neither sanctioned by religion nor socially advantageous.

Kinship preferences in adoption is indicated by the patterns of who adopts whom as shown in Table 44.

Table 44

Adopter	Adoptee												
	Br	BrSo	DaSo	SiSo	BrSo So	SiSo So	FaBr So	HuBr So	SiDa	WiSi DaHu	FaBr DaHu	FaFa BrSo So	Total
Male	4	8	3	—	3	—	—	—	—	1	1	1	21
Female	6	3	5	3	—	1	1	2	1	—	—	—	22
Total	10	11	8	3	3	1	1	2	1	1	1	1	43

Irrespective of the sex of the adopter, the adoptee is usually his or her brother (younger) or brother's son, or daughter's son. As is evident, there is a definite preference for agnatic relatives as adoptees, although non-agnatic kin are also adopted. Besides the availability of certain kin as adoptee, the merits of the boy and the degree of love and affection towards him are also vital considerations influencing adoptions. Cliques and pressure groups (in the kin group) also influence the adopter's choice of a specific kin as adoptee. In general, respondents advocated that there is a preference for the brother's son since he is the nearest agnatic relative. It is also relevant to note that the Code of Manu considered the daughter's son as the best substitute for a son. The patterns of adoption in Gokul more or less follow such a Code.

The adoption of a son requires the fulfilment of certain conditions as laid down in the Hindu Adoptions and Maintenance Act, 1956. The adoptee shall be deemed to have cut off his ties with the family of birth and possesses all rights of a real son in the adopted family. The adoptee is prevented from marrying any one within the prohibited degrees of relationship of his family of birth and also the family of adoption. The new law of adoption states that the child to be adopted must be actually given and taken in adoption by the parents or guardian concerned or under their authority with intention of transfering the child from the family of birth to the family of adoption. The performance of *datta homam* (adoption ritual), required under the Hindu law prior to 1956, shall not be essential to the validity of adoption. However, the adoption ritual is still being followed in Gokul. It was observed that the adoptee instead of severing connections with his family of birth continues to have frequent social interaction with the natural kin. He maintains greater love and affection, help and cooperation towards his natural parents and siblings than his adoptive kin.

Maintenance

The new law of maintenance generally has the support of the Brahmans. Nevertheless, they are critical of those provisions which compel individuals to maintain and support illegitimate children. In addition, this law falls short of their expectations for the fulfillment of kinship obligations, as the eldest son, in reality, is expected to take care of and maintain his younger unmarried brothers and sisters, and widowed sister or daughter as well as his aged parents. This kinship responsibility is not recognized by the law of maintenance. In the absence of adequate social security programmes of the State, kinship still plays a paramount role in helping the socially and economically dependent or handicapped individuals. Under such circumstances, according to the respondents, the law should recognize these kinship obligations, and provide to concerned persons with certain privileges and concessions in payment of taxes, etc. Without such incentives it is believed, one is likely to neglect his dependents because of the increasing cost of living. The Hindu Minority and Guardianship Act of 1956 influences the Brahman more or less the same way as it does the Lingayat.

The land reform legislation abolishing absentee landlordism hit especially hard the upper class Brahman families which mainly depended on the rent received from land. By putting ceilings on the size of land holdings this law tends to break the extended kin group.

Welfare State and Kinship

Since the majority of Brahmans are employed by Government or semi-Government institutions and organizations, social security[2] schemes such as pensions, provident fund, life insurance and the like, have influenced the kinship dependency and the interpersonal relationships. Retired persons, those in economic crisis and others in need of help need not depend exclusively on relatives. On the other hand, the young men in the city have another story to tell. They say the high cost of living in the city, the social demands of the city life, the opposition from the wife to help the patrilateral kin, are some of the major reasons why they cannot always fulfill the expectations of dependent relatives. However, conflicts on this account do not appear serious. Adjustments between generations are being made, and kinship obligations and expectations are being fulfilled at least partially if not wholly. As a matter of fact, in 39 cases, aged parents received money from their adult sons.

Among the several social welfare programmes of the State,[3] the one regarding liberal and technical education merits consideration. Brahmans value educational achievements since they are the main asset not only for earning livelihood but also for ensuring social prestige. In these contexts family and kinship no longer play the same role as they did in the past. The number of schools and colleges have been rapidly increasing, especially after independence, as well as the number of free tuitions and fellowships offered by the State to the needy and deserving students. Caste based charity organizations provide free boarding and lodging facilities, scholarships, and other privileges, to caste members studying in the various educational institutions. However, by and large in the selection and appointment to various positions in government and nongovernment organizations the candidate's qualifications and experience would be taken into account rather than his caste or kinship affiliations. Hence in the modern urban society kinship tends to recede to the background, at least in formal organizations.

Modern technology, educational institutions, the new values spread through the media of mass communications, and secular egalitarian policies of the state have been influencing the younger generation in the modern urban milieu far more now than ever before. Agencies external to the family and kinship increasingly impinge on individuals and instil in them the new aspirations and ambitions which are far advanced from the point of view of the older generation. In the context of the operation of these factors one can understand the eagerness on the part of the "self-made" man who builds his own career to separate himself from his kin. This tendency to dissociate oneself from one's kin may occur because one has had little help or encouragement from one's relatives in shaping his career. So he is not always enthusiastic about shouldering too many kinship obligations when he achieves a higher position in life.

---

12   See, Moorthy, 1954.
13   See, India, Govt., 1956.

State activities relating to the public health services, maternity homes, social security programmes, new housing schemes, and various other social welfare measures may seem to have been supplementing kinship functions in the modern urban society. Indeed, India, as it is evident from her Constitution, is commited to the ideals of a welfare state. But as Nels Anderson rightly observes, "Most of the developing countries have their programs of collective security and welfare, but only in exceptional cases are these programs effective. The principal weakness is the lack of financial support, which can hardly be expected until industrialization advances and unemployment sufficiently reduced so that reserve funds can be accumulated".[4]

In the absence of sufficient social security programmes and social welfare services, kinship still has an important role to play in Indian cities. Although the social policy and planning of the state have been responsible for sponsoring several welfare programmes after Independence, they have only supplemented, and not completely replaced, the kinship functions. It is for these reasons that one observes a strong kinship orientation and kinship dependency influencing the personality structure. Nimkoff echoes similar views when he says that "The rate of industrialization is slow and the economic dependence on the joint family is still very great, an important factor no doubt in the continuing high prestige which the joint family enjoys".[5] The pre-eminence of extrafamilial kinship, despite spatial and social mobility, is indeed remarkable.

The foregoing analysis demonstrates that the effectiveness of the same legislation or the same welfare services is different on each communities depending upon the factors of caste, education, occupation, the stage of economic and sociocultural development of the community and the degree of internalization of modern values. The customary law and values seem to be more dominant than the statutory law of the modern state. Furthermore, whenever the law sets new social ideals which are far ahead of the current social norms, it is natural that in the initial stages such law may be opposed by the conservative elements and its effective functioning may not be possible.

Society is always in a state of flux. It often changes faster than the law. Therefore, the law should be constantly modified to meet society's changing needs and values. But sometimes law may be faster than society in initiating changes, as is the case in Kalyan and also in Gokul. Many of the social institutions as they have existed may turn out to be contrary to constitutional ideals and the spirit of democratic socialism. This means that new laws which flow from the ideals and the spirit of democratic socialism may at times conflict with the existing social institutions. Social legislation assumes all the greater significance as an instrument of planned social change; and this it has to bring about by promoting the goals of social justice and individual welfare as laid down in the Directive Principles of the Constitution.

---

14   Anderson, N., pp. 83–84.
15   Nimkoff, *S.B.* Vol. VIII. No. 2, 1959, p. 38.

Social Problems and Social Policy

Law cannot altogether ignore the social problems associated with family, kinship, and community. Most of the laws are enacted to protect society against social evils and to subserve social telesis. Often they suffer owing to their own defective nature, lack of sufficiently strong or efficient machinery for implementation, shortage of funds or personnel, absence of the necessary social consciousness in the community and lack of appreciation of the objectives of the law and the impediments of superstitions and misconceptions among people.

Problems of social welfare and law have been intimately connected in the modern society. Since the varied needs of individuals in the modern urban milieu cannot be adequately or fully met by kinship or by the traditional voluntary philanthropy—religious or otherwise—it is the major concern of the modern welfare state to satisfy ever increasing social demands. A close cooperation between the voluntary and government welfare agencies is essential for the proper implementation of social welfare legislation and other welfare programmes. Laws by themselves are not enough. "An efficient administration alerted by an informed and watchful public opinion are as necessary .To secure due obedience to the law it must be known to and approved by the public on whose behalf, it is enforced."[16] In the two suburbs of Dharwar, nearly 65% of the people do not know the law. The percentage of those who are ignorant of law is much higher in Kalyan than in Gokul. Those who know the law, know it vaguely. Since ignorance of the law is no excuse and every responsible citizen should know the law; it is incumbent on the State to spread legal knowledge through the mass media.

It is often assumed that the function of law is not only to reflect the current social needs and ideals or merely adjust to the changing social system but also to introduce new social ideals. In the task of moulding the social institutions through legislation and welfare programmes the modern welfare state may have to arouse the social consciousness of the people. Hence for every new legislation it becomes imperative to create an appropriate sociocultural environment accompanied by intensive efforts to mobilize public opinion, and to bring about the necessary social preparedness through education and other social forces. Litwak points out that "If law is to act on human behaviour, it should provide an environment which will enable the deviant or potential deviant to internalize the values embodied in the law or it should provide an environment which will force the deviant to confrom by systematically placing blocks in his achievement of his deviant values, whenever he violates the law."[17] It is needless to say that the provision of suitable environment is more important than a mere environment of blocking the achievement of deviant values by the violaters of law.

Although law has different ways of effecting social control through punish-

16   India, Govt. 1956a p. X.
17   Litwak, 1960 b, p. 208.

ment, therapy and education, it is mainly through the appropriate social milieu that law as social engineering can give leadership or direction, form and continuity to the planned social changes in the best interests of society. In such an endeavour public cooperation is of paramount importance. The needs of the community and the ideals of the members for whom the law is intended need to be taken into account in the formulation of social policy. Besides giving recognition to the sub-culture variations, some kind of uniformity in legislation is considered desirable from the point of view of national interests. The consensus of public opinion seems to be that the complexity and the legal jargons can be made much less formidable to the common man. People express the need for free legal aid to the poor and also the need to establish separate courts to decide family and matrimonial disputes so that waste of time and money can be minimized. Legislation and welfare activities of the State and also the efforts of the voluntary welfare agencies have not as yet made their impact on safeguarding the interests of family and kinship in these two suburbs of Dharwar. In the absence of adequate welfare services, kinship still plays a dominant role. Despite modernization of the Hindu law it is amazing to find the persistence of customary law of marriage, family and kinship.

CHAPTER EIGHT

Modernization and Kin Network

IN THIS FINAL CHAPTER we summarize, sometimes at the risk of repetition, our main findings in this study and offer some additional comments on certain issues of modernization and kin network. Based on empirical evidence presented so far, the summary which follows shall make it possible to discern the extent to which we have achieved at least provisional answers to the questions raised at the beginning of this inquiry. But prior to such a venture and in order to have a proper perspective of the major issues under investigation, let us have an overview of the processes of modernization and change in India. We shall also review the main findings of similar studies on family and kinship so that the results of our study might be placed within the total perspective of present knowledge of the effects of modernization on kin network.

Modernization

The process of modernization began in India under the aegis of British rule. The development of industries and the commercialization of agriculture led to the growth of cities. The new ideologies such as capitalism, liberalism and the principle of equality made considerable impact on the economic, political and social life of Indians. Democratic principles in particular questioned all disabilities and privileges based on kinship and caste.

The Industrial Revolution had its impact on the Indian society. New factories, mills and the industrial cities gradually came into existence. Relatively inexpensive and superior manufactured goods tempted the Indians to accept the material innovations. Industrialization although slow during the British period gave a death blow to the traditional Indian handicrafts and village industries Agriculture was commercialized to meet the needs of modern industries. Interdependence in the economic and social spheres increased. Modern roads, buses, and railways broke the relative social isolation of the people, facilitated frequent contacts, and established new customs of mutual visits. The changes in the transport system and the modern urban way of life tended to weaken the rigid caste taboos as regards ceremonial purity, inter-dining and other forms of social intercourse and affected the orthodoxy and conservatism of the Hindu.

The modern education provided by the British government and the Christian missionaries was undoubtedly the most important channel through which Western ideas flowed into India. This education not only laid the foundation of scientific, secular and democratic principles, egalitarian ideologies, nationalistic sentiments and a rationalist world outlook, but also began to question the caste stratified, authoritarian Hindu social structure, as well as British domination. The intellectual elite became leaders of the national socio-economic, religious and political reform movements and through them the modern ideas of individual liberty, equality and nationalism filtered into the different strata of Indian society.

The modern mass media accelerated this process. The press has been a powerful instrument in the dissemination of modern knowledge, in organizing the Indian national movement, in exposing social evils, in mobilising public opinion and in publishing the policies and programmes of democratic reconstruction of the Indian social system. Movies and radio have been potent factors in the spread of modern ideas among the masses, most of whom are illiterate. Besides being new sources of entertainment and knowledge, they have been one of the most effective agencies of propaganda. These have influenced young men and women considerably, and one can discern changes in their customs and costumes, etiquettes and ideas, speech and behaviour patterns.

The spread of female education, the movement for the emancipation of women, the equality of sexes and the equal recognition of the members of all castes through British law, the introduction of adult franchise and the democratic parliamentary political institutions brought significant changes in the life of the Indians. As a consequence of these socio-economic and political changes there was a reshuffling of the age-old social classes, and the new social classes unknown in the pre-British period emerged. The Russian Revolution, the two World Wars, British Rule and the struggle for national independence have significantly transformed the culture of India.

With Independence and the emergence of the Republic of India,[1] the tempo of modernization has received added impetus. Accelerated in speed, the modernization process has assumed a new direction and dimension which pervades the entiry country. This process has been influencing the different socio-economic classes, communities and regions differently. The national leaders of modern independent India have designed massive Five Year Plans[2] for national reconstruction and socio-economic development. Colossal projects for the planned industrialization of the country and community development programmes directed mainly at the modernization of agriculture, now in operation, are aimed not only at increased production but also at changing the attitudes and behaviour of the masses. Such forces of modernization are potentially capable of producing cataclysmic changes and are geared to the achievement of a democratic socialistic pattern of society. In fact, the spirit of modernism is being carried to the remote recesses of India.

The Preamble of the Constitution of India sets out the goal of the attain-

---

1 India became politically independent from British domination on 15th August 1947, and emerged as Republic of India on 26th January 1950, with the implementation of the new Constitution. For an account of modernization of India during the British period and after Independence refer, A. R. Desai, 1954, 1971.

2 Government of India's First Year Plan was initiated in 1951.

ment of justice—political, economic and social, and the equality and fraternity of all Indians. The Constitution guarantees fundamental rights to all the citizens irrespective of race, religion, caste, creed, sex or place of birth and establishes universal adult franchise, abolishes untouchability, provides special safeguards to the "schudeled castes and tribes" and special privileges to women and children. The directive principles of state policy[3] which form a part of the Constitution aim at an egalitarian secular social welfare society. During the last two decades there have been radical changes in land legislation, with a view to abolishing absentee landlordism; and in the Hindu law of marriage, succession, adoption and maintenance in order to give equal rights to women. National policies and programmes pertaining to agriculture and industry, education and health, housing, transport and communications, social security, and social welfare which are designed mainly to improve the standards of living of the people and to change their values and attitudes, have been responsible for the increased rate of modernization. Endogenous as well as exogenous factors have contributed to the acceleration of modernization of a traditional society.

Modernization is accompanied by an increasing tempo of sociocultural change in most developing societies of Asia and Africa. Hauser[4] and Eisenstadt[5] have maintained that in the so-called underdeveloped nations, modernization will result in frictions, disorganization and dislocation, social problems, cleavages and conflicts between various groups, and movements of protest, resistance to change. It is further argued that disorganization and dislocation thus constitute a basic part of modernization, and every modern and modernizing society has to cope with them.

Most of the sociologists tend to think that change is inevitable. But there seems to be no consensus among sociologists with regard to the nature, degree and direction of change. Kapadia,[6] I.P. Desai,[7] Ross,[8] and Gore[9] present different findings as regards the nature of change of family and kinship in urban India. The studies[10] of some African and Asian countries report the stresses and strains, a series of maladjustments and weakening of kinship ties among the natives living in the cities due to westernization. Some sociologists such as Wirth,[11] Zimmerman,[12] and Parsons[13] have observed the isolation and atomization of the nuclear family unit devoid of extra-familial kinship ties in

---

3   See, Constitution of India, 1956.
4   Hauser (ed.), 1957.
5   Eisenstadt, 1966, pp. 20–21.
6   Kapadia, 1959.
7   Desai, I. P. 1964.
8   Ross, 1961.
9   Gore, 1968.
10   See, Radcliffe-Brown & Forde (eds.), 1950; Unesco, 1956; Hauser (ed.), 1957.
11   Wirth, 1938.
12   Zimmerman, 1947.
13   Parsons, T. 1953, 1958, 1959, 1961.

the industrial urban societies. Recent empirical studies[14] however reveal the existence of a wider kinship network and mutual interaction among kin in England, Canada and in the United States of America.

What is happening to extrafamilial kinship in urban India? Contemporary Indian society is the scene of momentous changes affecting the entire economic, political, ideological and socio-cultural structure. Is this process painful and beset with stresses and strains, tensions and frictions and maladjustments?

As a result of the various forces of modernization, it is assumed that the joint family is distintegrating or should disintegrate,"[15] and in fact the Census of India, 1951, concludes that "the habit of breaking away from the joint-family and setting up separate households is quite strong."

According to Ross[16] industrialization and urbanization affect the family by separating adult children from their parents because of increasing geographical and social mobility. Modern education and employment, the new aspirations and freedom acquired by the son will affect the age of marriage, choice of mate, residential patterns, etc., which greatly reduce the authority and solidarity of the extended family. Dube[17] has noted the impact of modern science and technology on the Indian life and the shift in the emphasis of life from the sacred to the secular. He thinks that ever-widening opportunities of education and employment and other social forces have contributed towards weakening the bonds of kinship. Furthermore, he believes that the urban kinship system, while superficially retaining a lineal character, is becoming radial in content.

In view of the lack of factual knowledge about the traditional family structure in India and the changing family cycle, Gore[18] is correct when he writes. "The questions that may prove fruitful are not whether the joint family is being displaced by the nuclear family, but whether participants in joint as well as nuclear households show any changes in their role perception and in the acceptance of obligations."

While investigating the question of whether early industrialization and urbanization have modified family relationships in India, based on a research sample of a caste group in the Delhi area, Gore[19] concludes that "the sample as a whole still largely conforms to the pattern of joint family living in behaviour, role perception, and attitudes." Within this overall pattern of conformity, urban residence and education do seem to introduce a certain measure of variation. It is interesting to observe the existence of some elements of modernity as well as tradition such as a tendency to verbal "non-conformity" in replies to attitudinal questions, and a hesitant assertion of the importance of the conjugal

14   Firth, R., 1956, 1970; Young & Wilmott, 1957; Townsend, 1957; Sussman & Burchinal;
      Rodgers & Sebald; Robins & Tomenec; Reiss 1962; Sussman 1953, 1959, 1965; Litwak,
      1960; Bott, 1957; Sharp & Axelrod, 1956; Adams, 1968.
15   Chandrasekhar S.F., Vol. 21, 1943.
16   Ross, 1961, pp. 283–285.
17   Dube, 1963, pp. 202–203.
18   Gore, 1965, pp. 216–217.
19   Gore, 1968, p. 232.

tie, traditional patterns of behaviour in the acceptance of familial obligations, the patterns of segregation and subordination of women and so on, thus supporting the hypothesis of a "limited change".

Refuting the tempting assumption that, "industrialization is the independent variable and that family change is the dependent one", William Goode[20] suggests that "Family and industrial variables are independent though interacting." While analyzing social problems of urbanization Hoselitz and Moore[21] have pointed out that the transition from pre-urban to urban living necessarily involves frictions, which are manifested in social and personal problems. Though they concede the fact that the patterns of urbanization in the under-developed nations have not followed Western lines, and are not likely to do so in the future, they anticipate changes and predict that accompanying changes will be the frictions of change.

In the light of these arguments and findings let us summarize and evaluate the main findings of our study so as to arrive at some tentative conclusions. Throughout this study of the impact of modernization, the phenomena of both the changing and continuing norms, values, and behaviour concerning kinship are indeed striking. Therefore, in order to answer the questions raised in the initial part of this study we shall present the following summary under two major headings: (a) Change; and (b) Continuity.

Change

The following discussion will try to illuminate the pattern of influence of modernization on family and kinship among two castes in an Indian city, and will try to show that the patterns and effects of modernization have not been uniform in a developing society. In the absence of baseline studies of social systems of the Lingayats and Brahmans of this region, it is difficult to assess precisely the changes that have taken place since the turn of the century. Relying mostly on the responses of respondents aged sixty and above, and on the intergenerational data gathered from the two suburbs, it is possible to discern some changes in family and kinship.

Kinship fission, that is, separation from the extended or joint family and the establishment of nuclear families tend to increase gradually over the generations. When compared with the previous generation, the number of one's relatives in both recognized and operative terms has been diminishing. The circle of intimate kin is more restricted than before. Generation after generation there has been a declining trend in the frequency of exchange of services, mutual aid and cooperation, counseling and sympathy among extended kin. As reported by the respondents, filial piety, and respect and obedience for older relatives has been waning over the years.

A decline in the authority and decision-making power of the eldest male

20   Goode, 1963, pp. 368 ff.; Goode in Hoselitz & Moore (eds.), 1963, pp. 239, 252.
21   Hoselitz & Moore (eds.), 1963, p. 209.

of the extended kin network is inferred from changes such as the increase in the legal, civic and educational rights of sons and daughters, lessening control over choice of mates for children and economic independence and neolocal residential patterns of youngsters. The ceremony of ancestor worship is becoming relatively formal and nominal. There is a trend toward naming children on modern lines without a kinship basis. Nowadays, it seems that people are not willing to make sacrifices for any kin except their very close relatives.

The pursuit of higher education, the search for better jobs, and the new values and aspirations of the Brahmans have influenced to a great extent the rising marriage age of both sexes. Over the last three generations there has been a decrease in the incidence of interkin marriage. Gradually the rules of subcaste endogamy and hypergamy are being set aside. Those who belong to the younger generation tend to be more achievement-oriented, interested in the self rather than in the collectivity and assertive of individual rights.

Friends, neighbours and workmates have been competing with kinship groups. The increasing spread of education, occupational diversity and complexity, geographical and social mobility have been influencing traditional kinship values, and the behaviour patterns of the younger generation. The differences in ideas and ideologies, and in norms of family and kin behaviour between generations are widening.

Occupational roles are becoming increasingly different from kinship roles, removing the economic bonds of kinship cohesion. The modern urban occupational structure in India demands persons with special training and skills not normally provided by family and kinship. The differing family and economic roles break the traditional association between family and social status aspiration. Social status is determined more by the individual's merit and performance in the non-kin oriented educational and occupational organization. The intergenerational and intragenerational occupational mobility which has been on the increase for the last three decades does not facilitate joint economic enterprise among kin. This process appears to be an important factor in the transformation of kinship values and behaviour patterns.

As a result of increasing geographical and social mobility, people are more exposed to new cultures and new role models outside family and kinship. Increasing neolocal residential patterns tend to reduce the immediate surveillance and control by parents and the extended kin. Although the kinship systems of Lingayats and Brahmans are still strongly patrilineal it is becoming multilateral and radial in content. Social legislation, social security measures and other welfare activities of the state seem to minimize the importance of the traditional role of kinship. The solidarity of kinship tends to be gradually jeopardized as the Government of India sets a higher premium on individual performance and achievement than on status and kinship.

These changes seen mainly through the eyes of the aged informants are due to the internalization of the norms and values of democracy and individual liberty, increasing education and economic independence, nuclear residential patterns, weakening of religious and moral constraints, occupational heterogeneity, increasing geographical and social mobility, government legislation, welfare policies and programmes, new aspirations, increasng population and cost of living, and the "modern environment". The process of modernization and changes in the kinship system of Lingayats and Brahmans tend to be related. Since Brahmans are more modernized than Lingayats in our research sample it appears that the Brahman kinship has been affected more than the Lingayat kinship.

The differential impact of modernization on these two communities in the same city seems to be due to the differential capacity to internalize modern values and behaviour patterns. The different receptivity of modern values by these two communities may be largely attributed to the variables of caste, education, occupation, the subcultural value orientations and the variant "ethos" of the Lingayats and Brahmans.

In an effort to understand the process of change in urban India, it is difficult to isolate familial institutions alone when various other segments of Indian society have also been undergoing change. In modern urban India people tend to possess high achievement motivation. Life is becoming more and more secularized. Social mobility is increasing. Interpersonal relationships are becoming functionally specific to a greater extent. Aspirations to improve material conditions are quite strong. A majority of the urban population forms a part of many of the complex organizations. Modern urban man in a developing society is being increasingly influenced by advanced science and technology. More woman are attending schools and colleges, and are working. They express favourable attitudes toward family planning. As opposed to the traditional value systems and behaviour patterns, the modern man in urban India indulges in rational ends-means calculations, inculcates modern economic, political and social discipline and value orientations, and believes in the desirability and possibility of change. In other words, the process of acquisition of an image of limitless change as the normal character of life has been accelerated considerably in urban India. Such psychic initiation and interiorization of modern values, considered as an essential step in modernization, seems well under way in the cities of India. During the last two decades increasing empirical evidence[22] from other parts of India tends to support these generalizations. Significantly enough, these forces of modernization are potentially capable of producing cataclysmic changes. The initial impact of modernization and the concomitant changes in a developing society may not be radical initially. But one cannot ignore current repercussions of modernization and its future

---

22 The following are some of the major works documenting change in several aspects of Indian society: McClelland, D. C. & Winter, D. G., 1969; Lewis, J. P. 1964; Singer, M. 1972; Shah, A. M. 1972; Vatuk, S. 1972; Kapur, P. 1970; Epstein, T. S. 1962; Khare, R. S. 1970; Rudolph, L. I. & S. H. 1967; Rosen, G. 1966; Srinivas, M. N. 1966; Lambert, R. 1963; Smith, D. E. 1963; Taylor, C. et al. 1965; Harrison, S. 1960; Kuppuswamy, 1972; Clinard, M. B. 1966; Turner, R. 1962; Issac, H. 1964; Lynch, O. M. 1969; Jorapur, P. B. *IJSW* 31 : 4, 1971; Chandrasekhar, S. 1972; Bose, A. et al. 1972. Mandelbaum, 1970.

possibilities for vast changes as the tempo of modernization rapidly increases.

With the modernization of a traditional society, social scientists are tempted to think that the family will tend toward the ideal-type conjugal family which excludes a wide range of affinal and blood relatives from its everyday affairs and has no great extension of the kin network. The present study, however, suggests that despite modernization and some changes in urban family and kinship, the nuclear family, far from being isolated, and atomized, appears to be organically fused with the extended kin network. Both nuclear and non-nuclear families in the city maintain close ties with a wide range of blood and affinal relatives. Several traditional values, norms and behaviour patterns relating to family and kinship still persist. The summary discussion that follows, based on empirical evidence presented in the previous chapters, tends to support the important role of extended kinship in the urban setting.

Continuity

Compared to kinship systems in industrial urban Western societies[23] it cannot be said that the kinship system in Dharwar is of shallow geneological depth or of narrow range of kinship ties. Among the Lingayats the average depth of generations is six with a maximum of eleven. The average depth of generations is seven among the Brahmans. In both communities, compared to the Western societies, the number of Ego's kin tended to be stated more often in recognised and in operative terms.

A common feature is that one's intimate kin are derived not only from the nuclear family but also from beyond the orbit of the nuclear family. Besides the close kinship ties with parents, siblings and in-laws, it is not uncommon to observe reciprocal relationships with uncles and aunts, grandparents and cousins. Between the couple of the nuclear family and their kinfolk, the many rights and reciprocal obligations enjoined by religion and customary usage are still being maintained. The moral controls of kinfolk on the members of the nuclear family seem to be real.

A high frequency of mutual visits, and exchange of services and gifts is characteristic among kin. Even today, a considerable amount of mutual aid and cooperation, advice, sympathy, and other forms of communication (through letters and photographs) graphically illustrate the intertwining of the nuclear family with that of its widespread kin network. Youngsters have deep sentiments of filial piety and try to fulfill the wishes of their elders. In the important decisions of the nuclear family, parents and other intimate kin are closely involved.

Ancestor worship among these two communities reflects the continuing filial piety and strong kinship orientation cementing the present generation with the past and nurturing the link with the future. Performing rituals associated with ancestor worship is still a kinship obligation of paramount

---

23   Refer, Firth, 1956, 1970; Adams, 1968.

importance. Furthermore, the custom of naming children after their ancestors has been an important factor in fostering kinship sentiments.

The intimate kin largely control the choice of mate of their children. Caste endogamy is still persistent. A significant percentage of preferential kin marriages do take place, revitalizing kinship relationships. Customary Hindu law is more influential than the statutory law as regards marriage, the family, and inheritance of property. Despite the fact that the urban kinship system is becoming omnilineal, the patrilineage appears to have great weight.

Remarkably, in the urban milieu it seems that kin first and non-kin next is the principle widely upheld and scrupulously practised. Nepotism in its naked or disguised forms pervades modern organizations. Both in normal and in difficult times, making sacrifice and helping relatives are still considered norms. In the absence of adequate social security measures the major responsibilities of looking after the aged, the infirm, widows, orphans, the sick, and the unemployed still rest on the family and the extended kin network. What is more striking is the fact that in an overwhelming number of cases such kinship obligations are being fulfilled voluntarily, that is, without legal coercion. Indeed, such reciprocity among relatives constantly refuels and strengthens kinship cohesion.

It is evident from our data that unlike the situation in the highly industrialized countries of the West, kinship contacts in an Indian city are not merely statistical but largely normative in character. Furthermore, in spite of increasing geographical and social mobility, bonds of kinship are being maintained among members of the kin related families through the performance of reciprocal kinship rights and obligations and despite distance kin relations are kept alive.

In this process of modernization, the family and kinship are being transformed, however slight the changes may be. The family, in India as elsewhere, has withstood the test of time weathering several crises over the centuries. With the modernization over the last two decades, the family in urban India is adapting itself to changing circumstances. In order to meet the demands of complex modern urban life a modified extended family is emerging. The modified extended family structure as Litwak[24] points out involves a family relation consisting of a series of nuclear families joined together on an equalitarian basis for mutual aid. The modified extended family as opposed to the traditional extended family does not demand geographical propinquity and occupational dependence or a hierarchical authority structure for its viability. This family type is based on affectional ties and considerable mutual aid, and functions to facilitate the mobility strivings of its component member families and individuals. As a consequence, the nuclear family does not face the world as an isolated unit.

An overwhelming majority of the people in the two suburbs of Dharwar

---

24   Litwak, 1960, 1960a, *ASR*, Vol. 25, pp. 9–21, 385–394.

still consider the extended family as the ideal. In the relative absence of geographical propinquity, occupational involvement, and rigid authority structure characteristic of the traditional extended family, individuals and families are interwoven into a wider kin network, which is sustained through the frequent interactions among extrafamilial kin in the process of fulfilling a set of mutual rights and obligations. Despite modernization in the city of Dharwar, the family, whether nuclear or extended, appears to be strongly embedded in the extended kinship matrix. The extrafamilial kinship relations constantly reinforce and cement kinship cohesion.

The extended family in the modern urban setting in Dharwar does not seem to be structurally and functionally incompatible. It is not being atrophied. On the contrary, it is adapting itself to the new environment and by maintaining fairly close functional ties with extended kin it appears to be quite resilient.

In a study of a group of outstandingly successful industrial leaders in Madras city, Milton Singer[25] found that, while there were striking changes within three generations in residential, occupational, educational, social mobility and ritual observances, these changes had not transformed the traditional joint family structure into isolated nuclear families. On the contrary, he noticed that the urban and industrial members of a family maintain numerous ties and obligations with extended kin, although geographically distributed.

Furthermore, while a modified joint family organization is emerging within the urban and industrial setting, Singer also identifies the operation of adaptive processes such as the *compartmentalization* of the domestic and social sphere as "traditional and religious" and of the industrial sphere as "modern and secular"; the separation of ownership and control both in the organization of the family and in the organization of the industrial corporation; and the extension of the practices and principles of household management of the rural joint family to business management. In spite of some internal and external disturbances, it is remarkable to find, in the Madras sample, several approximations to the ideal structural congruence between joint family organization and the organization of industrial firms. Both studies in the Indian cities of Dharwar and Madras demonstrate that the extended family is adapting itself to the modern urban industrial environment.

It would be far from the truth if we stated that in the modern Indian cities extended kinship system is breaking up or that extrafamilial kinship relations are weakening, let alone that it is distegrating or disappearing. However, kinship in urban India is undergoing modifications and alterations, and it is adapting itself to suit modern environmental needs and pressures. The forces of modernization have not left kinship in tact. But the modified kinship still plays an important role in urban life. The modified extended family is neither incompatible with nor an isolated unit in urban India. On the contrary, with its numerous extended kin ties based on affection and mutual aid it seems to

---

25 Singer & Cohn (eds.), 1968, pp. 443–447, also in Singer, M. 1972.

have become a viable unit in the Indian urban setting. The process of modernization has a differential impact on the social structure of different subcultures within a country and even within a single region. Kalyan and Gokul provide one such example.

The urban milieu in Dharwar indicates that the patterns of modernization in developing societies have not followed exactly the similar lines in the Western nations. It is reasonable to presume that they are not likely to do so in the future. Likewise, the effects of modernization do not appear to be universally similar. Since different developing societies have different sociocultural systems, one can expect differential impact of modernization.

The analysis of the dynamics of family and kinship among the Lingayats and Brahmans who have been exposed to the total complex forces of modernization reveal some significant facts. While considering the crucial aspect of the relatively slow rate of modernization in India, one should also take note of the sociocultural system, which has been remarkably different from that of Western society. It is reasonable to expect then, that this very difference in the value system of Indians and the differing nature and rate of modernization would lead to differences in the nature of change in family and kinship in urban India.

The pattern of modernization in most of the less developed countries of the world is by no means the same. Interestingly enough, even within a country such as India there have been marked regional and even local differences not only in the nature and rate of modernization but also in the way in which traditional patterns of family life are being adapted and transformed. Moreover, we should realize that the relationship of modernization to family and kinship is not one of simple cause and effect but is rather an intricate interrelationship.

In general, the rate of modernization in India so far has been relatively slow. Consequently, change in the kinship system has been slow. The present study suggests that the possible stresses and strains, sociocultural maladjustments and conflicts are being kept at a minimum possible level through the lubrication of traditional sociocultural constraints on the one hand, and the slow rate of modernization on the other. It appears that in India the traditional value system acts as an insulating mechanism. The traditional social structure seems to absorb the latent social frictions and conflicts which are supposed to follow in the wake of modernization.

In the city of Dharwar, the process of modernization and the consequent changes in family and kinship have been gradual. But now the tempo of modernization tends to increase. The younger generation is internalizing modern values to a great extent. In due course, through the modern media of mass communications and transport, modern values and behaviour patterns are bound to infiltrate the rural areas as well. What is happening in Indian cities today may happen in other parts of India in the years to come. But what is most striking is the fact that the traditional social system is adapting itself to the new environment. While there have been some changes in the values and behaviour patterns of the urbanites, significantly traditional values and behaviour also persist. In the adaptive process of compartmentalization of the traditional-religious and modern-secular ways of life, a good deal of harmony and equilibrium seem to have been maintained.

Concluding Comments

It would be fallacious to assume that a traditional society such as India has remained static and unchanged until recently. For centuries, gradual change in Indian society has been taking place. Religious and social reform movements, and various other internal forces have been responsible for changes in family, caste system, values, and life styles. These changes that occurred from time to time are reflected in the law codes and literature. It is evident that even before Indian society encountered foreign cultures, it was subject to change. Besides endogenous factors of change, the impact of exogenous variables such as the Islamic, British and other cultures have been of tremendous importance. During the nineteenth and twentieth centuries, and more so after India gained Independence from the British in 1947, it is only the nature and rate of change that have become significantly different.

Underlying the fundamental unity of the Indian culture, there is a wide variety of values and norms in different regions and among varied caste groups thus providing legitimizing principles for several alternative forms of behaviour. In this context, it would be misleading to think of the traditional Indian society as a homogeneous social structure.

A classical theory of social change posits that old and new cultures are always in conflict where mutual adjustment is hardly possible, and states that in this process, the new replaces the old. Furthermore, a linear theory of social change besides using "tradition" and "modernity" as polar opposites postulates that traditional social institutions and behaviour patterns are obstacles to modernization. Contrary to this theory, the foregoing analysis makes it clear that tradition and modernity can coexist without manifest conflict and that mutual adaptation is possible. The data also demonstrate that acceptance of some modern values and behaviour need not necessarily lead to the rejection of the traditional modes. Innovations may only increase the range of alternative choices. Paradoxically enough, the same people may use bullock cart and automobile, magical practices and modern medicine, caste beliefs and scientific knowledge. The net result of the interaction of processes of modernization and traditional social structure is frequently an intermingling and synthesis of tradition and modernity in which each to a certain extent is buttressed by the other, rather than a collision of diametrically opposed entities. In this complex process traditional values and behaviour need not become obstacles to modernization.

In a succinct analysis of tradition and modernity Gusfield[26] observes that "the abstraction of a 'traditional society' as a type separate from a specific historical and cultural setting ignores the diversity of content in specific tradi-

26 Gusfield, *AJS*, Vol. 72. No. 4. p. 355.

tions which influence the acceptance, rejection, or fusion of modernist forms".
Empirical data from Japan, India, Indonesia and some African countries
suggest that traditional structures can provide skills, values and sources of
legitimation which are capable of being utilized in pursuit of new goals.

Diversity of content in traditional cultures is crucial in that a specific
traditional culture may possess values more compatible with modernization
than another. Another traditional cultural system may be more firmly attached to its older form than another. A given cultural system is composed of
several dimensions and each dimension responds differently to modernization.
Far from being mutually exclusive and conflicting systems, tradition and
modernity seem to be often mutually reinforcing. The fusion of traditional and
modern values and behaviour without significant tensions and conflicts makes
us realize the fact that modernizing processes need not necessarily always
weaken or destroy traditions.

In India the desire to be modern and at the same time to preserve tradition
acts as a significant force for national planning action. The process of blending
tradition and modernity does not seem to be always in conflict. Modernization
depends upon and frequently finds structural support from tradition. In this
process of synthesis, tradition may be modified and changed. Innovations may
be adapted to a specific traditional culture. In this intricate process of change
both tradition and modernity may undergo transformation. It is evident that
modernization is not a universal and uniform process with the same consequences. On the contrary, as revealed by the present study, there is a variety and
mixture in tradition as well as in modernity, and also in the changes that follow
as a result of the interaction of the two.

This complex process of change is remarkable in that there appears to be
no manifest conflict between the young and the old, who normally stand for
change and continuity respectively. This empirical research suggests that: (a)
in an Indian city kinship has mainly been resilient. The family without being
isolated and atomized is organically fused with the extended kin network and
thereby the extrafamilial kin relationships do not tend to be attenuated.
(b) Furthermore, the patterns of modernization and effects of modernization
have not followed the same lines as in the Western nations and are not likely
to do so in the future. (c) In addition, the transition from traditional to modern
living need not *necessarily* involve stresses and strains, sociocultural maladjustments and conflicts, movements of protest and resistance to change. However,
this does not imply that modernization is a smooth process without any social
frictions and conflicts. It does mean, however, that given the relatively slow
rate of modernization and a traditional social system such conflict and friction
need not dislocate social life.

In a developing society one can also discern differences in the adjustments
of various castes and class strata to the patterns of modernization. These
differences no doubt suggest the independence of family and kinship variables.
But it is rather difficult to know precisely how the complex interaction of these
two takes place. This research merely attempted to outline some of the major

trends of modernization and the way they have been interacting with family and kinship in an Indian city.

If similar studies are conducted among other castes in other cities of India and in cities of different developing countries it would, no doubt, contribute to a broader comparative perspective and a greater insight into the intricate interacting mechanisms of modernization and family and kin network. Such an endeavour will go a long way toward producing a sophisticated theory of modernization and social change.

APPENDICES

APPENDIX (i)

Kinship Terminology: Terms of Address and Reference

Fa	Appa, Tande
FaFa	Ajja, Mutya, Tata
MoFa	Hennajja
FaFaFa, MoFaFa	Muttajja
Fa^eBr, Mo^eSiHu	Doddappa, Dodappa
Fa^yBr, Mo^ySiHu	Chikkappa, Chigappa, Kaka
MoBr (elder or younger)	Sodarmava, mava
Mo	Avva, Tayi, Abbe
FaMo	*Ajji*, Amma
MoMo	Hennajji, Hennamma
FaFaMo, MoFaMo	Muttajji
FaSi (elder or younger)	Sodaratte, atte
Mo^eSi, Fa^eBrWi	Doddavva, Doddamma
Mo^ySi, Fa^yBrWi, Hu^eSi, HuFaSi	Chikkavva, Chigavva, Chikkamma, *Kaki*, Sannavva, Kakki, *Abbachi, Abachi*
^eBr, FaBrSo(elder), MoSiSo(elder), Hu^eSi-Hu, Wi^eSiHu, HuFaSiSo(elder)	Anna
^yBr, FaBrSo(younger), MoSiSo(younger), Hu^ySiHu, Wi^ySiHu, HuFaSiSo(younger)	Tamma
FaBrSo (elder and/or younger)	Dayadi
FaSiSo(elder), MoBrSo(elder), ^eSiHu, Hu^eBr (w.s.), Wi^eBr	Bhava
FaSiSo(younger), MoBrSo(younger), Hu^yBr, Wi^yBr, ^ySiHu	Maiduna, Maidana
^eSi, FaBrDa(elder), MoSiDa(elder), WiBr-Wi(elder), Hu^eBrWi, MoBrWi	Akka
^ySi, FaBrDa(younger), MoSiDa(younger), WiBrWi(younger), Hu^yBrWi	Tangi
FaSiDa(elder), MoBrDa(elder), Hu^eSi, Wi^eSi, ^eBrWi	Attige, Attigi
FaSiDa(younger), MoBrDa(younger), Hu^y-Si, Wi^eSi, ^eBrWi	Nadini
So, BrSo(m.s.), SiSo(w.s.), HuBrSo, WiSiSo	Maga
BrSo(w.s.), SiSo(m.s.),	Sodaraliya, aliya
SoSo, DaSo	Mommaga, mammaga
Da, BrDa(m.s.), SiDa(w.s.), HuBrDa, WiSiDa	Magalu
BrDa(w.s.), SiDa(m.s.)	Sodar-sose, sose
SoDa, DaDa	Mommagalu, Mammagalu
DaDaDa, SoSoDa, SoDaDa, DaSoDa	Marimagalu
FaSiHu, HuFa, WiFa, FaSiSo(elder), MoBrSo(elder), Wi^eBr(m.s.), ^eSiHu(m.s.)	Mava
MoBrWi, HuMo, WiMo, FaSiDa(elder), MoBrDa(elder)	Atte
Hu	Ganda, Yajaman, Maneyata, Hiriya
WiSiHu (elder or younger)	Shaddaga
Wi	Hendati, Maneyaki, Yajamani Kutumba
HuBrWi	Oragitti, Varagitti, Negenni

DaHu, HuSiSo, WiBrSo, FaSiSo(younger),
MoBrSo(younger), BrSo(m.s.), SiSo(m.s.)   Aliya
Sowi, HuSiDa, WiBrDa, FaSiDa(younger),
MoBrDa(younger), Wi^{y}Si, ^{y}BrWi   Sose
SoWiFa, DaHuFa   Beegaru
SoWiMo, DaHuMo   Beegati
Step-mother (FaWi other than Ego's Mo)   Malaavva, Malatayi
Step-father (MoHu other than Ego's Fa)   Mala-appa, Malatande
Co-Wife (Another Wi of one's Hu)   Savati
Step-daughter   Mala-magalu
Step-son   Mala-maga
Step-sister (elder)   Mala-akka
Step-sister (younger)   Mala-tangi
Step-brother (elder)   Mala-anna
Step-brother (younger)   Mala-tamma

APPENDIX (ii)

Subcastes

Lingayat Subcastes	No. of Households	Brahman Subcastes	No. of Households
Jangam	7	Vaishnava	73
Panchamsali	52	Smartha	33
Totiga	13	Konkanastha	9
Hugar	6		
AdiBanajiga	24		
Jadar (Sivachar)	6		
Ganiga	1		
Turkar	2		
Madivala	1		
Navaliga	3		
Total	115	*Total*	115

APPENDIX (iii)

Bedagu and Gotra

Bedagu (Kalyan)	Gotra (Gokul)	
Honnabuttiyavaru	Agasthya	Kaudinya
Honnajajannavar	Atri	Kaushik
Honnakorennavar	Bharadwaj	Manubhargava
Honnavali	Gargya	Shandilya
Muttinapendenavaru	Gautama	Srivatsa
Malibagi	Harita	Vasistha
Paduvanagi bagi	Jamadagni	Vishnuvardha
	Kashyap	Vishvamitra

APPENDIX (iv)

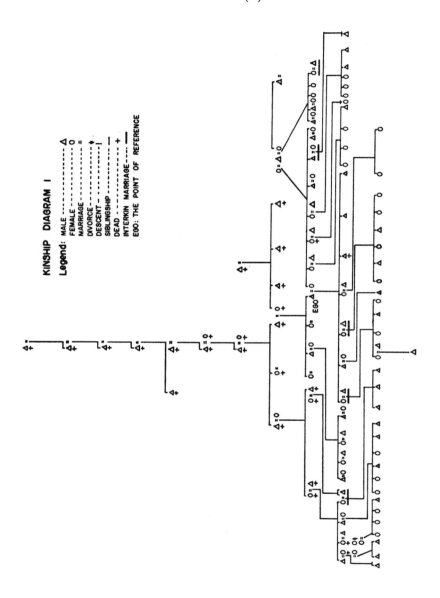

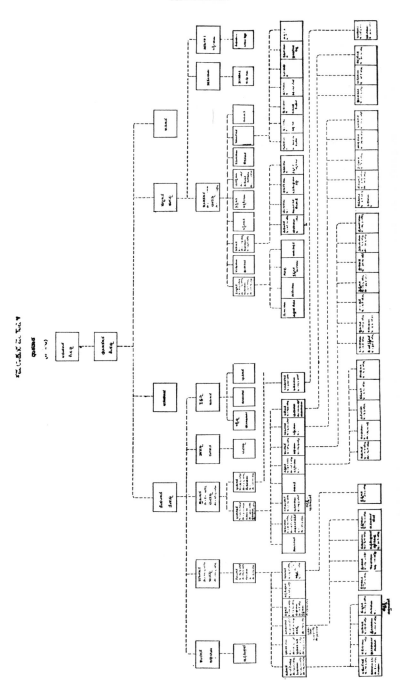

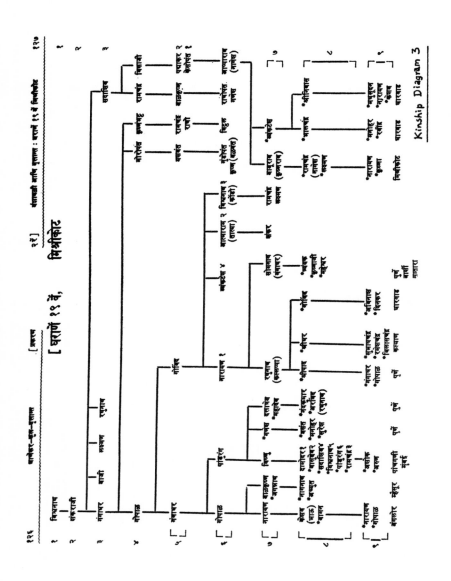

Kinship Diagram 3

APPENDIX (v)

Glossary

Aheru: wedding gift
Bagi: exogamous group among Lingayats
Balaga: relatives
Banajiga: a subcaste among Lingayats
Bandhu-balaga: relatives (refers to consanguines)
Basava: socio-religious reformer of the 12th century. He is said to be the founder of Lingayat
    sect.
Bedagu: exogamous group among Lingayats
Beegaru: affines
Dasara: festival in honour of Goddesses of Wealth and Learning.
Dattahomam: adoption ritual
Deepavali: festival of lights
Dharma: righteousness, religion, morals, law.
Dhoti: cloth worn by men
Gotra: exogamous group among Brahmans
Hiriyarahabba: rite in commemoration of ancestors among Lingayats
Jangama: a subcaste among Lingayats
Kalluballi: kinship
Konkanastha: a subcaste among Brahmans
Math: religious establishment
Munjive: the ceremony of initiation among Brahmans
Muyya: exchange of gifts; counter-prestations
Nagapanchami: festival in honour of the Lord of Snakes
Panchayat: a council of five members which is expected to settle disputes and safeguard the
    interests of a caste group.
Punya: religious merit
Sagotra: belonging to the same exogamous group among Brahmans
Sapinda: Agnate or cognate who shares in "Pinda", i.e., rice-ball offering made to the ancestors.
Saree (sari): cloth worn as main garment by women
Sati (satee): Hindu widow who immolates herself on her husband's funeral pyre
Smartha: a subcaste among Brahmans (worshippers of Lord Shiva)
Sraddha: rite in commemoration of ancestors among Brahmans
Taluk: territorial subdivision of a district for revenue and administrative purposes
Udaki: a secondary union between a widow and widower or divorcees
Upanayana: the ceremony of initiation among Brahmans
Vaishnava: a subcaste among Brahmans (worshippers of Lord Vishnu)
Vamsha: Lineage

APPENDIX (vi)

Abbreviations of Journal Titles

AA	American Anthropologist
AJS	American Journal of Sociology
ASR	American Sociological Review
BGM	Bombay Geographical Magazine
BJS	British Journal of Sociology
CSSH	Comparative Studies in Society & History
DCB	Deccan College Bulletin
EW	Economic Weekly

IJSW	Indian Journal of Social Work
IJCS	International Journal of Comparative Sociology
JAAS	Journal of Asian and African Studies
JKU	Journal of the Karnatak University
JMF	Journal of Marriage and the Family
J.Psy	Journal of Psychology
JRAI	Journal of Royal Anthropological Institute
JUB	Journal, University of Bombay (Students' Union)
KHR	Karnatak Historical Review
Man	Man: Record of Anthropological Science
MI	Man in India
MFL	Marriage and Family Living
SP	Social Problems
S.B.	Sociological Bulletin
SOC	Sociologus
SSR	Sociology and Social Research
SF	Social Forces

BIBLIOGRAPHY

Adams, Bert N.
    1968   Kinship in an Urban Setting. Chicago: Markham.
Anderson, Nels
    1964   Our Industrial Urban Civilization. Bombay: Asia.
    1963   Aspects of Urbanism and Urbanization. *IJCS*, Vol. 4. No. 2.
Anshen, Ruth N. (ed.)
    1959   The Family: Its Function and Destiny. New York; Harper.
Arensberg, C. and Kimball, S. T.
    1948   The Family and Community in Ireland. Cambridge, Mass.: Harvard University Press.
Bell, Norman W. and Vogel, Ezra F. (eds.)
    1960   A Modern Introduction to the Family. London: Routledge and Kegan Paul.
Bendix, R.
    1967   Tradition and Modernity Reconsidered. *CSSH*, Vol. 9. No. 3.
Bendix, R. and Lipset, S. M. (eds.)
    1953   Class, Status and Power. Glencoe, Ill.: The Free Press.
Black, C. E.
    1967   The Dynamics of Modernization. New York: Harper.
Bose, A. and Desai, P. B. and Jain, S. P. (comp.)
    1972   Studies in Demography. Chapel Hill; University of North Carolina Press.
Bott, Elizabeth
    1957   Family and Social Network. London: Tavistock.
Bottomore, T. B.
    1962   Sociology: A Guide to Problems and Literature. London: George Allen & Unwin.
Burgess, E. W. and Locke, H. J.
    1953   The Family. New York: American Book Co.
Chandrasekhar, S.
    1943   "The Hindu Joint Family". *SF*, Vol. 21.
    1972   Infant Mortality, Population Growth and Family Planning in India. Chapel Hill: University of North Carolina Press.
Chekki, D. A.
    1963   "The Study of Kinship in Anthropology". *JKU*; Vol. VII .
Chekki, D. A.
    1958   "Social Reformers in Karnatak". *JUB*.
Clinard, M. B.
    1966   Slums and Community Development. New York: The Free Press.
Cormack, M. C.
    1961   She Who Rides a Peacock. Bombay: Asia.
Derrett, J. D. M.
    1963   Introduction to Modern Hindu Law. Bombay: Oxford University Press.
Desai, A. R. (ed.)
    1971   Essays on Modernization of Underdeveloped Societies. Bombay: Thacker.
    1954   Social Background of Indian Nationalism. Bombay: Popular.
Desai, I. P.
    1956   "Joint Family in India—an Analysis". *SB*, Vol. 5. No. 2.
    1964   Some Aspects of Family in Mahuwa. Bombay: Asia.
Desai, M. N.
    1945   The Life and Living in Rural Karnatak. Sirsi: The Anand.
Desai, P. B.
    1957   "Dharwar: Origin and Early History". *KHR*, Vol. 7. Nos. 1 & 2.
Dhekney, B. R.
    1959   Hubli City. Dharwar: Karnatak University.

Dube, S. C.
　　1963　"Men's and Women's Roles in India: a Sociological Review" in Women in the New
　　　　　Asia, ed. by Barbara E. Ward. Paris: Unesco.
　　1958　India's Changing Villages: Human Factors in Community Development. London:
　　　　　Routledge & Kegan Paul.
　　1955　Indian Village. London: Routledge & Kegan Paul.
Dumont, Louis and Pocock, D. (eds.)
　　1957　Contributions to Indian Sociology, No. 1. Paris and The Hague: Mouton & Co.
Dumont, Louis
　　1957a Hierarchy and Marriage Alliance in South Indian Kinship. London: Royal
　　　　　Anthropological Institute, Occassional papers No. 12.
Durkheim, Emile
　　1947　The Division of Labor in Society. Tr. by George Simpson. Glencoe, Ill.: The Free
　　　　　Press.
Eisenstadt, S. N.
　　1966　Modernization: Protest and Change. Englewood Cliffs: Prentice-Hall.
Embree, J. F.
　　1946　A Japanese Village: Suye Mura. London: Kegan Paul.
Enthoven, R. E.
　　　　　"Lingayats" in Hastings (ed.) Encyclopaedia of Religion and Ethics, Vol. 8.
Epstein, T. S.
　　1962　Economic Development and Social Change in South India. New York: Humani-
　　　　　ties.
Evans-Pritchard, E. E.
　　1951　Kinship and Marriage among the Nuer. Oxford: Clarendon Press.
Fairchild, H. P. (ed.)
　　1961　Dictionary of Sociology. Paterson, Littlefield Adams.
Firth, Raymond et al.
　　1970　Families and their Relatives. New York: Humanities Press.
Firth, Raymond (ed.)
　　1956　Two Studies of Kinship in London. London: The Athlone Press, University of
　　　　　London.
　　1936　We, The Tikopia. London: Allen & Unwin.
Fortes, Meyer
　　1949　The Web of Kinship among the Tallensi. Oxford: University Press.
Freedman, Maurice
　　1958　Lineage Organization in South Eastern China. London: University of London.
Garigue, P.
　　1956　"French Canadian Kinship and Urban Life". AA, Vol. 58.
Bombay Government
　　1959　Gazetteer of Bombay State, Dharwar District. Bombay: Government Publications,
　　　　　Revised edition.
　　1884　Gazetteer of the Bombay Presidency, Dharwar, Vol. XXII. Bombay: Government
　　　　　Press.
Geertz, Hildred
　　1961　The Javanese Family: A Study of Kinship and Socialization. Glencoe: The Free
　　　　　Press.
Ghurye, G. S.
　　1950　Caste and Class in India. Bombay: Popular.
Goode, William
　　1963　World Revolution and Family Patterns. New York: The Free Press.
Gore, M. S.
　　1968　Industrialization and Family Change. New York: Humanities.
　　1965　"The Traditional Indian Family" in Nimkoff, M. (ed.), Comparative Family
　　　　　Systems. Boston: Houghton & Mifflin.

Gough, Kathleen E.
1956 "Brahman Kinship in a Tamil Village". *AA*, Vol. LVIII, 5.
Gusfield, Joseph R.
1966 "Tradition and Modernity: Misplaced Polarities in the Study of Social Change". *AJS*, Vol. 72, No. 4.
Harrison, S.
1960 India: The Most Dangerous Decades. Princeton: Princeton University Press.
Hauser, P. M. (ed.)
1957 Urbanization in Asia and the Far East. Calcutta: Unesco Research Centre.
Homans, G. C. and Schneider, D. M.
1955 Marriage, Authority and Final Causes: A Study of Unilateral Crosscousin Marriage. Glencoe: The Free Press.
Hoselitz, Bert F. and Moore, Wilbert E. (eds.)
1963 Industrialization and Society. Chicago: Unesco-Mouton.
Hsu, F. L. K.
1949 Under the Ancestors' Shadow. London: Routledge & Kegan Paul.
Hutton, J. H.
1946 Caste in India. Cambridge: University Press.
India, Government
1962 Census of India 1961. New Delhi: Government of India.
1961 The Third Five Year Plan. New Delhi: Government of India, Planning Commission.
1956 The Constitution of India. New Delhi: Government of India.
1956a Social Legislation: Its Role in Social Welfare. New Delhi: Planning Commission, Government of India.
1956b Report of the States Reorganization Commission. New Delhi: Government of India.
India, Government
1952 Census of India. New Delhi: Government of India.
1908 Imperial Gazetteer of India: "Dharwar Town", Vol. XI. Oxford: Clarendon Press.
Ishwaran, K.
1971 The Canadian Family. Toronto: Holt, Rinehart & Winston.
1970 Change and Continuity in India's Villages. New York: Columbia University Press.
1968 Shivapur: A South Indian Village. London: Routledge & Kegan Paul.
1966 Tradition and Economy in Village India. London: Routledge & Kegan Paul.
1964 "Kinship and Distance in Rural India". *IJCS*, Vol. V, No. 2.
1959 Family Life in the Netherlands. The Hague: Uitgeverij Van Keulen.
Issacs, Harold
1964 The Ex-Untouchables. New York: The John Day.
Jong, Josselin De, J. D. B. DE
1952 Levi-Strauss's Theory on Kinship and Marriage. Leiden: E. J. Brill.
Jorapur, P. B.
1971 "Intergenerational Occupational Mobility". Indian Journal of Social Work, 3 : 4.
Kannan, C. T.
1961 "Intercaste Marriage in Bombay". *SB*, Vol. X, No. 2.
Kapadia, K. M.
1962 "Caste in Transition". *SB*, Vol. XI, Nos. 1 & 2.
1959 Marriage and Family in India. Bombay: Oxford University Press.
1947 Hindu Kinship. Bombay: Popular.
Kapur, P.
1970 Marriage and Working Women in India. New York: Humanities.
Karve, Irawati
1953 Kinship Organisation in India. Poona: Deccan College. "The Kinship System and Kinship Terms in Karnatak". *DCB*, Vol. X, pt. 1.

Khare, R. S.
    1970   The Changing Brahmans. Chicago: University of Chicago Press.
Kuppuswamy, B.
    1972   Social Change in India. Delhi: Vikas.
    1956   "A Statistical Study of Attitude to the Caste System in South India". *J.Psy.*
Lambert, R.
    1963   Workers, Factories and Social Change in India. Princeton: Princeton University
            Press.
Lang, Olga
    1946   Chinese Family and Society. New Haven: Yale University Press.
Lerner, Daniel
    1964   The Passing of Traditional Society. New York: The Free Press.
Levy, Marion J.
    1966   Modernization and the Structure of Societies. 2 Vols. Princeton: University Press.
Lewis, Oscar
    1958   Village Life in Northern India. Urbana: University of Illinois Press.
Lewis, J. P.
    1964   Quiet Crisis in India. Garden City, New York: Doubleday.
Linton, Ralph
    1959   "The Natural History of the Family" in Anshen, R.N. (ed.), The Family: Its
            Function and Destiny. New York: Harper.
Litwak, Eugene
    1960   "Occupational Mobility and Extended Family Cohesion". *ASR*, Vol. 25 No. 1.
    1960a   "Geographic Mobility and Extended Family Cohesion". *ASR*, Vol. 25 No. 3.
    1960b   "Divorce Law as Social Control" in Bell, N. and Vogel, E. (eds.), A Modern
            Introduction to the Family. London: Routledge & Kegan Paul.
Lowie, R.
    1950   Social Organisation. London: Routledge & Kegan Paul.
Lynch, O. M.
    1969   The Politics of Untouchability. New York: Columbia University Press.
Madan, T. N.
    1965   Family and Kinship: a Study of the Pandits of Rural Kashmir. Bombay: Asia.
Malinowski, B.
    1955   Sex and Repression in Savage Society. New York: Meridian.
    1963   (1913) The Family among the Australian Aborigines: a Sociological Study.
            New York: Schocken.
Mandelbaum, D. G.
    1970   Society in India (2 Vols.). Berkeley: University of California Press.
Mannheim, Karl
    1940   Man and Society in an Age of Reconstruction. New York: Harcourt Brace.
Marriot, McKim (ed.)
    1955   Village India. Chicago: University Press.
Mayer, Adrian C.
    1960   Caste and Kinship in Central India: A Village and its Region. London: Routledge
            & Kegan Paul.
McClelland, David C.
    1961   The Achieving Society. Princeton: Van Nostrand.
McClelland, D. C. and Winter, D. G.
    1969   Motivating Economic Achievement. New York: The Free Press.
McCormack, William
    1963   "Lingayats as a Sect". *JRAI*, Vol. 93. pt. 1.
            "Sister's Daughter Marriage in a Mysore Village". *MI*, Vol. 38. No. 1.
    1959   "The Forms of Communication in Virasaiva Religion" in Singer, M. (ed.),
            Traditional India: Structure and Change. Philadelphia: The American Folklore
            Society.

Merton, Robert K.
   1962   Social Theory and Social Structure. Glencoe: The Free Press.
Mogey, J. M.
   1956   Family and Neighbourhood: Two Studies in Oxford. Oxford: University Press.
Moorthy, B. M. L.
   1954   Social Security in India.
Morgan, L. H.
   1870   "Systems of Consanguinity and Affinity of the Human Family". Smithsonian Contributions to Knowledge, XVII.
Morrison, W. A.
   1959   Family Types in Badlapur. *SB*, 8 : 2.
Mulla, D. F. revised by S. T. Desai
   1960   Principles of Hindu Law, 12th edition. Bombay: Tripathi.
Murdock, G. P.
   1949   Social Structure. New York: Macmillan.
Needham, Rodney
   1962   Structure and Sentiment: A Test Case in Social Anthropology. Chicago: University Press.
Nimkoff, M. F. (ed.)
   1965   Comparative Family Systems. Boston: Houghton & Mifflin.
   1960   "Is the Joint Family an Obstacle to Industrialization?" *IJCS*, Vol. 1. No. 1.
   1959   "Some Problems Concerning Research on the Changing Family in India". *SB*, Vol. VIII, No. 2.
Owens, Raymond
   1971   Industrialization and the Indian Joint Family. Ethnology 10.
Parsons, Talcott et. al. (eds.)
   1961   Theories of Society, 2 Vols. New York: The Free Press.
   1959   "The Social Structure of the Family" in Anshen, R. (ed.), The Family: Its Function & Destiny. New York: Harper.
   1958   "The Kinship System of the Contemporary United States" in Essays in Sociological Theory: Pure and Applied. Glencoe: The Free Press.
   1953   "Revised Analytical Approach to the Theory of Social Stratification" in Bendix, R. and Lipset, S. M. (eds.), Class, Status and Power. Glencoe: The Free Press.
Piddington, Ralph
   1961   "A Study of French Canadian Kinship". *IJCS*, Vol. 2, No. 1.
Pocock, D. F.
   1955   "The Movement of Castes". *Man*, Vol. LV.
Ogburn, W. F. and Nimkoff, M. F.
   1950   Sociology. Boston: Houghton & Mifflin.
Prabhu, P.
   1955   "Social Effects of Urbanization on Industrial Workers in Bombay". *SB*, Vol. 4. No. 2.
Prabhu, V. R.
   1953   "Dharwar: A Study in Indian Urban Landscape". *BGM*, Vol. 1. No. 1.
Radcliffe-Brown, A. R. and Forde, D. (eds.)
   1950   African Systems of Kinship and Marriage. London: Oxford University Press.
Reiss, Paul J.
   1962   "The Extended Kinship System: Correlates of and Attitudes on Frequency of Interactions". *MFL*, Vol. 24. No. 4.
Rivers, W. H. R.
   1968   Kinship and Social Organisation. London: Athlone Press. (1914)
Robins, L. N. and Tomanec, M.
   1962   "Closeness to Blood Relatives outside the Immediate Family". *MFL*, Vol. 24. No. 4.

Rogers, E. M. and Svenning, Lynne
    1969   Modernization Among Peasants. New York: Holt, Rinehart & Winston.
Rogers, E. M. and Sebald, H.
    1962   "A Distinction between Familism, Family Integration, and Kinship Orientation".
            MFL, Vol. 24. No. 1.
Rosen, G.
    1966   Democracy and Economic Change in India. Berkeley: University of California
            Press.
Ross, Aileen D.
    1961   The Hindu Family in its Urban Setting. Toronto: University Press.
    1959   "Education and Family Change". *SB*, Vol. VIII, No. 2.
Rudolph, L. I. and S. H.
    1967   The Modernity of Tradition. Chicago: University of Chicago Press.
Schapera, I.
    1955   "Kinship Terminology and the American Kinship System". *AA*, Vol. 57.
    1966   (1940)   Married Life in an African Tribe. Evanston, Ill.: Northwestern University
            Press.
Shah, A. M.
    1972   The Household Dimension of the Family in India. Berkeley: University of Cali-
            fornia.
Shah, B. V.
    1962   "Gujarat College Students and Selection of Bride". *SB*, Vol. XI, Nos. 1 & 2.
Simmel, G. (Tr. ed. K. H. Wolff)
    1950   The Sociology of Georg Simmel. New York: The Free Press.
Smith, D. E.
    1963   India as a Secular State. Princeton: Princeton University Press.
Singer, Milton
    1972   When a Great Tradition Modernizes. New York: Praeger.
Singer, M. and Cohn, B. (eds.)
    1968   Structure and Change in Indian Society. Chicago: Aldine.
Sorokin, P. A.
    1957   Social and Cultural Dynamics. Boston: Porter Sargent.
Srinivas, M. N.
    1966   Social Change in Modern India. Berkeley: University of California Press.
    1962   Caste in Modern India and other Essays. Bombay: Asia.
    1962a   "Changing Institutions and Values in Modern India". *EW*, Feb.
    1955   India's Villages. Calcutta: West Bengal Government.
    1955a   "The Social System of a Mysore Village" in McKim Marriot, Village India.
            Chicago: University Press.
    1952   Religion and Society among the Coorgs of South India. Oxford: University Press.
    1942   Marriage and Family in Mysore. Bombay: New Book.
Stephens, W. M.
    1967   "Family and Kinship" in Smelser, N. J. (ed.), Sociology. New York: Wiley.
Sussman, M. B.
    1965   "Relationships of Adult Children with their Parents in the United States" in
            Ethel Shanas and Gordon F. Streib (eds.), Social Structure and the Family:
            Generational Relations. Englewood Cliffs: Prentice-Hall.
Sussman, M. B. and Burchinal, L.
    1962   "Kin Family Network: Unheralded Structure in Current Conceptualizations of
            Family Functioning". *MFL*, Vol. 24. No. 3.
Sussman, M. B.
    1959   "The Isolated Nuclear Family: Fact or Fiction?" Social Problems 6 : 333–340
            Spring.
    1952   "The Help Pattern in the Middle Class Family".
            American Sociological Review. 18 : 22–28.

Taylor, Carl C., Ensminger, D., Johnson, H. W. and Joyce, J.
  1965   India's Roots of Democracy. Bombay: Orient Longmans.
Toennies, F. (Tr. ed. C. P. Loomis)
  1957   Community and Society. East Lansing: Michigan State University Press.
Townsend, P.
  1957   The Family Life of Old People. London: Routledge.
Turner, R. (ed.)
  1962   India's Urban Future. Berkeley: University of California Press.
Unesco
  1956   Social Implications of Industrialization and Urbanization in South Asia. Calcutta:
         Unesco Research Centre.
Vatuk, Sylvia
  1972   Kinship and Urbanization: White Collar Migrants in North India. Berkeley:
         University of California Press.
Ward, Barbara E.
  1963   Women in the New Asia. Paris: Unesco.
Warner, L. and Lunt
  1941   The Social Life of a Modern Community. New Haven: Yale University Press.
Weber, Max
  1958   The Religion of India. Glencoe: The Free Press.
  1950   General Economic History. Glencoe, Ill.: The Free Press.
Weiner, Myron (ed.)
  1966   Modernization: The Dynamics of Growth. New York: Basic Books.
Williams, W. M.
  1956   The Sociology of an English Village. London: Routledge & Kegan Paul.
Wirth, Louis
  1938   "Urbanism as a Way of Life". AJS, Vol. 44, No. 1.
Young, M. and Willmott, P.
  1957   Family and Kinship in East London. London: Routledge & Kegan Paul.
Zimmerman, C. C.
  1947   Family and Civilization. New York: Harper.

INDEX